GRANDPA THE SNIPER

The Remarkable Story
of a 1916 Volunteer

Frank Shouldice

The Liffey Press

Published by
The Liffey Press Ltd
Raheny Shopping Centre, Second Floor
Raheny, Dublin 5, Ireland
www.theliffeypress.com

© 2015 Frank Shouldice

A catalogue record of this book is
available from the British Library.

ISBN 978-1-908308-80-1

Cover design by Alan Dunne Design.

Printed in Spain by GraphyCems.

Acknowledgements

It has It has been a long-fingered wish to fill in the gaps Grandpa left behind. Born in the West of Ireland with a humility that made him a reluctant witness to the achievements of his life, I set out to learn more and write his untold story. Numerous people have helped in ways big and small to bring this book to a conclusion, and any personal satisfaction I have in completing it implicitly acknowledges the contribution of others. Since embarking on the first days of research my mother Jean has, as always, provided steadfast and generous support. Thanks Mam.

Grandpa was not, of course, only my grandfather – writing about somebody so central to all our lives required a show of confidence from my brothers Ronan and Killian (an uncompromising auxiliary proofreader) and my sister Darina. They let me just get on with it and I am grateful to them for entrusting me with the freedom to handle a theme and subject of deep personal significance to all.

Grandpa's story is intertwined with that of his brother Jack. I have in mind Jack's daughter Ena, whom my Dad and I have met at many Easter commemorations, and Jack's son Chris Shouldice, who has done extensive work over the years to keep this story alive.

My publisher David Givens has been supportive about this project from the very start and I greatly appreciate his calm editorial eye as well as the encouragement of all at The Liffey Press. Alan Dunne brought fresh ideas to designing the cover and gave welcome assistance to processing images for the book.

A debt of gratitude is due to Professor Diarmaid Ferriter for taking time out of a very busy schedule to read the manuscript, to historian Paul O'Brien for his genial assistance to my irregular queries, to Lyn Ebenezer, Jim Fleming, Chris Impey, Sean Reynolds, Niall Bergin, Aoife Torpey, Mary Murphy, the Sheerin Family, Mary Lynch, Gregory O'Connor, Lar Joye, Patsy McGarry, Sheila O'Leary, Maeve O'Leary, Kathleen O'Donovan, Clodagh O'Donovan, David Fitzpatrick, *The Western People*, *Roscommon Herald*, Paddy and Ciaran Holohan, The 1916 Four Courts Relatives Committee, Gethin Jones, Alex Hickey, Barry Feely, Tracey Huxley, Gwynedd Archives (Dolgellau), Ballaghaderreen GAA Club, Andrew Durkin, S4C Cymru, Caoimhe Nic Dhábhéid, Alwyn Jones, Anwyn Jones, Einion Thomas, Bob Nicholson, Al Ryan, Tom Quinlan, Oisín MacGreal, photographers Lorraine Sherry and David Pierce and my RTÉ colleagues Paul Maguire, Paul Murphy, Aoife Hegarty and David Nally.

Day-to-day research has generated countless queries and requests at a variety of librarians' desks with responses helpfully provided by Keith Murphy at the National Photographic Archives, his colleagues at the National Library of Ireland, Dublin City Library (Pearse Street), National Archives of Ireland (Bishop Street), Collins Barracks, National Military Archives at Cathal Brugha Barracks, Gwent Archives and the National Archives of Britain in Kew, London.

Devoting time and energy to such a personal project inevitably means drawing time and attention from elsewhere. The plight of golf widows is well documented but the church of temporary neglect has disciples in many other pursuits that don't involve small white balls. Progress may yet be made on the various small jobs to be done around the house, but for her perseverance, kindness and much more my wife Rachel deserves special gratitude.

◆

Frank Shouldice
Dublin, October, 2015

For Da

1.

Boys, Oh boys, sure that's the reason why
We're in mournin' for the Pride of Petravore[1]

We are chasing history, summoning ghosts. Grandpa might have left us 41 years ago but he is the reason Dad and I are at a book launch of *Crossfire: 1916 in Focus*, Paul O'Brien's vivid reconstruction of the role played by the Four Courts garrison during the Easter Rising.

The wine reception at the Law library on Church Street is crowded. Public interest in 1916, for so long a minority sport, is gaining momentum. The library itself is located just fifty yards from where the Jameson distillery malthouse once stood, the very site where Grandpa wrote himself into a page of Irish history. We pick up a copy of the book and I go to the index at the back. Flicking through I find an entry with his name and read through a passage:

> Taking up his sniping position, Shouldice took careful aim at the British gunner. Squeezing the trigger of his rifle, he emptied the magazine into the British position, killing the gunner and firing ceased from the target building.[2]

I am staggered and wonder how this is the first I know about it.
'Da, did you know Grandpa was a sniper?'
'What?' says Dad.
I read him the passage.
'Show me,' he says incredulously, leaning in closer.
And there it is, in black and white. Grandpa the sniper.
Dad sits back, thoughtfully fingering his glass. Clearly, I am not the only one caught by surprise.

2.

'While Dublin was undergoing strange experiences on Easter Monday, crowds of people were making their way by road and rail to Fairyhouse for the annual races of the Ward Hunt Union, one of the most delightful, as it is certainly one of the most sporting of fixtures, especially when favoured by such fine weather as on Easter Monday' – Irish Life, 12 May 1916

Rewind to December 10, 1974. The precise details are unclear but the scene is etched in memory. A collision of images coalesce into short sensory sequences. Glasnevin cemetery. Grandpa's coffin draped in a tricolour. A tall larch tree bending protectively over the mourners. A uniformed firing party, rigid to command, prepares military-style for one last send-off. A volley of shots. Blackbirds scatter.

Children would cover their ears at the report of gunfire. It's an alien sound but at Glasnevin it feels different. The crack and echo is personal and when the circling blackbirds resettle on branches above it starts to sink in that Grandpa has taken his leave.

His legacy is honour. He leaves us his earthly goods and he leaves us a name. His story is untold because that's how he left it – fully incomplete. Like many others who took part in The Rising and subsequent War of Independence, he was averse to self-promotion and would never single himself out for attention.

I was named after my father and grandfather so there were three Franks in our house. My family had taken to calling me Fran but I protested at the loss of a missing consonant until full title was restored. Grandpa's departure cut our complement of Franks to two. I was 11 at the time.

Although he was reticent about those tumultuous years, how fortunate that Grandpa turns out to be both a steady hoarder and diligent archivist. He keeps personal records in a tan leather suit-case with two metal fasteners. In it he stores personal letters, official records, diaries, newspaper clippings, the holster of his Webley revolver – he surrendered the gun to local gardai in 1972 for safe-keeping. Everything is left for somebody to find. He even keeps a 1920 hurling match ticket from Dublin v Tipperary, a Croke Park fixture which gained infamy as Bloody Sunday.

When retracing Grandpa's journey I encounter the past behaving in concentric circles – even Bloody Sunday has a personal relevance previously unknown to me. I learn that the match, a fund-raiser for Volunteer dependents, was organised by his brother, Jack.

Frank and Jack's heavy involvement in the Easter Rising and War of Independence plucks national history from the abstract and connects us to it. Small things acquire fresh significance. Like a blue and white mushroom basket resting on the floor of Grand-pa's empty bedroom. Using a ball of twine wrapped around the basket's thin metal handle it served as a semi-hydraulic rubbish bin. When the basket was full he would open the sash window and, letting the twine out as a pulley, lower it to the ground for collection afterwards. Visitors were often intrigued by an airborne mushroom basket suddenly hovering into view.

As I would later discover, the same practice was used by Irish prisoners nine decades ago. In Wakefield and elsewhere[3] they found themselves in cells one floor above conscientious objectors, Englishmen who refused to go to war. The 'conchies' as they were known were treated as the lowest form of life and were denied all privileges. Taking pity on the men below them the Irish prisoners would use a piece of string as a lifeline, a conduit from cell window to cell window, to secretly pass on food, letters and encouragement.

Frank and Jack were both sacked from the British-run Civil Service for taking part in The Rising. Significantly, neither man took part in the Civil War. Both were aghast, if not repulsed by it, and refused to undo what they had achieved. How regrettable that many more of their ex-comrades did not feel the same! Even though they tried to move on with their lives they lost good friends on both sides, most notably Harry Boland who was fatally wound-ed after being shot by government troops in Skerries.

Brothers in arms:
Frank and Jack Shouldice

Although reinstated to the Civil Service after independence in 1922, the Shouldice brothers took the most difficult position in the great Treaty divide – to remain unaligned. Like others who chose not to take sides in the Civil War they felt they lost out in later years. No room for neutrals in the sharing out of spoils. For Grandpa, promotion to Higher Executive Officer was a snail-like and frequently delayed process; Jack retired as a Junior Executive Officer at the Department of Agriculture in 1950, the same position he held when first dismissed in 1916. The oversight did not go unnoticed.

As garrison secretary of the 1st Battalion Dublin Brigade Jack Shouldice made a point of encouraging his men to commit their recollections of 1916-22 to posterity through the Bureau of Military History in Rathmines. The effort was hugely worthwhile and we are indebted to contributors for treasures that would otherwise be lost. Unfortunately, Grandpa never made any statement to the Bureau. Why he opted out of public record is not quite clear although he was a private man and such reticence was entirely in character. His dear friend and comrade Tom Sheerin made no statement either.

And so Grandpa has packed his old suitcase and left it behind. Decades later its contents will become my guide to tracing the past. A life passes more privately through the intermittent pages of his diaries, the entries less regular and less legible in later years. Not that every diary entry reflects a political awakening – bringing a new dog home in January 13, 1949 he writes:

Pup named Biro (mother was Parker).

His self-effacing modesty is truly admirable but such deep silence has almost come at our expense. It is frustrating that so many questions remain unasked but I am very grateful that he stored his own collection and deeply proud of what he did.

Often it is thanks to the personal accounts of veterans and access to official records I can locate Grandpa and *situate* him retrospectively in the course of his own history. It falls to others to tell his story. He may have played down his role – or even covered his tracks – but he is unmistakably present. And each quiet discovery is a reminder that he – and others like him – had no idea of the immodest impact of their actions.

Grandpa was 23 years old when he and Jack (33) started out for North King Street on Easter Monday. What followed were the events to shape his life. Grandpa used to take my older brother Ronan to Easter commemorations at Dublin Castle and Arbour Hill. Years later he brought me to Arbour Hill where firing parties would honour the living of 1916 and offer a cordite requiem for the dead. In open space behind Arbour Hill – in use then as a jail and still in use now – a memorial was unveiled for the 50th anniversary of The Rising, the wording of the Proclamation inscribed on curved Wicklow limestone along with the names of 64 Irish Volunteers and Citizen Army members killed during Easter Week.

The Irish Army don't do firing parties at Arbour Hill commemorations any more, part of the gradual de-militarisation of Easter Week. Management of that legacy is firmly in official hands. Not that the veterans were ever thanked for what they did. Back then, Grandpa would attend these events with his ageing comrades, a defiant gathering of proud, long-coated, be-medalled gentlemen ever-declining in number. They would present themselves to honour lost patriots and friends. The occasion would also afford these men the opportunity to recall, however imperfectly, when they never felt so alive. Around them were the only ones who could know what those moments were really like. Under the brims of their homburg hats these men would stand in silent reminiscence, flanked by the people with whom they shared the singular, strange sensation of making history.

*'Young men of character, having begun within the last
twelve or eighteen months, to refuse entering Constabulary
service notwithstanding the general want of employment'*[4]
– RIC Inspector General Duncan McGregor, 1848

Henry Shouldice joined the Royal Irish Constabulary (RIC) when policemen were leaving the force in droves. It is the height of the Famine and the RIC stands sentry to epic misery, overseeing evictions and protecting despised rate collectors while much of the country, particularly the West of Ireland, is ravaged by death and starvation. The lucky ones are the ones who get away.

The harsh extremities of policing in 1847 sees a surge in RIC men retiring before pensionable age. As W.J. Lowe points out, the number of policemen killed in action from 1847-49 is double the RIC casualty rate from the entire 1841-1914 period.[5] Into this turbulence steps young Henry, aged 20, fitted out for uniform a year later when he begins his career as Sub-Constable.

Originally from County Clare his duty through tumultuous times takes him all around Connacht with postings to Newport, Castlerea, Boyle, Delphi, Ballintubber and Rosses Point. Though he looks taller he is registered on RIC books at 5 foot 7¾ inches, not untypical of the height of RIC officers at that time. In his early days he shows great commitment to the job, enthusiastic enough to take Thomas Shannon to court in December 1855 for allowing 'a pig to wander about the streets in the town of Boyle.' Shannon is fined sixpence for his trouble.

Twenty years later Henry is back in Boyle to marry his Sligo-born wife, Christina Meighan. His dedication to upholding the law is rewarded by promotion to the rank of sergeant. Through his career he prosecutes numerous cases at the petty sessions courts but the tables are turned in November 9, 1876 when he is named defendant in a case taken by RIC Sub-Inspector John Smith. Henry is charged that he did 'allow and suffer one James Brennan a prisoner to escape from the custody of the Police out of the Police Barrack of Westport.' The case is dismissed but being prosecuted by his own superiors may have soured his relationship with the job. It is his last listed appearance in court and Sergeant Shouldice retires from the RIC three years later, aged 52.

Christina gives birth to a dozen children. Frank Joseph Shouldice, born in Ballaghaderreen, County Mayo – now County Roscommon – on October 15, 1892, is eighth of the brood. Although a large family, mortality and tragedy shake the household. Patrick Henry dies in 1878 from diphtheria, aged two years; sister Mary and Patrick Henry II also die in early age.

The family home is St. John's Terrace, off Main Street, Ballaghaderreen, known far and wide as a market town well lubricated by public houses. Christina is some-

Henry Shouldice (top) and Christina Meighan

how listed as a licensed publican on the 1901 census but there is no family pub. When Frank is six the county boundaries are redrawn by the Local Government Act and Ballaghaderreen finds itself shunted from County Mayo into County Roscommon.

Significantly, Ballaghaderreen's credentials remain rooted in Mayo when it comes to football. The local GAA club switches temporarily into County Roscommon in 1905 but moves back to Mayo after just one season. Ballaghaderreen GAA club has played under the Mayo County Board ever since, lending the town a somewhat amorphous dual identity even if Frank insists on addressing all letters home to Ballaghaderreen, County Mayo. Whatever the posi-

Jack in London

tion at official level he always refers to it as a Mayo town and considers himself a Mayo-man first and foremost.

It is, like most of Connacht, blighted by emigration. His oldest brother Jim (aged 19 years) sets sail for the United States. Jack, ten years older than Frank, makes his way for London, aged just 15, and gets a job as a messenger boy. Over there, Jack plays football for St Patrick's GAA club and gets acquainted with Harry Boland. He also links up with Peadar Kearney (who composed *Amhrán na bhFíain*) and Sam Maguire (after whom the All-Ireland football championship is named). Maguire is instrumental in Jack joining the clandestine Irish Republican Brotherhood (IRB).

It is unusual, but not unique, that an RIC sergeant would end up with four republican children – three sons and a daughter – taking up a cudgel against the authority to which he devoted his life. However Henry dies in December, 1900 and is spared ever having to wonder where he went wrong. Having served 31 years in the force his annual salary of £72 and 10 shillings translates into a pension of £68 per year, the sum paid annually to Christina, his widow.

Returning to Dublin in 1907 Jack gets a job in the Civil Service. A year later he wins an All-Ireland medal with Dublin, playing for county club champions Geraldines who beat Kerry champions (Tralee Mitchels) in the home decider and then defeat Hibernians of London in the final outright. The feat earns Jack the sobriquet as the first Mayo footballer to win the All-Ireland, albeit for Dublin.

When Frank finishes his schooling at St. Nathy's in Ballaghad-erreen he too sets off for the bright lights of London in March 1909, aged 17. It is a monumental change from provincial town to cosmopolitan city but necessity makes a virtue of adventure. He gets a job as a boy clerk in the Surveyor of Taxes Office and plays football and hurling with the Milesians club in south London. He also visits a number of photographic studios where he seems to

Earliest shot of Frank at school (top left corner). His younger brother Bertie is looking over the teacher's right shoulder.

enjoy getting his portrait taken. Looking directly to camera he strikes a confident and assured pose although the vanity of going to photographic studios is almost comically out of character to anyone who knows him.

A year later he moves back to Dublin to take up a temporary clerk position at the Irish Land Commission. Putting greater effort into playing ball than into any career path he moves to the Department of Local Government in November 1912, taking up the post of assistant clerk at the National Health Insurance Commission (Ireland).

His younger sister Ena (christened Christina) also moves from Ballaghaderreen to live and work in Dublin. Jack, Frank and Ena are a close trio and they move within a circle of mutual friends. Another brother, Bertie, who works as an assistant at Flannery's general store in Ballaghaderreen, sometimes comes up to visit them.

For much of this time the two brothers live in digs at The Crescent in Fairview, a half-circle row of three-storey Georgian houses. The Boland family are neighbours living at Number 15 – Jack is already friends with Harry from their time in London. Although elegant in appearance Marino Crescent was constructed out of spite. Developer Charles Ffolliott and landowner Lord Charlemont

The Shouldice family of Ballaghaderreen: (Standing L-R) Patrick, Mary, Jack, Ena, Frank; (seated) Bertie, Christina, Lily

had a bitter fall-out. Ffolliott then built The Crescent in 1792 on land between Dublin Bay and Donnycarney, reportedly to block Charlemont's view of the sea.

Whatever about any nascent political interest there is plenty of time for sport. In the argot of Gaelic football, Jack and Frank are both 'very handy.' Despite their age difference the brothers are teammates with Dublin inter-county seniors and on April 9, just two weeks before The Easter Rising, they're on the bus to Athlone to line out for the final of the Croke Cup. Dublin beat Roscommon in what proves to be the last ever match in the competition. Everything, including sporting life, is overturned by war – it will be two years before Frank receives his Croke Cup medal. By July, ten players from the All-Ireland-winning Geraldines team will be locked up in British jails.

In later years Frank will switch colours to play inter-county football with Mayo but through his twenties he finds time for handball, billiards, cards, drink and dancing. We might presume turn-of-the-century Dublin to be grey but weekend dances often go until 4.00 a.m. and 5.00 a.m., after which the stragglers might shuffle into the Pro-Cathedral for early Mass before finally collapsing into bed.

Behind the scenes Jack and Frank are heavily involved with a growing republican movement. Frank follows his brother into the IRB, a secret organisation rooted within the National Volunteer movement. Both are active in recruiting IRB members, with Jack more prominent before The Rising and Frank afterwards. In a statement to the Bureau of Military History, Patrick Cassidy of Ballaghaderreen, who fought with the East Mayo Brigade, tells how he first got involved:

> Frank Shouldice took me into the IRB in Ballaghaderreen in 1918 and a circle was organised there. They were all Volunteers and we had four or five men from each Company, usually the officers. I was Centre of the Circle and we paid a subscription of threepence a week towards the funds. We met fairly regularly. We held discussion as they were at the moment and considered what could be done to intensify the fight against the enemy.[6]

Similarly, Seamus Doyle, who fought at Mount Street Bridge in Easter Week:

> About the spring of 1914 Jack Shouldice asked me to join the IRB. I was sworn in by him . . . the Centre,

Dublin GAA football team c. 1915 – Frank (standing, fifth from right); Jack (seated, third from left).

as far as I remember, was Bulmer Hobson, although I remember Cathal Brugha presiding at some meetings.[7]

The nightmare of war in Europe drags on far longer than anyone anticipates and acrimonious disagreement breaks out among the Irish Volunteers over recruitment to the British Army. The issue is so fundamentally divisive that it splits the nationalist movement. In return for the promise of Home Rule the majority move with John Redmond to the newly-formed National Volunteers which continues to supply manpower to Britain's war effort. The Irish Volunteers, now a smaller rump, remains firmly opposed to recruitment of any kind.

Historians are dubious that nationalist obeisance to the Crown might ever have been rewarded by Home Rule but Frank and Jack are not the only ones running out of patience with Redmond's long game. They stay with the Irish Volunteers. Headed by Chief of Staff Eoin MacNeill the Irish Volunteers is fully infiltrated by the IRB, for whom armed insurrection is a political necessity. MacNeill is not a member of the IRB.

The Irish Volunteers continue to drill and stage manoeuvres in the open – the Ulster Volunteer Force (UVF) has already made a political virtue of armed resistance. Audacious military-style training hardly goes unnoticed by the Dublin Metropolitan Police (DMP), particularly when some of the Volunteer's manoeuvres are staged as mock battles outside police headquarters at Dublin Castle itself.

As early as June 1914 the Royal Irish Constabulary (RIC) Inspector-General reports to the Chief Secretary's office:

> In Ireland the training and drilling to the use of arms of a great part of the male population is a new departure which is bound in the not distant future to alter all the existing conditions of life. Obedience to the law has never been a prominent characteristic of the people . . . if the people became armed and drilled effective police control will vanish. Events are moving.[8]

And move, they certainly do.

The very structure of the Government in Ireland belies its administrative faults. As its executive manager, Chief-Secretary Augustine Birrell, commutes regularly between Dublin and parliament in London; Lord Lieutenant Ivor Wimborne – a first cousin of Winston Churchill – is titular head with more of a symbolic role so it means much of the day-to-day administration falls to Under-Secretary Matthew Nathan. His posting to Ireland begins in August 1914 after stints as Governor of Sierra Leone, Gold Coast, Hong Kong and Natal. What he fails to see coming in Ireland will eventually hit him.

It is to Nathan that DMP Chief Commissioner Walter Edgeworth-Johnstone reports his concerns:

> These recruiting meetings are a very undesirable development, and are I think causing both annoyance and uneasiness among loyal citizens . . The Sinn Féin party are gaining in numbers, in equipment, in discipline and in confidence and I think drastic action should be taken to limit their activities. The longer this is postponed the more difficult it will be to carry out.[9]

Throughout 1915 and 1916 the DMP and RIC provide daily reports of restive nationalism across Ireland. The DMP opens a surveillance file on 'Movements of Dublin Extremists' which features many recognisable names – Tom Clarke, Padraig Pearse, Thomas McDonagh, James Connolly, Ned Daly, Eamon de Valera, Arthur Griffith, Sean T. O'Kelly, Michael O'Hanrahan, The O'Rahilly, Con Colbert, Eamonn Ceannt, Sean MacDiarmada, Eoin MacNeill, Bulmer Hobson, Piaras Béaslaí, Joseph McGuinness, Tom Byrne, Diarmuid Lynch, Frank Fahy, Barney Mellowes and J.J. O'Connell.

The level of observation and the resources required to maintain it are quite staggering. On a random day for example

Striking a pose in 1914

13

– June 1, 1915 – these 'Secret' records – signed off by DMP Chief Superintendent Owen Brien – notify the Under-Secretary directly that:

> . . . about 34 Sinn Féin Volunteers without rifles assembled at 41 Rutland Square at 8.20 p.m. and afterwards in charge of Joseph McGuinness went for a route march in direction of Fairview.[10]

Tom Clarke's tobacconist's shop on Parnell Street is watched at all times. On June 29, for instance:

> At 75 Parnell Street James Murray, Con Colbert, John T. Kelly, T.C., and F. Fahy. Clarke was not in the place during the day being engaged in fitting up his new residence, 10 Richmond Avenue, Fairview. JJ Walsh going into D.B.C. Restaurant, Sackville Street at 1.45 p.m. JJ O'Connell left Amiens Street Terminus by 3 p.m. train en route to Carrickmore. RIC informed. Wm Mellowes returned from Tullow at 6.30p.m. P. Ryan (Sinn Féin) in Volunteer Office, 2 Dawson Street at 8p.m. Denis McCullough returned to Dublin last evening from Carlow.[11]

But the men under observation are not always unarmed.

> The annual pilgrimage to Bodenstown took place yesterday. Two special trains conveying those taking part left Kingsbridge for Sallins at 11.15 a.m. and 11.45 a.m. About 1,500 persons travelled by these trains which included contingents of the Sinn Féin Volunteers, Citizen Army and National Boy Scouts. About 70 of the Volunteers and Citizens Army carried rifles.[12]

By Easter 1916 the RIC's complement is down to 9,302 officers, about half the strength of the previous decade. The RIC has been discouraged from trying to enlist new officers lest it competes with the British Army for badly-needed recruits.

Three months before The Rising the British Censor's office detects a marked shift in sentiment in Ireland towards war in Europe. From January 9-22 – and it is a sign of things to come – 377 items of transatlantic mail are intercepted from the postal service. Many of them originate from or are bound for Ireland. Discussing the American mails, the War Office writes to General L.B. Friend, Commander-in-Chief of the British Forces in Ireland.

> Examination of a large proportion of the inward Irish mail has revealed a flood of anti-English and pro-German correspondence, reflecting the general sentiments of the Irish in the United States . . . the letters were transferred for the most part to MI5 and that section is occupied in the following up the various clues suggested by the intercepted material. To have stopped a large quantity of enemy United States newspapers and other propaganda is also an advantage.
>
> We have lately received from your staff officer a further list of suspect names and every effort will be made with the help of that and its predecessors to make the Censorship fruitful from an Irish point of view. Believe me.[13]

But even this intensive level of surveillance seems pointless when Volunteers are allowed to brazenly carry out drilling and military training in the open. On St. Patrick's Day 1916 – just five weeks before The Rising – the Irish Volunteers bring Dublin city centre to a standstill. Gathered at Parnell Square, Commandant Ned Daly leads Dublin Brigade's 1st Battalion down to College Green where the men, armed with new rifles, hold up traffic for two hours and go through full manoeuvres. It's a rehearsal for the real thing.

4.

'I dressed hurriedly while my mother and father
got out my rifle and some sandwiches'
– Vol. Patrick J. Kelly, 'G' Division, 1st Batt.,
Dublin Brigade on Easter Monday

As an Irish Volunteer Frank joins 'F' Company of the Dublin Brigade's 1st Battalion. His older brother Jack – also known as John – is First Lieutenant. During Easter Week 'F' Company is part of a 312-strong garrison at the Four Courts commanded by Ned Daly. All have read and re-read thinly-veiled instructions in the 'Headquarters' Bulletin of the *Irish Volunteer* newspaper:

> Arrangements are now nearing completion in all the
> more important brigade areas for the holding of a very
> interesting series of manoeuvres at Easter.[14]

For several weeks Jack Shouldice has been taking stock of the streets around Smithfield. Instructed on a need-to-know basis he and other officers have attended evening lectures on urban warfare and taken classes on street-fighting. Volunteer meetings are usually held in St. Colmcille's Hall in nearby Blackhall Street. On Good Friday Jack goes for an unleisurely stroll down Church Street and North King Street along with Capt. Fionnán Lynch and Second Lieut. Diarmuid O'Hegarty.

Lynch told a BBC interview 50 years later they did it to size up the neighbourhood 'which was to be our charge during the week. We looked over our area, looked for material for barricades and so on so we should know something to do to occupy when we'd take up our positions.'[15]

Through Easter Saturday the men prepare themselves for what is to come. The vast majority go to Mass and receive Holy Communion; many also take the opportunity to make what they feel could be their last confession.

The authorities are also on edge. In a memo to Under-Secretary Nathan, DMP Chief Commissioner Edgeworth-Johnstone spells out the anxiety within the Irish administration over what may yet unfold.

> Dear Sir Matthew,
>
> We got information last evening about 9pm that there was to be a general mobilization of I. Volunteers to be followed by an attack on Dublin Castle. Needless to say I did not believe the latter statement.
>
> However the Sinn Féiners began to assemble with arms at Kimmage, Blackhall Place and the T W Union people at Liberty Hall. I thought it was wise to take no chances so had a good reserve of our men and 300 military standing by until 11.45pm when the bodies at their three centres dispersed.[16]

All Volunteer preparations go awry when Chief of Staff Mac-Neill discovers that Easter manoeuvres are a cover for an IRB-conceived insurrection. Aghast to find military plans so far advanced, MacNeill, for one, gives up all hope that this could succeed when news comes through that a shipment of 20,000 German guns on the *Aud* is scuttled off the Kerry coast after interception by the British Navy. Furthermore, Roger Casement is arrested. Tragedy piles upon farce when three Volunteers – wireless operator Con Keating, Dan Sheehan and Charlie Monahan – who travel to make radio contact with the *Aud* – drown after driving off the pier in darkness at Ballykissane near Killorglin. The driver, Tommy McInerney, 33, survives.

Fionnán Lynch is one of a number of armed Volunteers impatiently awaiting orders at a safe house in 44 Mountjoy Street (known then as the Munster Hotel). He recalls Sean Connolly, an Abbey actor, bring them news of the *Aud* and seeing Sean MacDiarmada, one of the signatories to the Proclamation, reeling at the news.

Irish Volunteer officers, 1916.
Jack Shouldice (standing)
and Miceál Ó Corcáin

Special Branch detectives from Dublin Castle's 'G' Division – better known as 'G' men – then call to Number 44 to make enquiries about Con Keating who used to reside there. In this way the hotel's restless guests hear about the accidental death of three comrades. It's all very frantic and it feels like their bold plans are unravelling. The safe house in Mountjoy Street is deemed unsafe and the uneasy dwellers disperse across the north inner city.

MacNeill realises the IRB has completely infiltrated the Irish Volunteers. He refuses to accept he heads an organisation he does not control. With German guns at the bottom of the Atlantic MacNeill takes an advertisement in the *Sunday Independent* to formally scotch Easter manoeuvres 'as any failure to obey it may result in a very grave catastrophe.'[17] His cancellation order causes huge confusion among the already agitated thousands who had readied themselves for something momentous. It causes turmoil within the movement.

Most Irish Volunteers are puzzled by the cancellation. To have got themselves mentally prepared to risk everything only to be stood down by leadership at the last minute, feels like a body blow. For many, the U-turn is an inexplicable loss of nerve.

Speaking to the Bureau of Military History in 1948, Jack said he felt 'surprise and disappointment'.

> The countermanding order caused complete disorganisation.[18]

Only retrospectively can Fionnán Lynch sympathise with Mac-Neill's dilemma:

> Looking back on it one can understand poor MacNeill's attitude because he was not let into all the secrets at all and was opposed to being used as a front by the IRB.[19]

It is not too hard to guess what Frank made of the news from Tralee or of MacNeill's order. In the tense, muddled lead-up to The Rising he and Jack take their orders from the IRB. High-level IRB meetings continue at the Gaelic League headquarters in Parnell Square throughout Easter Sunday with 'F' Company acting as sentry for MacDiarmada, Pearse, Clarke, Ceannt and McDonagh.

But there's still time for a kick around. A group of Volunteers heads up to Phoenix Park late Sunday morning. Gerald Doyle, who played for Geraldines GAA club with Frank, Jack, Harry Boland and Maurice Collins, recalls Jack telling the group he believes The Rising will go ahead, despite MacNeill's instructions. Late on Sunday evening they discover this to be true. The officers are told manoeuvres will proceed at noon the following day.

In another part of Phoenix Park – the Vice-Regal Lodge – a very different meeting runs late into the night. Lord Wimborne, Viceroy of Ireland, pushes a hesitant Under-Secretary Nathan into action. He wants the Irish Volunteer leadership arrested under Britain's Defence of the Realm Act (DORA). With German guns intercepted, Casement apprehended and a rebellion seemingly thwarted, Wimborne insists that the charge of 'hostile association' with the enemy (Germany) will now stick and that the authorities can finally move against these 'militant extremists'. Nathan agrees to telegram Birrell to seek an immediate clampdown but the horse has already bolted. The next London-bound telegram will tell the Chief Secretary that Dublin city centre is under rebel control.

On Easter Monday Frank and Jack set out from their digs in The Crescent, Fairview. They drop by the Bolands' house on the way. Kathleen Boland recalls:

> Harry, who had been attending a Convention of the G.A.A. in Croke Park – he was, as my father had been,

Chairman of the County Dublin Committee – came home and said to my mother, 'I have to go out. The other boys are going.' She asked, 'Who are they?' He replied 'Jack Shouldice, Frank Shouldice and many others.' She replied, 'Go, in the Name of God! Your father would haunt you if you didn't do the right thing.[20]

Their sister Ena is at home in Ballaghaderreen for the Easter holiday but Kathleen Boland, Harry's sister, knows that ammunition is hidden in Ena's flat nearby on Addison Road. Kathleen collects it and hands it over. Over on the southside their Geraldines teammate Gerald Doyle gets a call at 9.30 a.m. to make for Larkfield in Kimmage. It is a journey of remarkable poignancy.

My father had joined the British Army about seven or eight days before the Rising. He had been a member of Redmond's Volunteers and the first time I ever saw him in uniform was on the Easter Monday morning as I myself was leaving the house to report to Larkfield, Kimmage. He had come from Wellington Barracks, South Circular Road, and we just met and passed each other with a casual 'Good morning!'[21]

Fionnán Lynch recalls a welcome sense of resolution to what was becoming a stop-start rebellion. On Easter Monday:

We all arrived at 44 Mountjoy Street . . got the guns down from the ceiling. The guns and ammunition had been stored away behind a timbered ceiling in the bathroom. We, I'm afraid, left the house in a bit of a mess for poor Mrs McCarthy and went off with our guns and ammunition . . .

Mort Ó Conaill went with Lynch to pick up about a dozen Howth rifles.

I was told to bring all the stuff down to Blackhall Place, which I did quite openly, laying four or five rifles across the handlebars of a bicycle and holding them up at the end. I made three journeys in all and met several soldiers and policemen going off to Fairyhouse Races, making for Broadstone Railway Station. After my third journey I was told I couldn't go back any more but was to take up my position in the company at about five or eight minutes to 12 o'clock.[22]

Gerald Doyle collects his friend John Traynor en route to Kilmainham and they march together to the South Dublin Union under the command of Eamonn Ceannt. Easter Monday is John Traynor's 19th birthday. Later that afternoon he will take a bullet during exchanges with British troops and die instantly.

Jack and Frank rouse other Volunteers on their way into town. They bump into Peadar Lawless, whom they also know through football. Jack offers to get him a gun but the 21-year-old declines and drifts home. By the end of the week Lawless will count among the 14 civilians on North King Street murdered by the South Staffordshire regiment while sheltering from gunfire.

While the majority of Irish Volunteers obey MacNeill's cancellation order, about one quarter of 'F' company – almost 30 men – muster at Blackhall Street in Stoneybatter. Others, confused by contradictory instructions, arrive late, bringing 'F' Company's strength to 52 men by the end of the week.

Rendezvous for the Four Courts garrison is 11.30 am and about 150 Volunteers make their way there. The city is quiet, diverted by the freedoms of an Easter bank holiday and a popular day's racing yet to come at Fairyhouse. Taking a detour to avoid Bridewell police station Sean Prendergast takes men from 'C' Company to St. Colmcille Hall.

> One could not fail to notice the hub-bub prevailing in the hall; men were to be seen engaged in looking over their rifles and revolvers, adjusting and arranging their equipment, sorting out their various possessions of ammunition and placing them into bandoliers, pouches, haversacks or ordinary coat pockets . . . some of these they had time and again been in the habit of doing preparatory to going on marches and manoeuvres. But on this morning there was more animation, greater bustle and flurry than was in evidence on any previous occasion. There was a feeling too of restrained excitement,

of controlled emotions; the very atmosphere breathed that was something hard to define or explain.[23]

Comdt. Daly tells the men the Irish Republic will be declared at noon and the Volunteers will have to defend it with their lives. Anybody who wishes to withdraw is given the option to go home.

From Blackhall Street the garrison is spread around the Four Courts with a group of men despatched to blow up the magazine fort in Phoenix Park. Barney Mellowes, who would join Grandpa in a jailbreak from Usk three years later, joins the foray up to Phoenix Park. So too Garry Houlihan, who remembers taking the order:

> On Easter Monday Paddy Daly, who was the officer in charge of the attack, called at about ten o'clock with word that The Rising was to start at 12 o'clock. We were to take the Fort, but we were not to hold it and we were not to take life if possible.[24]

The Shouldice brothers are late for Comdt. Daly's historic address at Blackhall Street so they head straight to where 'F' Company is posted. The specific area they are to secure and hold is North King Street, just off Smithfield. It's an outer post that protects a key approach to the Four Courts. Jack has a garrison of about 20 men under his command. Between them they have about 16 rifles, four revolvers and six bayonets. Ammunition is limited. Local postmen, however, are not impressed. In fear of losing their jobs they insist they should be allowed through to do their rounds. They are verbally discouraged, then ordered away at gunpoint.

Makeshift barricades are erected in the surrounding streets using whatever comes to hand. Jack describes the build-up to the Bureau of Military History:

> Our barricades consisted of broken articles of furniture, cases, barrels full and empty, some with paraffin oil which constituted a menace to houses adjoining – but it was a sense of needs must. A hackney cab, carts with and without wheels, sacks of flour and meal from a local branch of the Blanchardstown mills in Brunswick Street. The owner of the hackney cab came along later

with a dilapidated cart and begged me for pity's sake to take it in place of the cab which was his only means of living. His request was granted. One local resident implored us to remove a barrel of paraffin oil which was placed against his house. It was removed later and put into the middle of that particular barricade where it was afterwards pierced with bullets but fortunately did not go on fire.

The Volunteer movement has been seriously ruptured over policy and strategy. By week's end about 1,800 men and women, a fraction of the numbers potentially available, take up arms against British rule. Thousands more 'await orders' following MacNeill's countermand. The flip side is that the military authorities also see the Chief of Staff's published notice and presume any thoughts of rebellion have evaporated. They are soon caught unawares.

By double fluke, the understrength rebels are thwarted in their attack on an undermanned Dublin Castle. Unknown to the Volunteers there's an important meeting upstairs. Under-Secretary Nathan is in discussions with Major Ivor Price, Director of British Military Intelligence in Ireland and Arthur Hamilton-Norway, Secretary of the Irish Postal Service. Dublin Castle wants all telegraph links in Munster cut so the arrested Casement can be brought to Dublin and ushered quietly onto London without fuss. Hamilton-Norway is unaware at this point that his workplace, the GPO, is about to turn into the epicentre of modern Irish history.

Their discussion doesn't get far when they hear shots ring out and James O'Brien, a 45-year-old Dublin Metropolitan Policeman falls, believed to be the first casualty of The Rising. The DMP Chief Commissioner decides to withdraw his unarmed civilian police force to barracks and let the military deal with it.

With key points in the capital under Volunteer control, Nathan, Price and Hamilton-Norway realise the very heart of British administration in Ireland is under attack. Nathan tries to call London direct but he finds the telephone line cut. Managing to get past the cordon at the Castle gates the Under-Secretary reaches the nearest telegraph office. Chief Secretary Birrell gets a telegram delivered to his Elm Park home in London.[25]

Insurrection broke out at noon today in Dublin when attack made on Castle but not pressed home. Soon the large hostile party occupied Stephen's Green and various parties have held up troops marching from barracks firing on them from houses. City Hall, Post Office, Westland Row station occupied by Sinn Féiners. Some railway bridges blown up and telegraphic communication generally interrupted. Have information of two policemen one officer and half a dozen soldiers killed but casualties may be much more numerous. Situation at present not satisfactory but understand troops now beginning to arrive from Curragh.

Nathan

One of the original ambitions for the Irish Volunteers' 1st Battalion is to seal off Broadstone railway station, thereby cutting Dublin's rail links to the West of Ireland. However the confusion over mobilisation has seriously reduced numbers and they simply don't have enough men to take it. They stick to the plan of tight, inter-connected defences. Piaras Béaslaí, Vice-Commandant of 1st Battalion, told an RTÉ television interview many years later:

A portion of 'F' Company, under the command of Lieutenant John Shouldice was stationed at the intersection of Church Street and North King Street. There was a public house at the corner closed and shuttered with the name Reilly over the window which it was decided to occupy. After knocking and getting no answer the Volunteers decided there was nobody there and broke in. I was standing by at the time. Lieutenant Shouldice thought it prudent to ensure that none of his men would be tempted by the liquor. He ordered that all the bottles to be smashed on the ground and this was done.[26]

In his account to the Bureau of Military History Liam Archer, Section Commander of 'F' Company, adds colour to the detail:

We were subjected to a considerable amount of abuse from the residents of the locality, they being of a class which had supplied a large number of recruits to the British regiments.[27]

When the situation threatens to boil over Archer recalls being told by Béaslaí to fix his bayonet.

> I complied, but no sooner had the bright steel appeared when a buxom fishwife, clothed in all the purity of her holiday attire of a white apron and voluminous shawl, promptly stepped from the path in front of me and proceeded in the traditional Dublin manner to work herself into a frenzy by beating her ample bosom with her fists and calling upon me to 'put it through her for the sake of her son who was out in France'. We steered a wide course round the angry dame . . .

Half an hour after the proclamation of the Irish Republic at the GPO the Volunteers at Church Street trade gunfire with a passing group of Lancers escorting a consignment of ammunition to Phoenix Park.

In a rare interview in 1966, Grandpa told John Cauhlan of Boston radio station WNAC:

> There was a bit of excitement there the first day after the British Lancers had charged down O'Connell Street and they were scattered. Some of them rode down the streets from the centre of the city, from where the General Post Office is. They made a terrific clatter, the horses, and we saw we were in the middle of it right away. [28]

According to Béaslaí:

> Volunteers, thinking they were being attacked, fired on them. One Lancer galloping up the up Church Street, firing wildly, and was shot down. The lance of this man was converted by us into a flagpole and planted at the centre of the cross made by Church Street and North King Street. The flag on this pole was not a tricolour but green with a gold harp, a flag provided by Daly on the order of the military council who thought it would more appeal to the public than the tricolour which was

popularly regarded as the Sinn Féin flag. The public house became known as Reilly's Fort and outside on the street fluttered the green flag amid a network of crudely made barricades.

But up at Phoenix Park the order to blow up the army's magazine fort without taking lives 'if possible' has not gone according to plan. The fort commander's family is held captive while the raiding party goes about its mission. With the explosive charge set the raiders withdraw quickly. Instead of the family taking cover as instructed, their teenage son races from the fort to raise the alarm. There is no option but to stop him and no time to think any further. Whatever the purity, even innocence, of rebellion, Garry Houlihan offers an unsentimental insight into the profound consequences of following through on romantic ideals:

> Before we reached the park gate leading in to the Chapelizod Road we noticed a lad of about 17 years of age running from the fort. He went to the policeman on duty in the middle of the road opposite the gate and ran on towards Islandbridge. When he reached the corner of Islandbridge Road he ran towards a house. I followed him on my bicycle and when the hall door opened I fired at him from the gate and shot him.[29]

The young victim, Gerald Playfair, dies from his wounds later that day.

Jack Shouldice's men settle into defensive positions around Reilly's Fort – today a pub called The Tap – at the junction of North King Street and Church Street. They hold a strategic position with the intention of impeding any British troops coming north-south down Constitution Hill from the railway station (now a bus garage) in Broadstone. Reilly's Fort can also block east-west troop movements from the city centre to the Four Courts.

The key vantage point is the granary tower of the Jameson malthouse (since demolished) on Beresford Street. Jack sends his brother Frank and a handful of other sharpshooters up to man it.

Jameson's Distillery in the 1920s – Malthouse situated
centre right of photo (Courtesy of Irish Distillers Pernod Ricard)

'I was transferred to Bow's Distillery under NCO Frank Shoul-dice where I remained until Friday night,' recalls Patrick O'Hanlon. 'I remained (there) until Friday night when we left the building to defend the barricade at North King Street and Bow Lane left uncovered by our wounded comrades.'[30]

The mechanics of The Rising are detailed brilliantly in the late Max Caulfield's definitive work *The Easter Rebellion*, first pub-lished in 1963. Charles Townshend's more recent study (*Easter 1916: The Irish Rebellion*) adds valuable context while Paul O'Brien examines individual battlegrounds in his highly instructive series *1916 in Focus*.

After their opening exchange with the Lancers the next con-frontation at North King Street is more a question of hearts and minds. Insurrection unearths sustained opposition from unex-pected quarters. The way Jack remembers it:

> On the Monday and Tuesday a good number of the lo-cal residents, especially those who had relatives fighting for England in the European war were very antagonis-tic and their womenfolk especially made our fight none the easier. However we gradually got the sympathy or,

if not, the respect of the great majority of the people when they saw for themselves that we were conducting The Rising in a fair and clean manner and with such small numbers against the might of England.

For Chief Secretary of Ireland Augustine Birrell, still in London, update bulletins on The Rising are played out in the shocked staccato of urgent telegrams. The early suggestions from Dublin Castle are that the outbreak is coordinated and more widespread than first thought. Serious flare-ups are reported in Athenry, Enniscorthy, Ashbourne and north county Dublin.

> 25/4 2.22 pm Troops from Curragh. City Hall cleared, Customs House, Trinity College Dublin and several houses on the Green. Otherwise situation in Dublin not much altered since yesterday's telegram.[31]

Awoken from its torpor, the House of Lords registers shock at this 'bolt out of the blue'. Viscount Midleton is not placated by government assurances of order being restored.

> We had a statement to us yesterday afternoon in which it was said that the position in Dublin is 'well in hand'. What does that mean? The previous day, at about twelve o'clock, some of the most important spaces in Dublin were occupied by the Sinn Féin organisation . . . It appears to me to be a situation well in hand on the part of the rebels.[32]

Under-Secretary Nathan keeps Prime Minister Asquith informed.

> 26/4 10.25 am The Sinn Féin position around General Post Office has not yet been attacked but troops are being concentrated for its envelopment . . . House to house fighting is necessarily slow and the troops from England who are all now landed had to overcome a good deal of opposition of this sort on road from Kingstown . . . GOC has asked for further brigade from England

and I trust it will be possible to send this without delay to end present intolerable position.

26/4 11.55 am. Liberty Hall practically destroyed by naval guns and now occupied by military . . . Martial Law has been proclaimed in Dublin city and county.

Jack Shouldice may have his hands full with concerned mothers and truculent postmen but the War Office in London is already mindful of hearts and minds further afield. Casement, now under arrest, is not named in a communiqué from the Under-Secretary but it's clear that he's the big catch and Whitehall has its eye on political reaction the other side of the Atlantic. U.S. President Woodrow Wilson has yet to enter World War One. The last thing London wants arising is grounds for further delay.

26/4 12.14 pm Lord Lieutenant considers it most important that identity of prisoner captured on 21st should be published in Ireland and I am informed that it would be of greatest value to us if this were known at once in America. If War Office will agree please sanction our publishing in Ireland and if possible arrange for publication in America.

Meanwhile, the military operation continues with RIC antennae twitching for fresh ripples outside Dublin. Nathan keeps Birrell advised.

26/4 1.30 pm Cordon of troops now complete near centre of town on north side of river. Last two battalions of troops from England will arrive this afternoon. Small rising Ardee. More serious at Swords and Lusk. . . GOC has asked for additional brigade from England.

26/4 4-5 pm Casualty list received from military now shows following casualties since commencement of operations. Killed 6 officers and 24 men. Wounded 11 offices and 70 men. In addition to three police reported yesterday as killed. One has been wounded.

26/4 8.15 pm No considerable advance has been made in Dublin . . . some of those from England are at Kingsbridge and some held up for a time near Ballsbridge. Have overcome resistance there . . two battalions on their way from Kingstown . . . Most serious report is that 1500 Sinn Féiners from Athenry marching on Athlone. General office informed but cannot spare troops till Dublin dealt with.

While the insurgents and the military are gearing up for full engagement, disorder in the capital offers rich pickings for looters and opportunists. The days do not pass without their own Dublinesque comedy.

The *Evening Herald* reports:

A boy with a hockey stick was seen playing with a golf ball in O'Connell Street. When the ball disappeared he searched the thoroughfare for it with a pair of field glasses. Each of these articles had been looted.[33]

Twenty-five year old Patrick J. Kelly mans the stockade opposite Linenhall Barracks off North King Street.

During the afternoon a woman came to the barricade. She was heavily laden. The load she carried was covered by a shawl. I challenged her and asked what she had. She replied bread for the children. I insisted that she show me what she had. She threw open her shawl and exposed a vast array of silverware, trays, teapots, coffee sets etc. I was at a loss what to do so I allowed her enter a tenement house on Lisburn Street.[34]

At the malthouse 'F' Company member Mort Ó Conaill recalls:

A Dublin cabby came along to me at the distillery on the Wednesday and told me that his horses were starving. I told him he could take what he wanted from the grain stores, which he proceeded to do. He took a 16-stone sack which he hoisted onto his back and thus burdened he made his way down a rickety stairs and went with his sack down the street. We heard no more about him.

Michael O'Flanagan, one of four brothers in action in Easter Week, is posted to Church Street. From the barricades he recalls a resonating image that same afternoon:

> We noticed four or five men and women coming from the direction of Mary's Lane. Between them they were carrying a piano which we concluded they had stolen from some business premises. We called on them to halt but they refused to do so. We fired a few shots over their heads as a warning and they dropped the piano and made off. [35]

Intermittent and uneasy lulls in between bursts of fierce activity off Church Street also leaves plenty of time for half-truths to prosper. There are numerous rumours of the entire country rising up and foreign allies at hand. Charles Shelley of 'G' Company 1st Battalion is almost convinced that 'the Germans had landed and were advancing along the Naas Road.'[36]

By Thursday evening Chief-Secretary Birrell is finally on his way. At twelve minutes to midnight the Home Office telegrams Nathan.[37]

> 26/4 11.48 pm I have just shown your wire to the Prime Minister and took instructions to General French from him with the following result. The following troops will leave Liverpool tomorrow for Kingstown. One field artillery brigade, one infantry brigade, one field company, RT Divisional Squadron and Divisional Headquarters. The remainder of the Division will be concentrated at Liverpool and will be sent off as the situation demands and as transports become available. Kindly inform General French of these arrangements. The Prime Minister wishes the wire here to be kept open during the night and I have arranged accordingly.
>
> Power.

5.

*'The work of the snipers was marvellous – not
many shots were wasted but had a damaging
effect on the morale of the soldiers'*
– Lawrence Ginnell, MP North Westmeath, 1916[38]

The rebels, as they become known, are unrepresentative and unrepentant. For 'F' company the first few days at Reilly's Fort are relatively quiet. Miraculously, bread production continues nearby at Monk's Bakery with armed Volunteers stewarding the hungry queues. The real storm is yet to come and, as John J. Reynolds details in *Four Courts and North King St. Area in 1916*, it is a time of escalating tension.

> The street lamps were all extinguished, leaving the streets in pitchy darkness. The officers went round all the posts, picquets (sic) were sent out, and the sentries were relieved at regular intervals, and all approaching the barricades were challenged until the watchword was given. Throughout the night sounds of desultory firing could be heard in distant parts of the city, and nearer, from the Mendicity Institute and the river front.[39]

Frank and several others stationed up high in the malthouse have easy access to the distillery but Jameson state immediately after The Rising that its stock and its furnishings were left untouched with the exception of a box of quality cigars which found its way to men stationed at the Four Courts. It was a lasting taste for Volunteer and IRB man Con O'Donovan.

> The memory of those cigars regaled me for a whole twelvemonth in Dartmoor and Lewes prisons, where even the smell of cigarette smoke was unknown.[40]

In a departure from its editorial attitude, the *Irish Independent* notes:

> To the credit of the insurgents it must be said that they took no part in looting the city, but, on the contrary, made some efforts to prevent it.[41]

Elsewhere in the city, publishers of the *Irish Life* recount their own travails:

> Our office was in the occupation first of the Sinn Féin-ers and after of the military. Both parties, we are bound to say, behaved like gentlemen and did not commit an atom of wanton damage and very little damage of any sort.[42]

With a portrait of a medal-laden General Maxwell adorning its cover, the editorial, titled 'The Week of Fools', describes their insurgents' actions as 'an honest, however perverted, sense of patriotism'. The matter arises during a House of Lords debate two weeks later when Mayo-born Home Ruler Lord MacDonnell seeks to clarify:

> It is an extraordinary characteristic of this outbreak that outrages were not perpetrated by the rebels. Property of which they took possession was not interfered with. Where there was looting it was done by the people from the slums of Dublin, and I do not think any city in Europe can show slums of more sordid misery.[43]

Within days Frank, Jack and their comrades can hear heavy shelling in O'Connell Street from where huge fires illuminate the city sky. They can also sense superior forces amassing on the streets around them. Nathan telegrams the Home Office.

> 27/4 11.50 am Have just seen General Lowe who tells me that situation in Dublin much the same as last night but that cordon on both sides being completed and strengthened.

Later that same day telegrams are sent to the Home Office to the effect that things are quiet in Derry and Cork but a reported

Irish Life: The Week of Fools

600 Sinn Féin supporters are active in Athenry and Oranmore and 'some trouble is reported in Wexford'. Meanwhile in Dublin the military say 'progress has been made' in tightening the cordon around the GPO but 'strong resistance still continues and there have been various big fires'.

The barricades at North King Street and Church Street, however makeshift, prove very effective. Michael O'Flanagan is ordered to take a few men with him to bolster the line at Reilly's Fort. On arrival at the fortified pub he expresses qualms about how well it can be defended. O'Flanagan asks about an exit strategy and is told there is none. Once his men take up position at the windows live exchanges are continuous. 'As we were proving such an obstacle to enemy forces,' he writes, 'I realised they were prepared to sacrifice any number of men to dislodge us.'

The deadlock is down to a combination of resolute men well-positioned in and around Reilly's Fort and the naiveté of inexperienced troops fighting on tight city streets. It is due equally, as elsewhere in Easter Week, to the ineptitude of several British officers whose confidence in their own ability is matched only by their disregard for the young lives they squander.

Repeating the error made at Lower Mount Street, British officers at North King Street choose to go through obstacles rather than circumnavigate them, thus making a mockery of the numerical advantage they enjoy. It adds grievously to their own casualties. By the end of the week it will take a British force of some 20,000 men across Dublin to force about 1,800 Volunteers into submission. Frank and Jack could hardly have foreseen it at that stage but North King Street would become one of the most intense battle sites of The Rising.

6.

*'We were hoping we would be attacked because it
was such a sound position to defend'*
– John O'Connor, Irish Volunteer at Jameson Distillery[44]

Good Friday's homework is already paying off. The location of barricades and shooting posts indicate Messrs. Shouldice, Lynch and O'Hegarty have chosen well. Despite a shortage of manpower, their latticed network of key defensive placements makes it virtually impossible for British forces to advance.

In the early hours of Friday morning the new military commander arrives. General John Maxwell steps off a navy battleship at North Wall 'and found many buildings in Sackville Street burning fiercely, illuminating the whole city.'[45] He goes directly to British Army HQ at the Royal Hospital in Kilmainham where he is briefed by Brigadier-General William Lowe and Major-General Friend. They stick with the existing plan – a pincer movement that isolates rebel strongpoints in the city and connects a military line from north to south. The British military has vast resources at its disposal and the fight is conducted at such overwhelming odds it perplexes its strategists that it's taking so long to wrap it up.

The difficulty in closing the cordon around the Four Courts is that the streets are angular and tight and the rebels are firmly dug in. Manuals for trench warfare in Belgium and France never looked like this. There are pockets of very strong resistance across the river at Mount Street Bridge and artillery shells are circling the GPO, but in the north inner city the Army can't connect the dots from Capel Street to the Four Courts because Reilly's Fort is in the way.

Volunteer Liam O'Doherty remembers how difficult it was for those inside.

General John Maxwell in Dublin (Courtesy RTÉ Stills Library)

It wasn't possible to move from one room to another except on hands and knees as every window was covered by snipers and owing to the constant fire kept up by them, it was impossible to lean out of the windows to locate them.[46]

Reilly's Fort covers the width of Church Street leading into Bolton Street but the malthouse offers height advantage and exposes the streets below to a withering crossfire.

John J. Reynolds describes the layout in *An t-Óglach*:

The iron stairway leading to the metal, hook-shaped grain elevator on the roof proved a fine point of vantage, being the highest position occupied by the Volunteers. The technical schools in the Bolton Street, Jervis Street Hospital and other elevated building being plainly visible, whilst close beneath was the narrow passage Stirrup Lane joining Beresford Street and Church Street.

The Volunteer fire from the top of the iron stairway, which was barricaded with the bags of bran taken from the Malthouse, as well as fire from the loopholes already formed in the Northern walls by the metal ventilators, swept North King Street beneath by lateral fire.

As the fighting intensifies, the malthouse post plays a key defensive role. In return, it becomes a target. 'F' Company's William Scully recalls that 'Frank Shouldice got a graze under eye in the malthouse trying to dislodge a machine gunner.'[47]

Down at ground level Jack hears of the near-miss.

> One particularly close call was that of my brother Frank who was sniping from a small opening at the top of the malthouse. His attention was called by someone inside the granary and as he turned his head to inquire the cause a bullet grazed his face, hitting the inside of the little window or opening.

An t-Óglach relates it vividly and although Grandpa is not named, he is obviously the Volunteer in question:

> In this post, which was under heavy fire – the metal elevator being riddled with bullets – the bags afforded secure protection to the snipers. A military sniper's bullet entering one of the loopholes brushed so close to the Volunteer in command as to raise an enormous swelling on his face without, however, incapacitating him from action.

A British machine gun nest on top of Jervis Street Hospital (since demolished) strafes the barricades on Church Street and plays havoc with Jack's ground position. With the lives of his brother and comrades at stake the nest becomes Frank's sole focus.

Whatever the strange alchemy that turns a civil servant into a marksman, Grandpa is now required to make that transformation. Some of the obvious attributes – calmness, a good eye, detachment and a steady hand – might win cuddly toys at a fun fair, but midway through the deadly realities of The Rising, hidden enemies all around are trying to take his life.

*Reilly's Fort, now The Tap public house on North King Street
(pictured in 1966)*

The Jervis Street machine gun post spits out spent cartridges, pinning Volunteers at ground level with uninterrupted fire. With the aid of binoculars Frank locates the machine gunner's nest. From his malthouse eyrie Grandpa, the sniper, finds his target with a succession of shots. The machine gun goes quiet, the threat removed.

John J. Reynolds records this key moment in *An t-Óglach*:

> The Volunteers in the Malt House at Beresford Street by means of a powerful field glass discerned a machine-gun on the roof of Jervis Street Hospital playing in May Lane direction. The snipers in the Malt House concentrated their fire on the gun and after some time it was silenced.

In 2014 Tile Films later made a very fine docudrama for TG4 called *A Terrible Beauty* in which brothers Frank and Jack feature significantly in re-enactments of 'F' Company's week. We are used to characters calmly shooting their quarry on screen, but it's a different sensation when that character is one of your own. Viewing it is an uncomfortable experience although any sense of guilt readily dissipates when life has been reduced to a choice of shoot or be shot.

In the film Grandpa (played by actor Colin Farrell) lines up the sight along his rifle and coolly eliminates a British Army machine-gun post. Four consecutive kills feels a little Ramboesque and di-lutes factual truth with dramatic licence. In real life, however, I am proud that Grandpa's comrades could count on him. I am also relieved that he got there first.

On a rare foray to the neighbourhood many later years Grandpa took my brother Ronan to the old distillery and pointed out where he fired from and where he was almost killed. The malthouse was still standing at the time, its pock-marked wall behind the stairwell bearing witness to where Grandpa's luck held out.

Thinking back on these events I wonder how he felt about it afterwards. Whether his reluctance to speak about it derived from seeing through field glasses what happened when bullets he fired entered another man's flesh and bone. The last look on the faces of his victims. At a less philosophical level it made me wonder when he learned to shoot. Where in Dublin might a budding sniper go to practice?

For nearly two years Volunteers were constantly training and drilling and learning to handle rifles in various halls around the city. But there had to be more to it than John J. Scollan's recollec-tions as Commandant of the Hibernian Rifles in Dublin:

> We improvised broom handles to act as rifles and with
> these we practised aiming at targets.[48]

Capt. Sean Prendergast, who became O/C of 'C' Company, 1st Battalion Dublin Brigade, ran a firing range for Volunteers, re-markably, right in the city centre. Using the basement of the Irish National Forester's Hall in 41 Parnell Square – presently derelict – Volunteers could fire away without fear of being heard. It all took place underground, beneath the hard clip of horses hooves and uphill trundle of heavy carts. Despite numerous raids of the build-

*British troops under sniper fire off Parnell Street, Dublin
(Courtesy Kilmainham Gaol Museum)*

ing by police and soldiers over the years the shooting gallery was never discovered.

Prendergast stated to the Bureau:

> I was placed in charge of the Company rifle range to instruct and supervise shooting practice. This was carried out in the basement of '41'. We fired with a .22 bore miniature rifle . . . at the rate of a penny for five rounds. Every parade night, which was generally on Thursday of each week, would see a number of men testing their skill . . .

> The portion of the basement set aside for shooting – a long narrow passage – could not boast any form of lighting, at least not where the target was, and so we had to procure candles, one of which had to be placed very near the target area. That was where the fun arose, as generally the rifle shots fired close to it snuffed out the candle. It was trying, yet funny, having to work under such conditions. But why complain when man had to be trained to shoot?[49]

There were exceptional cases – like Newry-born Patrick Rankin who trained at a rifle range in Philadelphia in 1914. Inspired by a clarion call made in person by Roger Casement at the Irish Club, the 27-year-old tradesman returned to Ireland, improbably smuggling 600 rounds of ammunition through customs along with his personally licensed 22-bore Stevens rifle.[50]

But Grandpa didn't have to go to Philadelphia – he didn't even have to go into town. 'F' Company held target practice in Fairview every Sunday at Fr. Matthew Park just off Windsor Villas. Frank and Jack lived nearby in The Crescent. The venue served as a training ground for the Irish Volunteers and Cumann na mBan while the Irish Citizen Army had their own firing range in Croydon Park up the road.

Local Volunteer Harry Colley, who joined 2nd Battalion, told the Bureau:

> Each Sunday evening at about four o'clock, we had rifle practice in Fr. Matthew Park. 'F' Company men were all very keen and usually all members of the Company attended and went through their courses with a Martini Mauser and .22 ammunition. We paid twopence for five rounds and were not allowed to spend more than fourpence owing to the scarcity of ammunition. Occasionally, if rifles were available, we would practice volley-firing on a swinging tin can.[51]

The Volunteers had another shooting range southside in Larkfield. At a time when Dublin Castle was alive to any threat of sedition it seems incredible that a political group growing paramilitary horns was allowed hold its own version of Sunday service – shooting practice in local fields.

Two years previously, James Nowlan, President of the GAA and future prisoner at Frongoch, told GAA players to 'join the Volunteers' and 'learn to shoot straight.'[52]

Judging by Colley's remarks to the Bureau of Military History, many took Nowlan up quite literally.

We started to play football every Sunday in Fr. Matthew Park after rifle practice.

With the insurrectionist temperature rising a store room in Fr Matthew Park became HQ for Dublin Brigade's 2nd Battalion. Just weeks before The Rising the DMP staged a raid. Colley recounts Lieut. Oscar Traynor and two brothers, Mick and Kit Ennis, standing at the park entrance with rifles loaded.

> . . . (he) ordered the police to halt. The rest of us he lined along with the wall with our revolvers which, at that stage, we always carried. I had a .32 revolver at that time and 12 rounds of ammunition. Lieut. Traynor sent out word immediately to gather in other Volunteers. The police halted and then commenced to advance. He stepped to the gate and called out in a loud voice, 'Halt, not one step further, or I order fire!' They halted, and then retired.[53]

When the call went out Colley and Traynor say that about 200 Volunteers – including Thomas McDonagh and The O'Rahilly – swarmed into Fr. Matthew Park from Fairview and beyond. We don't know if Frank and Jack were among them but we do know the DMP withdrew and never came back.

That standoff seems a long time ago. By Wednesday of Easter Week the Volunteers at North King Street must wonder if they will get out of this alive. They have inflicted and suffered loss and injury on a scale none of them have experienced before. There is no going back. John J. Reynolds is told by eyewitnesses how:

> . . . the whole burning area became a roaring furnace, the barrels of oil being projected high into the air and exploding with a loud report. At night a pin could be picked up by the glare overspreading the surrounding streets. On Friday the fire subsided, the dying flames flickering at intervals in lurid and fitful flashes before they were finally extinguished. Towards the end of the week the severest fighting was carried on in pitch darkness, which completely enveloped the narrow streets

now entirely deserted save by those engaged in the grim work of death.

But despite the risks and dangers all around them they are a collection of men and women bound and inspired by a rare unity of purpose. It registers with Ignatius Callender, a messenger for 'D' company, while making his own hazardous rounds.

> The spirits of the lads behind the barricades were simply astonishing, notwithstanding the anxious times through which they were passing. The want of sleep, the anxiety for dear ones at home and many other hardships they were always full of fun and enjoyed any joke passed on. They were wonderful![54]

From Dublin Castle, Under-Secretary Nathan keeps the Home Office apprised of developments.

> 28/4 10.31pm In Wexford Enniscorthy still held strongly by rebels . . . have no authentic information of situation in Dublin or of general disposition of troops.

The military cordon tightens but is still unable to breach North King Street. *An t-Óglach* captures the fatal drama as resistance reaches its fifth day:

> On Friday night within an ambit of a few yards round Reilly's Fort was fought a combat of frightful intensity. As the military approaching from Bolton Street attempted to push through to Church Street this Volunteer stronghold and the barricade in front bore the brunt of the first attack. Reilly's Fort was not visible, owing to a bend in the road, until a point is reached only some 50 yards from the building, when they at once came under close fire. Here they were met with a galling fusillade from Reilly's further back, and laterally, by the enfilading fire from the Malt House in Beresford Street.

Led by Lieutenant-Colonel Henry Taylor, two South Staffordshire battalions saturate the area. Launching attacks from their base in Bolton Street technical college they make use of an improvised armoured car that serves as a troop carrier. It's unbearably noisy for soldiers inside it but using the vehicle as cover to drop troops into position they force entry into the houses on North King Street. Once inside, they can tunnel through walls to advance unseen up along the street. Civilians cowering in Number 172, Sally Hughes' house, soon find themselves at the mercy of a military barely in control of itself.

The *Evening Herald* reports:

> Mr McCarthy, who was manager of the Lord Mayor's business premises in Dame Street, was shot dead in North King Street in the presence of his wife and child. He was in no way connected with the insurgents.[55]

A total of fourteen unarmed males unconnected with the Volunteers are separated from their families and murdered in these houses before the atrocity is swept under a very bloodstained carpet.

Peadar Lawless, who Jack and Frank met in Smithfield on Easter Monday, is shot dead alongside three other men in Number 27. According to War Office records, a British soldier at the scene remarked, 'The little man made a great struggle for his life and tried to throw himself out of the window, but we got him.'[56]

Little do the Volunteers nearby know what terror is being played out on innocents in the neighbourhood around them. Capt. Lynch told a BBC interview decades later:

> Shouldice's area especially, at the corner of North King Street, was under very heavy fire. The heavy fighting lasted until the surrender practically. The soldiers broke through from house to house, burrowed through and we discovered long afterwards of course – long afterwards – that every man found in the houses . . . who knew nothing about us and were not connected with the thing at all, were unfortunately shot by the military.[57]

When Jack subsequently hears that Peadar Lawless is among the victims he recalls with regret the young man's decision not to join 'F' Company on Monday. The case is raised specifically by Cork MP Tim Healy, quizzing Prime Minister Asquith.

> *Healy*: . . . if General Maxwell has called for any report on the murders of persons unconnected with the rebellion in North King Street, Dublin; will he ascertain if, at the Louth Dairy, kept by Mrs. Mary Lawless, 27, North King Street, from which no sniping or offence was directed at the military, a number of soldiers came to search the premises and, having turned Mrs. Lawless into the street, arrested her son and three other Louth men, named Finnegan, Hoey, and McCartney; whether a sentry was then placed on the premises; were these four men shot in the room and buried in the yard by the soldiers, no arms being found in the house or on the persons of the prisoners; were the bodies dug up by Mrs. Lawless and found to have been stripped of watches, rings, and money; if it is alleged that the troops were fired on from the house, why was Mrs. Lawless not arrested or her son given a trial? To what

The smouldering remains of Linenhall Barracks off North King Street
(Courtesy NLI Archive)

regiment did the sentry placed on the premises belong? And what opportunity will be given of establishing or investigating the facts by some independent authority?

Tennant: A court of inquiry is being held to investigate the occurrence and all the circumstances of the case.

Ginnell: Will it be an open court, to which the public will be admitted?

Asquith: I had better have notice of that question.

The 'inquiry' leads nowhere and the sad, irony endures that someone trying to escape violence should meet his fate in cold blood. 'If only he had joined us he'd probably have survived,' rues Jack for many years afterwards.

Unaware of the grisly murder of civilians only up the road, the Volunteers bring Friday to a boisterous, celebratory finale. They have held the line against all odds. Drunk with fatigue and a real sense of accomplishment they feel they can handle whatever comes next. Suddenly, from the malthouse above, a fine baritone breaks into 'The Pride of Petravore'. At ground level Jack recognises the choice of song and knows immediately his young brother's voice. It's followed by 'The Men of the West', picked up in chorus by men at the barricades. Rebel anthems peal into the night, further infuriating Colonel Taylor and his stalled progress.

Taylor calls for a fresh assault. Before dawn on Saturday he orders Major J. Sheppard to take four platoons from 'C' Company and swarm Reilly's Fort with a fixed-bayonet charge on the barricades. When Sheppard's men come into view they are met with a powerful volley from the barricade. Sheppard himself falls, wounded. The soldiers panic and break off into Beresford Street, all under Frank's watching eye from the malthouse above. Saying more than he ever said publicly about the event, Grandpa told author Max Caulfield many years later:

> Our fellows at Reilly's were firing into them and some more from six cottages then being built on waste ground on our left. About fifteen Tommies turned into Beresford Street right under me. I was on the iron

platform and all I had to do was fire down upon them. One by one we knocked them all over. It was a terrible slaughter and to this day I can't understand why they decided to rush things.

British soldiers search for arms in Tolka River, Ballybough
(Courtesy NLI Archive)

Assisting Max Caulfield's research for *The Easter Rebellion* Frank and Jack brought the author down to North King Street to explain the geometric frenzy of those six days and six nights in April, 1916. Tom Sheerin, Garry Holohan and Joseph Brady also met with Caulfield. The veterans spoke about facing Taylor's renewed assault and express some sympathy for the foot soldiers charging at them.

They do not see these troops as the real adversary. Rather, for many Volunteers, it is inept British Army officers who represent everything detestable about the Crown. 'If they'd kept boring through the walls, creeping up on us gradually we'd have stood no chance,' remarked Sheerin. 'Some officer, however, clearly lost his head and sent those lads out to their death.'

Watching it happen, Capt. Lynch was almost incredulous:

Some of the soldiers, who appeared to be either very stupidly led, or if they were led at all, they came through the last house before Cuckoo Lane. They turned into Cuckoo Lane on the double, about a dozen of them and this was completely under our fire. Frank Shouldice, Lieutenant Shouldice's brother, was in the malthouse just covering the place – absolutely. The lads were wiped out in no time.

It was of course a tragic thing in many ways. One had to be sorry for them. They were young boys. In fact Lieut. Shouldice told me when he went up to collect the rifles with the others he heard one lad saying, 'Oh Mammy, Mammy. . .' which was terrible.

Three weeks later Edgar E. James from Caerau in Wales writes to the *Glamorgan Gazette* to mark those fatal moments 'when my son, Trooper W.F. Moy James, 3rd Glamorgan Yeomanry, was mortally wounded' at North King Street.

Under fire from 'the Sinn Féiners, who had secretly congregated in the houses on both sides of the street' two soldiers were hit – one in the leg 'and my son, who was shot just above the heart. After falling he was carried into a house close by, and attended to by an old Irish lady whose tenderness will never be forgotten. He kept calling for water.'

The soldier, who died four hours later at Richmond Hospital, was aged 17.

Though clearly a rout – and a resounding success in military terms – the killing spree on Dublin streets that morning does not leave Jack Shouldice untroubled. Some 47 years after the event certain sounds and images will not go away.

When the last of those young fellows was knocked over, we leaped over the barricade in Beresford Street and ran out into the road and picked up their rifles and ammunition. One young fellow still alive was moaning pitifully for his mother but what could I do to help him?

7.

*'We had noticed a decided waning off in the sounds
of rifle shots that afternoon. It was quite easy for us
to distinguish between the report of the 'Howth' rifle
and of its smaller brother, the Lee Enfield. We all knew
that the supply of ammunition for the 'Howth' was
very limited, and wondered how long it would hold
out. But that rifle made a cheery sound for us, for we
knew that it was not being used by the English'*
– Con O'Donovan, Dublin Brigade
1st Battalion, 'F' Company

From that point on Lieut-Col. Taylor's men advance incremen-
tally but at very high cost. Volunteers on the outer barricades
at Church Street grudgingly pull back closer to Reilly's Fort but
'F' Company continues to hold the line from Church Street down
to the Four Courts. Given the sheer weight of numbers it is just a
matter of time. As General Maxwell notes in his 25-point report to
Field-Marshal John French:

> The troops had a trying time dealing with the numer-
> ous snipers, who became very troublesome during
> the hours of darkness. Owing to the considerable op-
> position at barricades, especially in North King Street,
> it was not until 9 a.m. on the 29th April that the Four
> Courts area was completely surrounded.[58]

With ammunition running out two young Volunteers – Patrick O'Flanagan and Edward Delamere – scamper down Church
Street to try re-supply the unit. On their way back O'Flanagan, 24,
is fatally hit in the doorway to Reilly's Fort. Jack tends to the dying
man inside the bullet-shattered premises. 'We managed to bring

his body into the shop and found that he was in possession of a number of slings of ammunition and two home-made grenades,' Michael O'Flanagan told the Bureau of Military History. 'Incidentally, Volunteer O'Flanagan was my brother.'

Piaras Béaslaí feels the same wonder decades later:

> I spent the night at the barricade above the church praying that the gallant band at Riley's Fort would be able to hold out. Day dawned and still the indomitable little band held their own. They were under fire most of the time for fifteen or sixteen hours. I was shocked at their haggard ghastly appearance showing the strain they had been under.[59]

Reilly's Fort cannot be defended any longer. Perilously low on everything that might keep them alive, Jack and Lieut. Maurice Collins, both teammates at Geraldines GAA club, weigh up the options and know they must withdraw. Jack writes:

> Through death, wounds and illness and, I may add, exhaustion after nearly two days of continuous defence of the position, our little garrison had been reduced to 7 or 8 wearied-out and almost stupefied men, some of us with practically no sleep since Wednesday. With no rest possible, ammunition nearly gone and no sign of reinforcements . . . it was decided to fall back to the next barricade on Church Street.

Frank and F.X. Coughlan protect the retreat with covering fire from the tower in St. Michan's Church. As Tom Sheerin tells Max Caulfied, 'We were simply past being frightened by then.'

Jack is ordered to rest along with his exhausted men at the Four Courts. Using scholarly tomes plucked from the law library as pillows they sleep instantly. The wounded are treated at Fr. Matthew Hall.

From North Brunswick Street the Holohan brothers – Patrick and Garry – make a strong attempt to recapture Reilly's Fort. The British troops who took it are now cut off from their regiment but hang in until reinforcements arrive. The chaotic pendulum of street fighting swings both ways through a Saturday afternoon pierced by sniper exchanges. The casualty rate climbs on both sides.

Béaslaí continues:

> The British then occupied the building and proceeded to pour a heavy fire on us. Then ensued a thrilling incident . . . the green flag on the lance remained standing through all the firing all night and was still there when the garrison of Reilly's Fort retreated. Eamonn Tierney, a Volunteer from London, climbed over the barricades, advanced under heavy fire to the North King Street cross, seized the pole and the flag and returned them to us.

Word reaches the Four Courts that surrender by Commander-in-Chief Pearse is imminent. All that's left to be discussed is terms. Comdt. Daly convenes his officers and tells them heavily that it's all over. The men are to lay down arms and give themselves up. Jack then hears that surrender will be unconditional.

> This was the cause of an outburst amongst the men and some of the officers who replied they would fight on sooner than surrender . . . the men who had protested, overwrought, and some in tears, then proceeded to smash their arms or render them useless for further action.[60]

In a series of interviews to mark the 50th anniversary of The Rising, Béaslaí, second in command at the Four Courts, told RTÉ:

> I went out and saw the place surrounded by British soldiers and Daly surrendering his sword to a British officer. He returned to the building, summoned me to a private room and showed me Pearse's order to surrender. Then he burst into tears.

Béaslaí saw that even though the Volunteers are raw with fatigue some remain strongly opposed to capitulating. Reluctantly, under Comdt. Daly's command, they hand in their guns. But Mort Ó Conaill notices Béaslaí himself in a vexed and emotional state.

When Béaslaí was being disarmed they tried to take his sword from him but he refused to hand it over. Breaking it on his knee he shouted, 'Long Live the Irish Republic!'

O'Connell Street in ruins at end of Easter Week
(Courtesy RTÉ Stills Library)

A couple of dog-tired Volunteers sleep through the historic moment. Having found a quiet nook of the Four Courts to rest their weary bones they somehow remain undiscovered. Nothing – not even the drama outside – disturbs their slumber. The two men awaken on Sunday to find their comrades gone and everything strangely silent around them. They dust themselves down and find their way home.

Back up at North Brunswick Street Garry Holohan is preparing his men for a fresh assault on Reilly's Fort. He has not received any order to surrender and his brother Patrick, commanding officer, is very sceptical when he hears it. Capuchin monks Fr Aloyisius and Fr Augustine intercede to arrange a temporary truce from 7.30

p.m. on Saturday to 10.00 a.m. Sunday. For all, it's an opportunity to remove the dead, treat the wounded and simply get some rest. When Patrick Holohan learns that Pearse's order is genuine he has to break the news on Sunday morning to his 58 unbowed comrades.

The Easter Rising is over and Under-Secretary Nathan finally dictates a telegram to the Home Office with words he's waited all week to say.

> April 30 – The surrender of part of Dublin rebels last evening.

Liam Archer remembers 'F' Company being ordered to line up for a march under escort to the Rotunda Hospital off Parnell Square. He recalls their wounded comrade, Arthur Shiels:

> . . . whose wounded arm was strapped to some form of suspension from the top of his bed, attempted to tear himself loose in order to reach the window and give one last cheer to our comrades. I do not think he succeeded in doing so and in silence and sadness he heard the muffled tramp of the remnant of our force entering captivity. This ended Easter Week for me.

Debris and cars litter O'Connell Street
(Courtesy Kilmainham Gaol Museum)

The Volunteers are under no illusion of how unpopular they are. In a strange twist that must have prompted its own soul-searching these captured Irishmen need the protection of British soldiers to save them from the ire of the people they were trying to liberate. 'Those British soldiers saved us from our own people,' a bemused Volunteer John O'Connor told RTÉ in 1966.

Fionnán Lynch recalls the day after surrendering:

> From the laneways the women and some men too were shouting at the military to bayonet them! The crowd were extremely hostile – there is no question about it we were not very popular at that stage of proceedings.

In warm sunshine 'F' Company's beleaguered fighters, who had held the line against the South Staffordshire regiment, join the Four Courts garrison in a march under bayonets to the Rotunda. The men have seen huge fires burning from afar but up close, Jack and others are struck by the sheer scale of destruction.

> From the GPO to O'Connell Bridge on both sides of the street the buildings were smouldering, also a good portion of Lower and Middle Abbey Street. The bodies of some civilians shot during the week were lying about also a few horses about O'Connell Street. The heart of the city presented a picture of utter desolation.

Volunteers from 'F' Company are marched through the Coombe, bound for Richmond Barracks (now Keogh Barracks), erstwhile base of the Royal Irish Regiment in Inchicore. Two drunks fall into step with the prisoners and end up in detention. Robert Holland tells the Bureau:

> We also had for some weeks an unfortunate seaman, a Swede, who was picked up on O'Connell Street during Easter Week. He had endless trouble convincing them he was not an Irishman as he could not speak a word of English.[61]

They are all left in the open at the Rotunda overnight. Patrick Rankin, who fought at the GPO, remembers:

When morning came there were three or four of my companions lying on top of me and others likewise. The church bells were ringing, calling the faithful. An old woman passed by saying, 'God bless you boys.' I thanked God for one kind person that morning.[62]

Mort Ó Conaill from Cahirciveen, County Kerry, sees Volunteers manhandled by British soldiers after surrendering. 'We were generally abused by the populace and pelted with refuse,' wrote Ó Conaill. Matters improve somewhat when the Dublin Fusiliers step in to escort the rebels back to Richmond Barracks but public anger has not subsided. For Rankin, the march down O'Connell Street, along the quays, through Kilmainham and on to Richmond, gives the Volunteers a presentiment that the worst is yet to come.

During the march not one person was to be seen at a door or window . . . As we arrived near the barracks things began to get a little bit more sharper as Dublin's worst was let loose from their stockades, the women being the worst. They looked like a few who were around during the French Revolution.

Irish Volunteers held at Richmond Barracks prior to deportation

Wearily, Patrick J. Kelly, a 25-year-old sharpshooter stationed around Church Street with 'G' Company, trudges into Richmond Barracks.

> Seated along the floor by the wall I noticed Comdt. MacDonagh and Comdt E. Daly. They looked tired and sad. As I looked at Comdt. Daly he gave me a sad smile and that was the last I ever saw of him.

All prisoners are fingerprinted by detectives from Dublin Castle's 'G' Division. Many are relieved of money, watches, jewellery, cigarettes by soldiers. Grandpa regards himself 'fortunate' not to have been fleeced. 'A whole lot of stuff and money was taken on other fellows, and claims for same have been sent in – but there's no result just yet,' he wrote to his mother, weeks later.[63]

Rankin also observes that none of the valuables are returned.

> I am sorry to say quite a few fell for this mean trick. One man beside me put a hand in his pocket to hand his watch over when I told him to wait until he was going to be shot.

> We were seated around the floor in the gymnasium when a party of 'G' men arrived, each with a large flower in the buttonhole of his coat. One would imagine that they were going to a wedding as they were all smiles.

Anyone identified as having a leadership role is taken aside for further questioning. Courts-martial await. The vindictive manner of some 'G' men, especially towards elderly Tom Clarke and Sean MacDiarmada, is observed by prisoners in bitter silence. These public humiliations are entered into a ledger of war where individual actions will be held to account. Balance will be restored in the form of retributions. On a date unspecified any 'G' man deemed to have acted with excessive cruelty towards prisoners at the Rotunda or Richmond will some day in the future pay with his life.

General Maxwell is keen to preserve the name of the British Army and limit any damage to his own professional reputation. In a summary of the conflict he refers to an 'ambush' at Mount

Captured Volunteers under escort along Eden Quay before being shipped out to jails in Britain (Courtesy RTÉ Stills Library)

Street Bridge. By this he means 31 Sherwood Foresters killed and 145 injured in sustained fighting with seven Volunteers under the command of Lieut. Michael Malone – Malone loses his life during exchanges of incomparable intensity.

Maxwell suggests instead that North King Street saw 'by far the worst fighting that occurred in the whole of Dublin. At first the troops, coming from one end of the street, were repulsed. And it was only when we made an attack from both sides that we succeeded, after twenty-four hours fighting, in capturing the street. The casualties were very heavy during this fighting. The troops were continually fired at from the roofs and upper windows of the houses.' For Fionnán Lynch, years later, Maxwell's backhanded compliment was 'the finest tribute that could be paid to my men.'

The Shouldice brothers are separated. Frank is lined up for deportation while Jack, as an officer, is taken to Kilmainham Jail to await his fate. Neither man knows what is ahead of them and it will be several weeks before one has any idea if the other is even alive. It will be more than year before they see each other again.

8

'I wouldn't have missed it for the world'
– Tom Sheerin, 1st Battalion, 'F' Company, Dublin Brigade

Having arrested and detained over 2,500 rebels the immediate difficulty for the British authorities is where to put them. Old Victorian jails in England and Wales are already full to capacity but the authorities are keen to trim the number of Irish suspects and deport whoever is left. Another pressing need is to conduct military trials of 88 officers (including Jack) – that number will grow to 187. Maxwell's enthusiasm for arresting suspects is creating a backlog.

The Home Office does not want its civil courts clogged up with hundreds of cases involving Irish republicans so it establishes an alternative legal process whereby the prisoners can be interned without trial. Emergency legislation introduced at the outset of World War One, the Defence of the Realm Act (DORA), offers a ready solution.

General Childs at the War Office in London cables General Byrne at Irish Command HQ in Dublin that Asquith wants 'combing out innocents processed with vigour. Home Secretary wants those who are to be interned got out of prisons and into camps as soon as possible.'[64]

General Byrne says 12 barristers are working full-time on the detainees and he hopes to 'get through combing out of the innocents at the rate of 150 a day.'[65] Once 'all the trumpery cases will have been eliminated' those that remain can be interned.

Grandpa and other Volunteers are arranged into groups and escorted to Dublin port. Joe Lawless, who had fought at the GPO with his company from Swords, recalls the more surreal aspects of the march through town.

Down the north quays we swung, glad of the opportunity to exercise our cramped muscles, through the eerie silence of the city around us, echoing the march of our tramping feet, gave a queer sense of unreality to the scene. Not a light was visible though it was now almost dark; no sign of any living soul could be glimpsed even at the windows of the houses. It seemed indeed a deserted city.[66]

The Irish prisoners are transported cross-channel from North Wall to Holyhead. With German U-boats active in the Irish Sea at the time torpedo attack presents a very real danger. However the lives of Irish Volunteers do not merit second consideration.

Lifejackets on the transporter *Slieve Bloom* are distributed to their captors but seldom to the prisoners, some of whom are quartered among frightened cattle. Man and animal would frequently submit to seasickness, often without water for relief.

Lawless recalls:

> The holds of the cattle boat on which we travelled were pretty crowded and intolerably stuffy, but hatches were fastened down and we had to make the best of it. Guards stood at the narrow companionways blocking most of what little air could get in that way and the final misery was the discovery after a little while that the water in the taps available to us had been turned off at the main supply.

Similarly for IRB man Capt. Liam Tannam of 'E' Company, 3rd Battalion, shipped out June 6:

> On the way down by Capel Street Bridge I heard some encouraging cries from some people. This came as a great surprise for my last memory of people had been an unhappy one. I had experienced some of the spitting through the windows of the GPO. We were embarked on a cattle boat in filthy surroundings and tightly crammed; almost everyone vomiting under these conditions.[67]

Frank Burke of 'E' Company is one of the lucky ones. He is handed a lifebelt.

> Our first thoughts naturally turned to submarines. It would have been so convenient to get rid of so many and blame the atrocity on the Germans! I fell asleep, not caring much at the time whether I was under or over the water. When I awoke we were in Holyhead. From there we were put on a train for Stafford Gaol.[68]

The rebels are dispersed in prisons around England, Scotland and Wales. The immediate reaction is to portray them as brave but misguided, an unflattering characterisation that sits plump and unchallenged for far too long. To a chorus of boos at the House of Commons Irish parliamentarian John Dillon declares, 'I am proud of these men. They were foolish, they were misled,'[69] a contradictory tribute replicated to bemused relatives by the Auxiliary Bishop of Dublin Dr Eamonn Walsh at a state commemoration of Easter Week in Arbour Hill in 2014.

While Lawless and Tannam are bound for Knutsford Prison after Holyhead, Grandpa and Frank Burke are bound for Stafford, a military prison near Wolverhampton. All Mort Ó Conaill remembers about getting the train from Holyhead to Stafford is that he could finally sleep.

> Inside the prison, ensconced in my cell, I was given a mug of lukewarm cocoa and some bread. It tasted delicious. I never enjoyed food or drink in the same degree before or since.

As home of the South Staffordshire regiment who suffered heavy casualties in Dublin – as well as executing civilians – some incoming prisoners face the ire of angry locals lining Stafford's streets. Patrick Colgan, who fought at the GPO, recalls one woman pelting them with herrings:

> When we got into the prison – a most forbidding place it appeared – a batch of prisoners were marched either side of a stairway and ordered to turn inwards. I was

a good bit back in the group . . . with the next group I went upstairs to the second landing . . . I stepped into cell 2/2. When the door closed on me I felt as if I was enclosed in a tomb. I tried the door, which was studded with bolts and closed flat with the wall. It was the first time since I left home that I felt defeated and depressed.[70]

Frank and his fellow prisoners are stripped naked and searched. When they get dressed undergarments are not allowed. They are placed alone in their cells and face an indeterminate period of solitary confinement. One of the sentries makes a point of pausing outside each cell while 'nibbling on a banana to annoy us.'[71] The first week it rains every day. Only when the weather is dry each prisoner is allowed one hour's exercise, walking the yard in a pre-ordained circle. No talking or communication is permitted. No mail is allowed, in or out and no visits either. The men are cut off from the world outside. Sometimes when parade is called the

Sketch by Irish prisoner Fionntáin Ó Múrcadha of cell at HMP Stafford, July 1916. Filling each other's autograph books with poems and drawings was a regular feature of prison life. Caption says, 'Home was never like this.'

prisoners find themselves inspected by visiting officials from Dublin Castle. The search for ringleaders goes on.

Frank has no idea that his brother Jack is being court-martialled in Dublin. The prisoners are being moved constantly from one jail to another. Good information is very hard to come by and the authorities are not disposed to keeping their charges – or families – up to date.

Already, however, there is a sense of public sentiment at home turning in their favour. Gerald Doyle, Frank's clubmate from Geraldines, is court-martialled after capture at the South Dublin Union. When Doyle is taken from Richmond he notices a crowd gathered outside the barracks. Arriving at Kilmainham there's an even bigger crowd outside the jail. The onlookers are moody and wordless before the shout goes out, 'Up the rebels!'

Doyle is sentenced to three years penal servitude in England. He is taken to North Wall to be deported. Standing on the boat another prisoner, William O'Dea, spots his fiancé on the quayside – the couple were due to marry on Easter Monday. O'Dea still holds the wedding ring in his pocket and asks a British Army sergeant to bring it down to his betrothed. In what could pass as a rehearsal for *Crocodile Dundee*, the sergeant kindly obliges, uniting the girl with the ring and raising a big cheer from those around her.

Gerald Doyle's next stop will be Portland Prison in Dorset where he will be joined by Lynch, Béaslaí, Richard Coleman and many others. In Portland they will experience night raids by a German zeppelins bombing the naval base nearby. His Majesty's homegrown convicts are moved to the basement cells for safety; the Irish prisoners are left where they lie.

9.

'Sir John Maxwell's work in Ireland is only half done.
A conspiracy which has been growing and spreading
for years – which, encouraged by the apathy of a feeble
Government has permeated nearly every department
of Irish life – cannot be destroyed by ten days fighting
in the streets of Dublin. Ireland needs a thorough
clearance of all her elements of disaffection . . . the fact
is that martial law has come as a blessing to us all'
– Irish Times, 10 May 1916

With Chief Secretary Birrell and Under-Secretary Nathan in disgrace the military in Ireland, under General Maxwell, takes control. Still smarting from a drubbing by what he sees as an unruly, disloyal rabble, Maxwell is keen to administer colonial justice in its swiftest, most lethal form. To quieten the revolutionary clamour he wants court-martials fast-tracked so that leaders of the insurrection can be executed as quickly as possible.

Within weeks fifteen men are executed by firing squad – Thomas Kent will be shot in Cork but all others are taken to the stone courtyard at Kilmainham. It is an act which, more than anything, transforms The Rising and its aftermath.

All courts martial are carried out *in camera* so that each case is dealt with quickly and invisibly. In one of the many thumbprints he leaves on Irish history post-Rising, General Maxwell signs the charge forms himself.

As First Lieutenant of 'F' company 1st Battalion Dublin Brigade Jack is deemed to have played a senior role. Under Schedule 43 'John Shouldice' goes before a court-martial on May 2 at Kilmainham Jail charged as follows:

Did an act to wit did take part in an armed rebellion and in the waging of war against His Majesty the King, such act being of such a nature as to be calculated to be prejudicial to the Defence of the Realm and being done with intention and for the purpose of assisting the enemy.

Jack pleads 'not guilty' to a court-martial presided over by Col. E.W. Maconchey. Years later in his account to the Bureau of Military History, Jack reflects:

The trials were obviously a farce. A young British soldier who was a prisoner in the GPO swore that he saw Con O'Donovan and myself (we were tried together) in the active fighting in the GPO. Con was in the Four Courts and I was in North King Street, Church Street area the whole week.

Detectives from 'G' Division confirm the two men as prominent Volunteers. Pending sentence, both men are placed in Kilmainham cell #88, next to Eamon de Valera. Located on the third floor the cell is vacated by Michael Mallin and Eamonn Ceannt who face execution the following day – in fact Jack and Con pass the condemned men in the passageway as Mallin and Ceannt are taken to cell #20 on the ground floor.

In a premature endorsement of Maxwell's response John Redmond tells the House of Commons:

This outbreak, happily, seems to be over. It has been dealt with with firmness, which was not only right but it was the duty of the Government to so deal with it. As the rebellion, or the outbreak – call it what you like – has been put down with firmness, I do beg the Government – and I speak from the very bottom of my heart and with all my earnestness, not to show undue hardship or severity to the great masses of those who are implicated.[72]

It is ironic but telling that the most perceptive parliamentary contribution comes from Attorney-General Edward Carson who, two years earlier, sourced guns in Germany for the Ulster Volunteer Force to oppose the British Government over Home Rule.

> It would be a mistake to suppose that any true Irishman calls for vengeance. It will be a matter requiring the greatest wisdom and the greatest coolness, may I say, in dealing with these men, and all I say to the Executive is, whatever is done, let it not be done in a moment of temporary excitement, but with due deliberation in regard both to the past and to the future.[73]

Correspondence between Field-Marshal French – relieved the previous year of his command at Mons – and General Maxwell suggests Asquith is quite satisfied with how things have gone. It also implies that captured rebels may be conscripted for the British Army.

> My Dear Maxwell,
>
> Your letter of May 1 – we are all very pleased with the progress of events in Ireland. I must agree with all you say, except with the disposal of these Sinn Féiners who are not to be severely punished. We shall have to think carefully before we mix them up with Troops in the field. As regards the Countess Markievicz I have put the matter before the PM and am now awaiting his decision which will be wired to you at once. Personally I agree with you – she might be shot . . . you shouldn't fear any political or other interference if I can possibly help it . . . I have communicated your messages to the King and have asked His Majesty to send a wire of congratulation to you and the Troops. You well deserve it. As regards your own position I have arranged with the GS that you are to be GOC in C in Ireland and are to have the military rank of General.
>
> As regards your wire reporting the Trial & Execution of the 3 rebel leaders and the punishment awarded to 3 others it is the PM's intention to announce this at once in the H of C and then the press can publish the news.

The PM expressed himself as 'Impressed' at the rapidity of the trial & sentences.

I pointed out that you were carrying out your instructions exactly & correctly and in strict accordance with Military and Martial law. He quite understands but asked me to warn you not to give the impression that <u>all</u> the Sinn Féiners would suffer death. I told him that the fact of 3 of them having been awarded a much less severe sentence was evidence enough of the attitude you were adopting towards them and that I thought it much better to leave you alone to your own discretion. He agreed to this.[74]

Facing shortages of manpower on the Western Front Asquith discusses a Military Service Bill to widen the net for conscription by adding married men, among other measures. The Bill is introduced at the House on the same day he announces Pearse, Clarke and McDonagh have been shot by firing squad. In a characteristically robust response Nationalist MP for North Westmeath, Lawrence Ginnell takes the floor and declares:

This Bill has been appropriately introduced by the announcement of a triple murder![75]

In fractious exchanges at the House of Commons Ginnell has little sympathy for the outgoing Chief Secretary.

Ginnell: Give Birrell a chance? We have got rid of him at last!

Mr Speaker: I must ask the Honourable Member to control himself.

Ginnell: We have got rid of him at last!

Mr Speaker: If the Honourable Member cannot control himself, I shall ask him to leave the House.

Ginnell: Give Birrell a chance!

Birrell: I rise to make a short, a very short . . .

Ginnell: The shorter the better!

Birrell: . . . personal statement.[76]

MP for North Westmeath, the redoubtable Lawrence Ginnell (centre) at Croke Park (Courtesy NLI Archive)

The firing party for the three Proclamation signatories is drawn from the Sherwood Foresters as a consolation prize for heavy losses sustained at Lower Mount Street.

From the cell he shares with Con O'Donovan, Jack feels an inevitability about it all.

> Every morning at dawn for the few days I was detained there I was awakened by the executions of two or three of our leaders at a time. We were in doubt as to our own fate until the following Monday or Tuesday when an officer came along to our cells and read out our sentences. Mine was 'that I was sentenced to death – a

pause – but the officer presiding at the court martial had commuted the sentence to five years penal servitude.'

Jack and Con are transferred to Mountjoy Prison along with others whose death sentences are commuted. They are photographed by the authorities on admission at Mountjoy with notes made of Jack having a 'scar + mole, right cheek'; Con with a 'long scar left side of heart, scar back + tail right eye.'

Unknown to them Mountjoy Governor M.F. Munro is desperate to join his younger brother Hector at the Western Front and even makes a fruitless appeal to the Under-Secretary via Lord Charnwood at the House of Lords. Under-Secretary Chalmers generously tells Charnwood he 'could not contemplate the loss of Mr Munro's services to the Prisons' Board.'[77]

The executions continue at Kilmainham, reverberating all over the city and heard in the cells of those next condemned. Not that everybody is kept awake. Capt. Fionnán Lynch told a BBC interview:

> After no sleep for thee or four nights in North King Street I was dead asleep even though there was no mattress or anything else in my cell. Except I had my shoes and an old hat on top of them under my head and a spare pair of socks under my hip. And my feet were in the sleeves of a shower coat. And I slept like a log.[78]

In parliament Redmond pleads for a stop to the executions. Prime Minister Asquith says that General Maxwell is in full command of the military courts-martial and the government has 'great confidence in the exercise of his discretion.' MP Ginnell interjects to demand immediate suspension of military courts.

> *Ginnell*: Cannot the Right Honourable Gentleman answer the last clause of the question – whether any more are to be executed before this House is afforded an opportunity of discussing the matter?

Asquith: I will answer that. I cannot give such an undertaking.

Ginnell: Murder![79]

The *Manchester Guardian* adds its voice in opposition, calling for a stop to the executions. In an editorial that is scathing of the process underway in Dublin:

> It is monstrous that a military tribunal, sitting in secret, should be allowed determine this great and critical matter in hot blood. The responsibility is for the Cabinet. There is no room for delay.[80]

Redmond's plea for restraint is brushed aside.
On May 4, Fionnán Lynch is hauled before his court-martial.

> They had to wake me up to sentence me. The one document contained both the sentence to death and the commutation to ten years penal servitude . . . and I fell asleep again within five minutes after being sentenced.

While Capt. Lynch sleeps Comdt. Ned Daly is taken out and shot. Then Willie Pearse, Michael O'Hanrahan and Joseph Plunkett. 'There were 18 of us tried that day,' recalls Lynch. 'But I know that when we paraded there were only 14 left and we were transferred the following evening to Mountjoy.'

Jack and Con O'Donovan pass the time in Mountjoy waiting to hear where they will serve their sentence. From their cells they can hear the sharp report of firing squads catch in the breeze across the Liffey from Kilmainham.

Fionnán Lynch is also sent to Mountjoy. He finds the name on his cell door reads 'Fenian Lynch' and delights in telling how 'a big stout warden came along and read the name and said with a great guffaw – "Ah begor," he says, "Fenian by name; Fenian by nature".'

10.

*'But it is not murderers who are being executed; it is
insurgents who have fought a clean fight, a brave fight,
however misguided, and it would be a damned good
thing for you if your soldiers were able to put up as
good a fight as did these men in Dublin – 3,000 men
against 20,000 with machine-guns and artillery'*
– John Dillon, House of Commons, 11 May 1916

Unknown to his family in Ballaghaderreen Frank is one of 208
prisoners to arrive at Stafford on May 1, 1916. He is Prisoner
#E29 in an antiquated prison already 123 years old. A total of 550
Irish prisoners, including Michael Collins, are incarcerated there.
Many of these men participated in The Rising but a sizeable minority did not. At a time when British military preoccupations are
elsewhere this hit-and-miss approach to deportations is facilitated
by General Maxwell's wide-ranging powers which make light work
of due process.

With Dublin – then the entire country – under martial law it is
a stressful ordeal for relatives and friends. Lists of prisoners' names
periodically appear in the national newspapers, saying where they
have been transferred. The first letter Grandpa gets is from his sister Ena, who is staying with the Bolands at The Crescent in Fairview. After many anxious days they finally find his name on a list
of deportations. Ena writes to Stafford but much of her letter is
blanked out by the censor.

Dear Frank,

We have been anxiously awaiting a line from you. Only
just seen by paper a few evgs ago where you were. Do
hope you are not ill from the treatment there.[81]

His mother Christina follows up, sending fresh eggs to Stafford.

My Dear Frank,

I will chance sending a few lines. I hope you will get this letter and write as soon as possible.[82]

When Ena receives a reply she writes back the same evening, telling him that Bertie (called by a pet name, Bob) was arrested during a raid on Ballaghaderreen by the Sherwood Foresters, brought to Richmond Barracks and sent onto Wandsworth Prison in London.

Bob and ten others, you can guess the crowd, were taken from B.* last Thursday week. There was a huge gathering at station and old Ballagh was weeping co-piously for its past sins (of omission)! Only got to see him on Monday last and the following day he went to England . . . Don't worry about Bob and Jack. There was a long letter from Harry today. Expect there's one at home from J. They went to Dartmoor last week. Saw J. in Mountjoy before he left. He wasn't looking too well I thought but however the rest will do him no harm. He said he felt alright . . . I wrote to Jim last week tell-ing him all that happened. He cabled to M. to know if you were all safe. She wired back. For the moment I can't remember his address but if you are writing send letter in c/o District Attorney's Office New York. That will find him and he'd be very glad to have a line from you. Tom McK is wandering round 'all on his ownio' and seems to have lost his usual gay spirits . . . did you know J got five years? Also Harry. A good thing they are together.[83]

*Ballaghaderreen

Such bleak times are leavened only by those who make light of it. Sheila O'Regan, a friend of Grandpa's, begins her letter with a suitable irreverence.

71

Prison yard at Stafford, 1916 – Michael Collins pictured walking left of centre

I know you are somewhere in England but the name of the hotel I do not know so I am just chancing this to Stafford. I only want to say a little word of comfort to you and may God bless your Irish heart . . . peace has stolen over our 'funny little isle' again, bearing with it a big dark wave of sadness that will roll away only when all our boys come home.[84]

With Sean MacDiarmada and James Connolly about to face the firing squad, MP Lawrence Ginnell cuts loose at the Commons.

What I have to say on this occasion must necessarily differ from that to which you have listened, addressing, as I am, an assembly stained with the blood of some of my dearest friends for no crime but that of attempting to do for Ireland what you urge the Belgians to do for Belgium.[85]

When Connolly is blindfolded and tied to a chair before being shot, Ginnell proposes a Hague Conference on the execution of wounded prisoners. The MP's wish to consult Washington rings alarm bells at Westminster. Foreign Under-Secretary of State Robert Cecil sees no reason to involve the Americans.

Ginnell: Can the noble Lord mention any other country where wounded military prisoners are shot summarily?

Cecil: I believe in all civilized countries people who are guilty of murder and treason are shot.

Ginnell: Is it not the fact that if that were the case some of those on the Treasury Bench would be shot?

At which point Independent Labour MP Charles Stanton interjects.

Stanton: Surely it is more merciful where a man is proven to be guilty to be shot, even though he be wounded, than to cure him and then shoot him![86]

Ginnell switches the debate to the murder of pacifist Francis Sheehy-Skeffington by Capt. Bowen-Colthurst (later found guilty but insane) but Stanton has had enough.

Stanton: Could we not put a cold water tap on the Honourable Member? He gets everyone's blood up.

MP Lawrence Ginnell will be a thorn in the side of British administration. A dog with a bone he courts – indeed thrives on – the hostility of the House by standing up for the seditiously unpopular. Despite attracting intense personal animosity he holds Asquith's government to account and will maintain that pugnacious vigilance when Lloyd George comes to power.

Jack and Con O'Donovan have eluded the firing squad and from their cell in Mountjoy they wonder what awaits. Rumours abound as to where the prisoners will serve their sentences – there's talk of being deposited at the Western Front or being sent to Tasmania. Days pass, waiting. In a belated effort to quell growing sympathy for the rebels the military authorities are pressured to soften the hardline response. Jack is one of 75 condemned insurgents to get a reprieve.

Taken from Mountjoy he is escorted to North Wall with Harry Boland, Con O'Donovan, Eamon de Valera, Frank Lawless and seven others. They are placed below deck on a cargo vessel and shipped, not to Hobart but to Holyhead. From there they are put on a train for a 15-hour journey but have no idea where they are going. 'There was twelve of us in the party and we sang our songs grave and gay as we travelled long to the west of England,' Harry writes to his mother, Kathleen.

> We had much speculation as to our destination. Some of us said Portland whilst others said Dartmoor. Shouldice and Donovan had many arguements (sic) over their geography and we passed through certain towns. Jack would say that's in Warwick, Conn would say 'twas in Staffs and so on we were all wondering where we were bound for. When we arrived at Plymouth we were told Dartmoor was to be our destination then we had much speculation as to how many Irish were here before us but we were the first contingent and I had the honour of being the first Irish man to cross the threshold.[87]

The association between the Shouldice and Boland families has strengthened through the Fairview connection. Like Frank and Jack, Harry and his older brother Gerry are connected with Geraldines GAA club. Harry is a better hurler and wins an All-Ireland medal with Dublin hurlers in 1909. Known for his drive and enterprise he sits on Dublin GAA's County Board when he is just 20 years old.

All four are members of the IRB. And like Frank and Jack, Harry, Gerry and their youngest brother Ned Boland all join the Irish Volunteers. When both Shouldices are stationed in North King Street for Easter Week, the Bolands are spread around – Harry in O'Connell Street, Gerry at Jacob's Mill and Ned at the Imperial Hotel. After the surrender Harry is sentenced to ten years penal servitude and Gerry bound for Frongoch. Ned manages to evade arrest.

According to Dartmoor records,[88] only one of the 11 men admitted with Jack has ever been charged by police before. Their present offence is written into the admissions book as 'Taking part in armed rebellion + waging war against H.M. The King.' Arriving on May 18, they are, Harry says, 'the most optimistic party that ever entered this establishment.'

Irish prisoners on wing at Stafford – Collins pictured fifth from right

They will have to bear out a dismal regime there for over six months, plenty of time to deconstruct the Virgil-inspired inscription at the entrance – *Parcere Subjectis* ('Spare the Vanquished'). Experience teaches them otherwise. 'There was not much love about Dartmoor,' Jack concludes.

Back in Dublin Lord Wimborne, Lord Lieutenant of Ireland writes a letter of fulsome praise to General Maxwell.

> I desire to take the earliest opportunity of expressing to you on my own part and that of the Irish Government our congratulations on the complete success of your efforts.[89]

But in the weeks that follow Wimborne's political career will join the footnotes of history. He will resign before the end of June, by which time his wholehearted endorsement of 'the conduct of officers, non-commissioned officers and men of the various units under your command' will require serious reappraisal after revelations of wanton killings in Portobello by Capt. Bowen-Colthurst and the murder of unarmed civilians in North King Street. In fact, Wimborne does get a second stint at Viceroy. However when he is removed from office a second time in 1918 he bites back at the establishment he was so happy to serve.

Frank can only wonder what he has left behind. Holed up with over 500 Irish prisoners at Stafford he has no idea of what happened to Jack. Like others in solitary confinement, he must hold himself together until there is a gradual relaxation of the rules. After about three weeks the punishment of solitary comes to an end.

Tom McKenna

Enforced silence is also lifted and the prisoners are allowed assemble together. Just as importantly, the embargo on post is also done away with. Smoking is permitted. Thanks to the 'National Aid' organisation, food parcels start coming in although it is brought to the organisation's attention by Prisoner G.71 (Duffy) 'a large number of parcels sent from Dublin to our men here never reach their destination.'[90]

His good pal Tom McKenna sends cigarettes via a Mrs Swan who is over visiting her son at Stafford.

> Dear Frank,
>
> I am sending on some chewing gum and also two books – 'The Channings' and 'The Wages of Pleasure' . . . Cheer up Frank. My earnest hope is that it won't be long till you are liberated and meantime it will be a pleasure to do anything which may tend to relieve the monotony or hardships of your present life.
>
> Your sincere friend, Tom.[91]

It is one of many kindnesses offered by family and friends over the next six years although McKenna, a young blade at the National Health Insurance Commission, is especially considerate and generous.

Morale lifts considerably when Lawrence Ginnell visits the prison to see conditions for himself. As MP for North Westmeath, a political maverick both fearless and irrepressible, he visits Stafford on June 15 and tells the men:

> We are proud of you; you have done more for the Irish cause than anyone else has done for years. We recognise you as martyrs and we want you to do the same again.

Prison staff report the MP's sentiments to the authorities. Detainees are offered a sign-out release form, distancing themselves from The Rising or from political activism in the future. In return, they will be allowed go home. With rumours circulating of an internment camp somewhere in Wales Frank writes an upbeat letter to his mother.

> We have now got a few mouth organs and a melodion and it's amusing to hear us play and sing rebelly songs as we march to and from our 'play yard'! Are we downhearted? No!!!
>
> The Govt. at present would release most of the fellows that these MPs 'take on' if they fill a certain form. But that form is a kind of 'going back' on our noble leaders who died for the cause – and pretending that you were led into the 'biz' like a child or a person blindfolded! Of course there's not much harm for suspects to fill them up seeing that they hadn't the 'pleasure' of being out – but the great majority here won't have 'em! . . . I got a nice barm brack and a few sweets from Tom McK yest. He has sent on a few fruit pcls also previous to this.
>
> The camp will be ok. I think tho' there will be a few extra restrictions – one lr per week out and a visit of ½ hour only in the month. At any rate I wouldn't miss it for anything. We'll have tons of football etc. I'm going to get my togs over – and if we don't have a team here to beat all the 'Shirkers' in Dublin – when we arrive it won't be from want of training!
>
> Larry Ginnell visited us a week ago and got a rousing reception. Carried round the yard and was presented with a nice buttonhole of 'the colours' which I saw by

the papers he wore in Parliament next day. A great old warrior indeed!![92]

I hope Lillie and yourself are feeling as good as your 'Gaolbird son'

Best love, Frank[93]

When Ginnell visits Wandsworth Prison he is again carried shoulder-high around the yard by Irish inmates. Regarded with disdain by British officials as an opportunist stoking a seditious cause, the authorities use Defence of the Realm legislation (DORA) to ban Ginnell from visiting any more Irish prisoners in England.

The Westmeath MP ignores the ban and travels to Knutsford Prison in Cheshire. At the visitor's gate he simply gives his name in Irish – Labhras MacFionngáil – but afterwards he is arrested and charged subsequently under DORA.

The episode turns a few heads in Wales where hundreds of Irish prisoners are interned. In an unusual show of Celtic solidarity, the *Carmarthen Weekly Reporter* questions why the MP was charged with 'giving a false name' when Labhras MacFionngáil is in fact his name in Irish.

> This decision opens up tremendous possibilities. There is a highly respected Calvinistic Methodist minister in Cardiff who is known to a limited circle as the Rev. Evan Rees . . . if he signed himself 'Dyfed,' there is evidently a possibility that he might under certain circumstances be charged under the Defence of the Realm Act with 'giving a false name'. At least if the authorities took up the same attitude towards Welsh that they do towards the Irish language this is what would happen.

Prompted largely by executions at Kilmainham the public mood at home shifts with unexpected swiftness. In the short interval between his arrest, detention, court-martial and deportation Fionnán Lynch says the 'change in atmosphere was simply astounding'. Rebuked by crowds on his way into prison, by the time he is shipped out from the North Wall the prisoners and their escorts are thronged by supporters in numbers that would have made escape 'quite easy.'

That transformation gathers momentum over the next weeks and General Maxwell continues to round up suspects into June. Tom McKenna writes of several mutual acquaintances picked up in Dublin.

> Fitzgerald was arrested as a suspect and detained 4 or 5 days in the Richmond before being released. 'Herr von Goltz' and Mce were also arrested as suspects and were sent to some detention camp in England. The former has been released but Mce not yet. D Hegarty had a similar experience to 'Von.'[94]

It is early days but Frank might sense that that the prisoners have gone full circle. On the 50th anniversary of The Rising his 'F' Company comrade John O'Connor told an RTÉ interview that when they left Dublin:

> We thought that was the end of it. We were all fully convinced we we'd never set foot inside Ireland again. We didn't know where we were going to go – we were discussing whether we'd be going to jails or concentration camps . . . another fella said we'd be deported to some island in the Pacific and I said that would've suited me grand . . .

But when word filters through to Stafford that John Dillon has spoken up for them in the House of Commons they knew something is happening. Encouraged, they listen out for news of Ginnell, Alfie Byrne and William O'Brien who they feel are fighting their corner at Westminster. Reports from Dublin, recalls O'Connor, are surprisingly positive.

> We felt we were coming back to life again. We felt we were not going to be outcasts when we went home. No matter how it would work, when we got home we would have the support of the people behind us.[95]

11.

'I doubt if any country in the whole world ever
possessed a Voluntary Army like the Irish Volunteers
of the Irish Citizen Army of Easter Week in 1916'
– Ignatius Callender, 'D' Company, 1st
Battalion, Dublin Brigade[96]

The world in 1916 is drawn in colonial colours, much of it blue and red. Officials sigh about a minor outbreak in Dublin involving a few wayward hotheads. Even so, reverberations from The Rising rumble like low-grade tremors across the British empire.

In his abject resignation speech outgoing Chief Secretary Birrell makes a self-serving plea that The Rising is but a blip. He assures that Ireland will demonstrate its loyalty by continuing to supply thousands of men to the British Army to help at the Front.

> It was said in this House that Ireland was to be the bright star of the Empire in the hour of her dire necessity. I hope it may even yet still be said to be so . . . This is no Irish rebellion. I hope that, although put down, as it is being put down, as it must be put down, it will be so put down, with such success and with such courage and yet at the same time humanity displayed towards the dupes, the rank and file, led astray by their leaders, that this insurrection in Ireland will never, even in the minds and memories of that people, be associated with their past rebellions or become an historical landmark in their history.[97]

However not everybody is convinced that The Rising can be digested so easily. Over the next weeks – then months – parliamentary time diverts increasingly into matters introduced as 'Disturbances in Ireland'. The extent of questioning and discussion on what exactly happened in Dublin preoccupies Question Time to the point that the casual observer would never know Britain is in military deadlock on a protracted and unprecedented scale with Germany.

Following an animated discussion on the use of cocaine in dentistry, the House of Commons hears 'A Royal Commission on the Rebellion in Ireland' penned by the fabulously named trio Hardinge of Penshurst, Montague Shearman and Mackenzie Dalzell Chalmers. The report sets out 'to inquire into the causes of the recent outbreak of rebellion in Ireland, and also the conduct and degree of responsibility of the civil and military executive in Ireland in connection therewith.'

This trio completes their final analysis with commendable efficiency. Interviews are conducted with 29 leading civil and military officials to fill a 126-page report. Despite much assurance in Westminster that Ireland remains loyal to the Crown the authors of the report pull no punches in their introduction.

> In dealing with the series of events which led up to the outbreak of the 24th April 1916, and in endeavouring to elucidate the causes of the rebellion in Ireland, the fact should be borne in mind that there is always a section of opinion in that country bitterly opposed to the British connection, and that in times of excitement this section can impose its sentiments on largely increased numbers of the people.

The Commission fully exonerates both the Royal Irish Constabulary (RIC) and Dublin Metropolitan Police (DMP) which it says gave 'abundant' warning to the administration in Ireland that unhindered open military drilling by the Irish Volunteers 'is having a very undesirable effect'. For 11 months prior to The Rising the DMP's very detailed 'Movement of Extremists' bulletins kept tabs on 230 known suspects within the Republican family, all of which was submitted daily to Under-Secretary Nathan at Dublin Castle.

Intelligence reports reveal that a rebellion in May 1915 was averted only by Eoin MacNeill's casting vote on the Council of Irish Volunteers. By November 1915 police reports describe the

Irish Volunteers as 'disloyal and bitterly anti-British and is daily improving its organisation.'

Yet the Chief Secretary is not the only one with questions to answer. Two weeks before The Rising Major Price, Director of British Military Intelligence in Ireland, submitted an eight-page report to Major General Friend at the War Office. The picture suggests low-level dissatisfaction and attributes a decline in military recruitment to growing opposition from Sinn Féin. Notwithstanding the anti-conscription campaign, however, Price characterises the Irish population as broadly loyal, concluding, 'the general state of Ireland is thoroughly satisfactory.'[98]

When the House of Lords discusses The Rising four weeks later Lord Beresford, a self-proclaimed Ulsterman, refers to Price's report.

> I think we must have an erratum in the dictionary to show the new meanings of the words 'reassuring' and 'satisfactory' – certainly in this sense they are totally different from the meanings which I was taught when I was a boy . . . I know my country well and am proud of my countrymen. They are a very impulsive though generous race and easily led and the people send over to govern Ireland were totally incapable of governing the country.[99]

As for The Rising itself, the Commission states:

> Apart from its general ultimate futility, the planning and conduct of the insurrection showed greater organising power and more military skill than had been attributed to the Volunteers and they also appear from all reports to have acted with greater courage. These things and the high character of some of the idealists who took part in the insurrection no doubt account for some of the sympathy which the beaten Volunteers have undoubted excited among a large – probably the larger part of the people of Dublin – and in many places in the country. There are also the deeper grounds of a passionate national feeling for Ireland of a long hatred of England.

The buck stops with Chief Secretary Birrell. When guns were landed in Howth in 1914, 'the Irish Government decided (as in the case of the arms imported at Larne) to take no action.' As far as the Commission is concerned Birrell was fully aware of police misgivings about increased Volunteer activity 'but he wrote no comment on their contents and no proceedings were taken.'

It continues:

> On the 7th April, 1916, public meetings of the Irish Volunteers were held for the purposes of protesting against the deportation orders and to enlist recruits. The speeches were very violent, threats being used that persons attempting to disarm the volunteers would be 'shot dead'.

Finding that Under-Secretary Nathan referred police warnings of paramilitary nationalism to the Chief Secretary and Lord Lieutenant Wimborne, the Royal Commission is singularly unimpressed with Birrell's ponderous response. Wimborne does not escape criticism either.

> On the (April) 12th the Chief Secretary wrote upon it, 'Requires careful consideration. Is it thought practicable to undertake a policy of disarmament, and, if so, within what limits, if any, can such a policy be circumscribed?' Upon the same day the Lord Lieutenant wrote upon it, 'This is a difficult point; could the disarming be satisfactorily effected?'

> No answer to the minute was returned to the Royal Irish Constabulary, and the file did not find its way back to the Inspector General until the 25th May.

Birrell's ignominy is complete when the House is reminded that the Chief Secretary was at home in London when The Easter Rising occurred. By the time Birrell set sail for Dublin the city was in flames and the rebels dug in for four days.

Conservative Unionist peer Lord Midleton asks the House of Lords:

I cannot conceive any Government, after all these warnings, being so blind as to allow such a state of things to
arise and to be paralysed by the absence of all its heads
when such difficulties were seen to be impending.[100]

With a judgment bordering on scorn, the Royal Commission
subsequently makes its displeasure quite plain:

> The general conclusion that we draw from the evidence
> before us is that the main cause of the rebellion ap-
> pears to be that lawlessness was allowed to grow up
> unchecked, and that Ireland for several years past has
> been administered on the principle that it was safer
> and more expedient to leave law in abeyance if colli-
> sion with any faction of the Irish people could thereby
> be avoided.

> Such a policy is the negation of that cardinal rule of
> Government which demands that the enforcement of
> law and the preservation of order should always been
> independent of political expediency.

The dye is cast. Chief Secretary Birrell ('primarily responsible
for the situation') and Under-Secretary Nathan ('did not sufficiently impress upon the Chief Secretary . . the necessity for more active measures') are left with little option but to resign.

Birrell falls on his sword even before the House debate begins.

> *Birrell*: I therefore, speaking for myself alone, say sor-
> rowfully that I made an untrue estimate of this Sinn
> Féin movement . . . the moment therefore that I was
> assured, as I was the day before yesterday by Sir John
> Maxwell, that the insurrection was quelled, I placed
> my resignation in the hands of my Right Honourable
> Friend the Prime Minister, who has accepted it.

The political careers of both men are in tatters although Nathan is reassigned as Governor of Queensland three years later.
Tidying up his personal effects in Dublin Castle, for reasons unclear he promises assistant Joseph Brennan, 'I will send you a photograph for yourself next time I have one taken.'[101]

Nathan's successor is Robert Chalmers who was Governor of Ceylon (now Sri Lanka) during the religious riots of 1915. Fearing that violence in Ceylon was getting out of control Chalmers' response was to declare martial law and order police and army troops to shoot anyone considered a rioter. MP Ginnell wants to know 'whether any of these executioners have accompanied Sir Robert Chalmers to Ireland?'[102]

For Birrell, Chief Secretary of Ireland for nine years, the Commission's report is just the opening salvo of a political onslaught. The *Irish Independent* in Dublin has little sympathy for him.

> Mr Birrell is taking the only course that was open to him by giving up the office which he had held but never administered.[103]

When the House of Lords discusses The Rising, Birrell is mauled. Lord Beresford puts it thus:

> I charge him with being directly responsible for having turned a peaceful country into a country seething with sedition and irritation and all the old angry sectarian and racial feelings . . . and this resulted in the Sinn Féin movement. Again and again were the Government warned about the Sinn Féin agitation. My noble friend Lord Midleton, to his lasting credit, never rested for months. He not only went to the Chief Secretary but he went to the Lord Lieutenant, to the Prime Minister and to all the other officials concerned. And what did they do? Nothing.[104]

His sentiments are echoed through the chamber. The Earl of Cromer doesn't hold back either.

> I cannot help thinking of what the Roman Emperor Augustus said after his defeat by the Germans. He said in his agony, 'Varus, give me back my legions'. I think we have a perfect right to say to Mr Birrell, 'Give us back the lives, the priceless lives, of those gallant young officers and men who have been sacrificed by your neglect of duty, by your want of foresight, by your culpable

optimism.' There was never a more senseless or more unjustifiable rebellion than this Sinn Féin movement in the course of history.

Birrell never returns to Ireland. He is awarded an honorary doctorate by the National University of Ireland in 1929. Fittingly enough, high seas prevent him travelling to Dublin for the presentation.

Despite his doughty backing of Maxwell's authority, Asquith visits Ireland on May 12 to see first-hand what is going on. That same day MacDiarmada and Connolly are executed, the last men to face the firing squad. Asquith is taken to Richmond Barracks and speaks with some of the rebel prisoners. Capt. Tannam relates the encounter to the Bureau of Military History:

> Asquith came along and interviewed quite a number of them and expressed the opinion that they were all very fine fellows, had fought a clean fight and acted like gentlemen and ordered that they be treated of the best. His order was taken literally by the chief cook . . . and from the date of Asquith's visit until I was shifted to Knutsford about the 6th June, we had eggs and ham for breakfast, tins of jam, genuine butter and porridge (if anyone liked it). For dinner we had roast beef or perhaps mutton and plenty of vegetables (far more than we could eat), more bread, jam, butter and tea. Tea was on a similar lavish scale, while the soldiers garrisoning the place were on the roughest of rations, and in carrying the stuff from the cook house to our quarters we were besieged by hungry soldiers, begging tins of jam, hunks of cheese or bread or anything that could be conveniently handled.[105]

Following his visit Asquith suggests many of the young detainees appear innocent. He instructs Maxwell to sift through the captives and send to England only suspects against whom there was a real case. Although the executions come to an end – it is August before Casement is hung at Pentonville Prison – Maxwell ignores Asquith's instruction. Participants in The Rising number approximately 1,800, yet Maxwell arrests over 3,000 suspects, deporting 2,519 of them to England. The Prime Minister's decision to entrust a political crisis to injured military pride proves a serious misjudgement.

Retrospective commendations by the Royal Commission lend the RIC and DMP greater authority in administering Irish affairs. RIC Inspector-General Neville Chamberlain insists on the continued necessity of martial law. David Harrel, former Chief Commissioner of the DMP, proposes 'strong repressive measures' as his fellow citizens 'are easily led and it is therefore the more incumbent on Government to nip lawlessness and disorder in the bud.'[106] With the police and military effectively handed *carte blanche* to restore order in Ireland it will be busy times ahead for 'G' Division, the Special Branch detectives at Dublin Castle.

Birrell and Nathan's departure prompts a clean sweep of the British regime in Dublin. Henry Edward Duke replaces Birrell as Chief Secretary of Ireland and is sworn into the job. Duke sets out his stall by demanding immediate renovation of his quarters in the Phoenix Park at the Chief Secretary's Lodge – now the residence of the U.S. ambassador to Ireland.

For Frank, Jack and over 2,000 Volunteers still uncertain of their fate, the career trajectory of high-level British politicians is of little immediate concern. However it's clear that the bloodlust at Westminster will not be satisfied by claiming the scalps of a few overseas administrators. For the opposition, criticism of Birrell's inertia dovetails neatly with a similar perception of Prime Minister Asquith as a ditherer.

The cumulative verdict is that the Easter Rising *was allowed* take place and that the response of Asquith's administration – whether in London, Dublin or beyond – was tardy and insufficient. Public mood in Britain is hugely exacerbated by drawn-out stalemate at the Battle of the Somme which claims a legion of victims, including Asquith's own son, Raymond. The battle, heralded as the turning point in a war that had already gone on way too long, begins on July 1. It will continue until November 14 and become a byword for waste and slaughter.

'Disturbances in Ireland' continue to occupy much of Question Time at Westminster while Britain strains to maintain the war effort in Europe. There is also the day-to-day business of administering its empire. So when the House of Lords discusses the Easter Rising on April 26, it follows with a debate on 'The Position in Mesopotamia'.

In terms of scale alone there is no comparison between the exigencies of World War One – for which the Britain mobilizes over seven million troops, loses an estimated 750,000 with an estimated 1.6 million wounded. However as London counts the imperial cost of the Easter Rising – 103 British soldiers dead (including 17 officers), 12 RIC officers, three DMP, 388 wounded and nine missing – there is a palpable and persistent unease about where this is heading. The capacity of Irish MPs to keep it on the wartime agenda means it is not going away. Questions, hundreds of questions, all demanding immediate answers. Dublin MP Alfie Byrne takes Home Secretary Herbert Samuel to task on whether an Irish melody called 'A Little Bit of Heaven' has been banned from being played in public places and if such a prohibition extends to all Irish airs. The Home Secretary replies that he issued no such order.

> It is possible that during the recent disturbances the playing of well-known Irish airs may have been suspended by the managers of places of entertainment. But if that was so, I trust that now the Irish melodies may be restored to their usual places in the programmes of the orchestras and in the favour of the audiences.[107]

The last prisoners are marched to North Wall in early June. Far from hearing irate Dubliners demanding they be bayoneted, the last batches leave with cheers ringing in their ears. The reverberations will be heard by Asquith – and later by Lloyd George – when they face Irish MPs fighting for their own survival with sharpened nationalist sensitivities.

12.

'I believe that it is important to commemorate the Rising and to honour those Irish people who made sacrifices for the generations that succeeded them. Their idealism is sadly lacking today, when we have a native government ignoring the 70th anniversary of the Rising. Ten years earlier they even barred a march commemorating the event'
– Sean O'Mahony, *Frongoch: University of Revolution*

For the first few weeks after the deportations Christina Shouldice has no idea where her sons are. The family in Ballaghaderreen nervously await news about Jack and Frank, seeking some sort of reassurance that they are still alive.

Jim, the eldest of the family, sends an urgent telegram from New York:

> Are you all safe answer immediately
> Shouldice District Attorney Office [108]

He also writes to Jack in Fairview so that the letter can be forwarded on via Mountjoy. He phrases the letter in a way to get past the censor although mention of sympathy in New York for the insurrectionists would disturb any interlocutor armed with a blue pencil.

> My Dear Jack,
>
> I have been waiting for a letter from you for while, telling me that you are all safe and that nothing has happened during those terrible days since Easter Sunday. Were you in Ballagh then? A letter of mother's received the other day said she expected you for the Easter Hols. I hope she wasn't disappointed. I cannot write much

of what I think about the revolution. However my heartfelt admiration goes out to those men who died or were ready to die for their country and I think that the trouble there has served to change the opinion of many people here, both Americans and Irish, as to the conditions in Ireland. They are commencing to see (the Americans) the likeness between their ancestors here in 1776 and the Irish of today. It was a terrible thing but it is good to see that there are yet men who are sufficiently devoted to an ideal to give their lives for it, and I am proud of them, whether they were foolish or not in what they did. I suppose there is a letter from you on the way – I hope there is as I have been quite anxious! I tried to get a cable over last week but I couldn't.[109]

He has better knowledge of the situation when he writes to Frank, c/o the Chief Postal Censor.

I suppose I must refrain from comments of any kind on the uprising, or what little chance there is of this reaching you will be spoiled. I will say it created an immense sensation in America. Have had no letter from home since it started, but had a cable on May 13th in answer to one of mine on May 12 saying 'All safe. Writing.' I have not yet got any letter though. Evidently Mother did not know. Five years penal servitude for Jack and you in England must have worried her awfully. It did and does worry me, but I am helpless out here.[110]

When postal restrictions are lifted at Stafford Frank sends a reply. Jim responds in earnest, referring to a 20,000-strong public meeting he attended at Madison Square Garden which raised some $30,000 in support funds.

I have just received your letter of May 29th and I need not tell you how glad I was to hear from you and I note with pleasure that you seem to be in such good spirits. Your letter helped to clear away a certain despondency under which I have labored lately when thinking of you there and your future. I begin to feel now that everything is for the best. I need hardly refer to my pride in

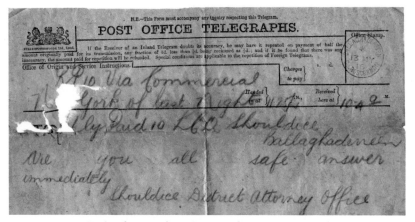

Jim's telegram from New York, May 13, 1916

you all, that you were not found wanting when the call came . . . I haven't heard from Jack. I understand he is in Portland. You know I suppose he got five years . . . I could tell you a lot of things but I suppose the censor would black them out, as he did a part of your letter with regard to something that Ena said – on the last page.[111]

Slowly, inexorably, news of the Easter Rising is spreading around the world. The first enquiries are from concerned friends now living abroad. Máire Merriman, a family friend from Ballaghaderreen, writes from the Traymore Hotel in Atlantic City where she is employed as a manicurist:

I hope you are all well and safe. We are awfully uneasy so please write soon won't you dear? I won't write any more now till I hear from you. Give my best regards to Jack and Ena and love for yourself. [112]

In the first weeks after The Rising hundreds of Irish prisoners are spread around Stafford, Wakefield and Knutsford prisons. Stretched to accommodate this sudden deluge the Home Office also designates Wandsworth, Glasgow, Perth, Woking and Lewes jails as holding centres.

Frank Joseph Shouldice is processed by two separate departments – Home Office and War Office – each issuing him with separate identifications (HO#316595; WO#1184B). He is now a statistical detail in the British justice system.

Conditions at Stafford are hardly luxurious but they could be worse.

> Our breakfast is served by our own men at 7.30 a.m. and consisted of cocoa and one slice of dark bread (not sufficient). Lunch 12.30, cabbage water, two ounces of horse flesh and one and a half potatoes (Bad). 5 o'clock cocoa and a piece of dark bread. On Sundays we got our cocoa at 3.30 so that the English staff could get leave off and the prisoners had to wait until 7.30 a.m. next morning for something to eat. The horse flesh was as hard as plug tobacco . . .[113]

Letters from home are heavily censored, prompting a cat-and-mouse tease for some correspondents. Grandpa's friends Aggie and Tess in Glasnevin tell him his teammates at Croke Park are standing by.

> Hello Frank
>
> What on earth took you over there, so far away from us all. Since we saw your name in the papers as being deported to Stafford we have been worried . . . the innocent prisoners are being released by the score, so perhaps before you get this you will have left your abode of rest – let's hope so in any case.
>
> You are sure of a céad míle fáilte on your return which we all hope will not be very long now. So hurry up. The bhoys are waiting for you in Jones Road.[114]

With Irish prisoners now allowed to send and receive letters small details of the broader picture begin to filter through prison walls. One of Grandpa's fellow inmates at Stafford is Herbert Pim, arrested in County Tyrone. On hearing that The O'Rahilly, 41, was fatally shot on Moore Street when Volunteers evacuated the GPO, Pim writes to the widowed Nancy O'Rahilly.

From that moment I ceased to feel anything. The tragedy and deaths before that made me weep and suffer but this news provided so great a shock that I found myself atrophied. It was a great relief to be arrested, to suffer a little personal inconvenience.[115]

MP Ginnell also writes to her in a loquaciously profound state of shock.

Dear Madame O'Rahilly,

I feared to write to you during the terrible time that has passed, feeling that it would be an intrusion amounting to desecration. Needless to say, my heart bleeds for you . . . I thought my heart would break. The soul of frankness and chivalry in the bloom of youth cut off. I was alone Mrs G. being in Ireland unable to return here. No on to speak to who could understand. When at length she returned, I threw myself on her lap and cried bitterly. English servants thought I had gone mad. [116]

A heavy volume of sympathetic correspondence floods the O'Rahilly home but an official letter from Secretary to the Chief Commissioner of Police at Dublin Castle would surely stand out, possibly the first instance of car clamping as an historical event.

Madam,

I am directed by the Chief Commissioner of Police to inform you that a motor car, the property of your late husband, which was found, partially burned, in Princes Street, outside the General Post Office, is now in possession of the Police having been conveyed to the Lower Castle Yard at a cost of 30/-.

The Car will be handed over to you or to any person authorised by you to receive it, on payment of the cost of conveyance incurred by the Police as stated above. [117]

Over the next weeks the Prison Commission in Britain tries to weed out the innocent as an antidote to Maxwell's enthusiasm for deporting suspects. Over 600 Irish prisoners are released from various British jails without charge and sent home.

However the discovery of two civilian bodies buried hurriedly in the basement at 177 North King Street opens fresh controversy about the conduct of the South Staffordshire regiment. The bodies are identified as local men, Patrick Bealen and James Healy. At an inquest into their deaths the coroner finds that Bealen 'died from shock and haemorrhage, resulting from bullet wounds inflicted by a soldier, or soldiers, in whose custody he was, an unarmed and unoffensive prisoner.'

Lieut-Col. Taylor, the officer in command at that time, does not attend the inquest but instead sends a statement:

> I cannot discover any military witnesses as to the man-
> ner in which the two men, Patrick Bealen and James
> Healy, met with their deaths, but I cannot believe that
> the allegations made at the inquest can be correct.

Dublin MP Alfie Byrne then brings to light four more civilians shot dead at 27 North King Street, including Peadar Lawless. The Lord Mayor of Dublin will travel to the House of Commons to demand an investigation. When details emerge of further civilian killings by the South Staffordshires Byrne raises the issue again on May 17:

> *Byrne*: To ask the Under-Secretary of State for War the
> name of the regiment and officers in charge in North
> King Street, Dublin, during The Rising; whether he is
> aware that fourteen men, unarmed, and not connected
> in any way with The Rising, were shot without trial and
> without any charge being made against them; and if,
> in the interests of justice and peace in Ireland, he will
> demand an explanation from those responsible for the
> incident?
>
> *Tennant*: This question, I think, is postponed.[118]

General Maxwell tries to douse the flames by putting civilian deaths down to collateral damage. In his official statement he says:

Whilst fighting continued under conditions at once so confused and so trying, it is possible that some innocent citizens were shot. It must be remembered that the struggle was in many cases of a house-to-house character, that sniping was continuous and very persistent, and that it was often extremely difficult to distinguish between those who were or had been firing upon the troops and those who had for various reasons chosen to remain on the scene of the fighting, instead of leaving the houses and passing through the cordons . . .

Some of these streets, for instance, North King Street, were found to be strongly held, rebels occupying the roofs of houses, upper windows, and strongly constructed barricades.

Under the circumstances related above I consider the troops as a whole behaved with the greatest restraint, and carried out their disagreeable and distasteful duties in a manner which reflects the greatest credit on their discipline. [119]

In a further statement to the *Daily Mail* General Maxwell holds 'the allegations of brutality seem almost exclusively concerned with the fighting in North King Street' but allows that 'possibly unfortunate incidents, which we should regret now, may have occurred' and that in the face of such 'treacherous assailants' some of his men 'saw red'.[120]

It was a phrase that stuck with some of the Volunteers. Reflecting on it fifty years later John O'Connor,[121] who fought at the barricades with 'F' Company, felt:

I thought it was an extraordinary excuse for an experienced general to make – that his men 'saw red' . . .

Maxwell discourages Field-Marshal French from visiting Dublin to 'give the troops & the situation time to settle down if this is possible' but privately admits 'there is no doubt there have been one or two most regrettable incidents!' He expects Capt. Bowen-

Colthurst's trial for the murder of Francis Sheehy-Skeffington to
be 'very tiresome' and reckons:

> . . . in all about four cases have come to light which
> may necessitate trial as much to give the accused a fair
> chance as anything else. With inexperienced officers,
> NCOs & young soldiers, the house-to-house fighting &
> sniping etc. gave many the jumps, but on the whole I am
> of the opinion the troops behaved with commendable
> moderation. The proof of this is that now fighting is over
> . . . One thing is quite certain, Great Britain does not
> understand & will not have Martial Law. It is a bogey
> but thank God we have the Defence of the Realm Act.[122]

But behind the scenes it's quite a different matter. The murders on North King Street prompt an internal army enquiry whose
findings are deemed too damaging to see the light of day. The
sensitivity of events leads to non-disclosure of records for 100
years – although in fact they are released in 2001. Edward Troup,
a senior official at the Home Office advises Asquith that the South
Staffordshire regiment abused the order to 'take-no-prisoners' by
summarily executing suspects. According to a memo marked 'Very
Confidential', individual cases, like the murder of Peadar Lawless
and three others at 27 North King Street, lead Troup to conclude:

> It is not unlikely that the soldiers did not accurately
> distinguish between refusing to make prisoners and
> shooting immediately prisoners whom they had made
> . . . it should have been made clear that it did not mean
> that an unarmed rebel might be shot after he had been
> taken prisoner: still less could it mean that a person
> taken on mere suspicion could be shot without trial.[123]

Yet as Max Caulfield points out, Maxwell knows more – much
more – than he lets on. He may blunder heavy-handed through
his term in Ireland but on this occasion he knows to stay quiet.
One of the guilty soldiers, a sergeant with the South Staffordshires,
even confesses to his superiors about what he has done. Maxwell

writes privately about it to the Secretary of State for War, Kerry-born Herbert Kitchener:

> In one case a sergeant acted like a madman, the re-deeming feature being he reported what he had done. It must be borne in mind that there was a lot of house to house fighting going on, wild rumours in circulation, conflagrations, and, owing to the darkness, a good deal of 'jumpiness.' With young soldiers and under the circumstances, I wonder there were not more.[124]

Troup feels 'the root of the mischief was the military order to take no prisoners.' He suggests that some of the victims were 'probably fighting or sniping' but he had 'little doubt that others were not taking any active part.' Had these killings occurred in England 'the right course would be to refer the cases to the D of PP' (Director of Public Prosecutions) but considering some Irish MPs were now on the warpath the political risk of 'hostile propaganda' made it more advisable to bury the controversy. He strongly advises against going public on the matter. 'Nothing but harm could come of any public inquiry that would draw further attention to the matter,' he writes. Duly notified, Asquith holds the official line when MP Byrne puts the same question to him in July.

Vainglorious celebrity. General Maxwell on cover of Irish Life

> *Byrne*: . . . if he is aware of the indignation in Dublin caused by the refusal to hold a public inquiry into the North King Street murders; if, to satisfy the demands for justice, he will call for the evidence submitted at the inquests of the victims and the jury's verdict on the same; if he will say why the Government refuse an open inquiry; and if he is aware that the refusal to accede

to this request is looked on with suspicion by the Irish people?

Asquith: I have nothing to add to the answer which I gave to the Honourable Member for East Mayo (John Dillon) on Monday last.[125]

And again a week later.

Asquith: I have nothing to add to the full answer I gave on this subject to the Honourable Member for East Mayo (John Dillon) on the 17th of this month.

Byrne: Will the Right Honourable Gentleman kindly answer the first question, Why the Government refuse an inquiry?

Asquith: No such inquiry was ever promised.[126]

Instead, victims' relatives in North King Street are put through an elaborate charade when presented with an identity parade of South Staffordshire troops in Straffan, County Kildare. Nobody is identified – it's hardly surprising seeing as those suspected of carrying out the killings are not present. The matter will eventually fade from public consciousness without anybody ever held to account.

The prisoners at Stafford settle into their own routine, wondering when they are to be moved on or possibly sent home. With solitary confinement lifted the daily regimen changes, allowing the prisoners out to the yard from 9.00 a.m. to 5.00 p.m. To fill the time Volunteers introduce the game of Gaelic football to Stafford yard, watched askance by British wardens and inmates alike. Until they get a proper football they use a bag stuffed with paper or rags. Thomas Doyle tells the Bureau:

Nearly every day there would be a football match between the prisoners, using a paper ball. One day the Governor was looking on. Two of our boys got hurt. Dinny O'Brien got his hip out and Mick Cahill his ankle out. The Governor said he would not like to be fighting against us. If they fought the same way as they played football, they would be dangerous to meet.[127]

As one of several inter-county footballers held captive, Frank finds the matches at Stafford take their toll, particularly on his footwear.

> My own were sent to the bootmaker here (they repair all our boots) but he couldn't do anything with them, probably on a/c of the desperate state I had kicked them into with our rag ball in a stoneyard – like the old times in St. John's B'Dereen!! So they supplied me with a fine pair of army bluchers, which are still alive and kicking.

> Did I tell you we do have big inter-house matches between the Dublin and Galway/Wexford crowds? Such excitement and enthusiasm amongst the 350, odd, spectators!! I'm captain of our crowd and we celebrated Wolfe Tone's anniversary (Bodenstown) on the 22nd by a big match for a set of 'The Colours' which we won . . .[128]

Over in Knutsford Prison Robert Holland of 'F' Company tells the prison doctor:

> At that time we had the making of an All-Ireland Gaelic Football Team – we had 20 each of 'Geraldines', 'O'Toole's, and 'Keating's GFCs . . . that hurling was well represented and there were some county, past and present champions in different branches of sport. I also told him if he tried the other prisons he would find that as far as the insurgents were concerned, they were a similar type . . .[129]

Replying with a unique insight into Irish society in 1916, the prison doctor tells Holland:

> I must admit that you men from Ireland have puzzled the medical men in attendance at the prisons . . . I have examined more than 600 of your men and in no case have I come across the slightest taint of venereal dis-

ease. We cannot understand this. Why, in the town outside the prison, I have four clinics weekly for men and women. [130]

The Ragballers' Gaelic football team in Stafford Jail
– Frank with an improvised 'ball' in centre

An old copy of the *Irish Independent* gets passed around at Stafford. The prisoners see an editorial condemn The Rising as 'Criminal Madness' and they wonder how representative a view this is.

> No terms of denunciation that pen could indict would be too strong to apply to those responsible for the insane and criminal rising of last week .. The leaders who organised and the prominently active spirits in this 'rising' deserve little consideration or compassion . . . we confess that we care little what is to become of the leaders who are morally responsible for this terrible mischief.[131]

But the Irish prisoners are not the only inmates at Stafford. Its role as a military prison makes it a holding centre for conscientious objectors court-martialled by the British Army. It's a strange mix, a group of defiant rebels bound together by a political cause and a set of defiant individuals fighting for personal beliefs. Patrick Rankin writes:

As we marched from our cells each morning for recreation we could see English prisoners in their cells who were doing terms for crimes connected with the war. Our men would be singing Irish songs and playing Irish marches on mouth organs and you would feel sorry for the poor prisoners standing in their cells but the obscure glass prevented them from seeing us. Very often we could see these soldiers marching up and down in full kids, in the blazing sun and this punishment would go on for hours. There were Canadians, Australians and South Africans there and we pitied them.[132]

When Joe Lawless is transferred to Wandsworth Prison – where Bertie Shouldice is already bound – he witnesses dreadful treatment doled out to the objectors.

We heard the 'Conchies', as they called them, being put through a gruelling course of squad drill in the exercise ground outside our cells, the NCO's in charge fairly revelling in the sadistic joy of making life an 'appropriate hell' for these poor beggars . . . on the other hand, we found the prison staff of Wandsworth quite decent to us, perhaps because they looked upon us as fighters, however misguided, and, as such, superior to the 'Conscientious Objectors' who, professing a repugnance to fighting in any shape or form, they looked upon and spoke of with contempt.

The Irish prisoners feel a real empathy for these unfortunates. At Stafford the conscientious objectors do laundry for all inmates. At the risk of getting caught, the Irish prisoners often leave cigarettes and matches in their pockets when handing clothes in for washing.

Frank Hardiman feels the same.

We were very much concerned with the brutal treatment they were getting. We could hear their cries and moans every night as they were beaten up and we were determined to do everything we could to make their treatment known outside, which we did.[133]

The Volunteers, uncharged and unconvicted, have plenty to complain about but they are reminded daily that there is another, altogether lower, category of inmate. Prior to internment, Joseph McCarthy from Wexford recalls Wormwood Scrubs so vividly that it reads like an extract from Dickens at his darkest.

> A file of about ten miserable prisoners passed slowly along in front of us. They were small in size, deformed – and some of them very lame, others of them hunchbacked – and each of them was carrying an iron ball which was chained to his leg. Their movements were deadly slow, their faces were drained of blood, flesh-parched and furrowed. Their eyes fixed on the ground, they looked neither left nor right but continued the snail's pace until they turned into a corridor.[134]

Following a court hearing over his ploy at Knutsford Prison, Lawrence Ginnell is fined £100 for a breach of DORA with the option of spending six weeks in jail. The Gaelic League backs his appeal at the end of which he is sentenced to three weeks and fined £50. When he does not pay the fine police raid his house and confiscate furniture. Suspended – but never silenced – by the House of Commons, the MP enters Pentonville and is hospitalised in Brixton before being released on November 21. However much he is reviled by the British establishment, the Irish Parliamentary Party and by Ulster Unionists, Lawrence Ginnell is one that Grandpa and his fellow prisoners regard as their champion. Through the summer of 1916 he will raise questions about internment on 41 separate occasions at the House of Commons.

The authorities will soon grasp another opportunity to curb Ginnell but even when handed spells in Mountjoy, Arbour Hill and Reading jails he continues to highlight prisoner-related issues. Indefatigable to the end, the next time Grandpa sees him in person will be late summer of 1916, a dapper, bearded gentleman striding his way across a muddy field in North Wales.

13.

*'I always believed, and still do, that the best men
Ireland ever had were in that lot in Frongoch'*
– John J. O'Reilly, 3rd Battalion, North Wexford Brigade

The British prison authorities cannot handle the situation indefinitely. Faced with such a sudden and sizeable addition to its inmate population the Home Office searches frantically for somewhere to accommodate the Irish detainees.

Officials find their answer in the thwarted dreams of Richard John Lloyd Price, a landowner and entrepreneur who came up with the idea of introducing Welsh whiskey to the liquor market. In 1889 Price built a distillery on his family's Rhilwas Estate, situating his enterprise in the townland of Frongoch in north Wales. A 22-mile Great Western Railway line to Blaenau Ffestiniog connects Frongoch to the nearest town, Bala, its single track used to transport supplies and merchandise in either direction. A large field between the Tryweryn and Mynach rivers becomes the birthplace of his dream, the short-lived Royal Welsh Whiskey.

As a landowner of considerable means Price pushed ahead with his project despite strong objections by the local Temperance movement. He even managed to get a bottle of spirits into royal hands when Queen Victoria visited Bala in September, 1889. A case of Royal Welsh Whiskey was delivered to Windsor Castle two years later. Whiskey connoisseurs were not convinced by the quality of the blend although local trout reportedly thrived on the barley wash entering Tryweryn waters.

Price's enterprise came to an unceremonious end when Welsh Whiskey Distillery Ltd went into liquidation in 1900, ending a shelf life of just eleven years. The business never reopened. Wartime demands for coal boosted the mining industry in Wales but

Royal Welsh Whiskey distillery in Frongoch, North Wales
(Courtesy S4C Cymru)

nobody had any use for a large distillery in the middle of nowhere. The disused building with its distinctive high redbrick chimney lay idle for years.

Unfolding turmoil in Europe brought improbable consolation to Lloyd Price when the Home Office purchased the property and adapted it to house German prisoners-of-war in 1915. Frongoch's main appeal is that because it connects, via Bala, to the national rail network, prisoners can be transported there under guard.

Located in Merionethshire (remapped as Gwynedd in 1974) it is a rural, under-populated Welsh-speaking townland of remote, natural beauty. The Germans feel no scent of milkwood charm about the place, instead enduring the severe cold and seeping damp of Welsh winters. The former distillery is not intended for human habitation but a delegation from the German division of the U.S. embassy in London visits on March 31 and deems the conditions acceptable.

Compared to wholesale slaughter in the mud of France and Belgium the German prisoners at Frongoch could hardly complain. Seven POWs die at the camp from typhus and are buried in St Driniol's Church of England cemetery not far from the distillery. All seven will be re-interred to the German War Cemetery in Staffordshire in 1963. The overgrown cemetery remains a resting place for two Irishmen, Joseph Martin Stenson of Maylough, County Sligo who died in 1900 and John Tierney, 34, 'believed to be a native of Waterford, Ireland.' Tierney drowned in Lake Tryweryn with his friend Ben Langridge in 1880. The two are buried together, their shared gravestone engraved:

> Farewell all I am gone before
> My love for you can be no more
> No grief nor sorrow for me take
> But love my friends for my sake.

Faced with the legal obstacle of how to incarcerate thousands of unconvicted men, Asquith's Government levers a mechanism under emergency legislation. Defence of the Realm Regulations (DRR) are brought into effect, enabling any suspect rounded up in Ireland by Maxwell to be transferred to the newly-established 'camp' as an internee. In a manner comparable to finding a legal basis for incarcerating newly-defined 'non-combatants' in Guantanamo Bay, Home Secretary Samuel uses the DRR to implement an entirely new judicial procedure.

Pressed by John Dillon, Prime Minister Asquith tells the House:

> The Government propose that orders of internment should be made under Regulation 14B of the Defence of the Realm Regulations. The men would be confined, not in prisons, but in an internment camp.[135]

It does not apply to Jack, Harry, de Valera or other Volunteer officers tried by court-martial. They continue to serve their sentences of penal servitude in convict prisons, even if the precise category of prisoner they are is far from clear.

For everyone else, including Grandpa, this is new ground. They face no charge so there is no trial. Instead, they may protest their innocence before a committee chaired by Justice John Sankey. If the Sankey Committee decides a prisoner is innocent, he will be released; if not, he stays at the camp until the Home Office says otherwise.

In keeping with the estimates of the number of combatants through Easter, Samuel has arranged for some 1,800 Irish prisoners to be held in the UK. The Home Office tells Sankey:

Irish internees line up at Frongoch Prisoner of War Camp
(Courtesy Daily Post)

It follows, therefore, that our 1,800 cases will be, so to
speak, picked cases . . . General Childs expressed the
opinion that there would not be a single case for release
amongst the whole lot.[136]

The following day Dillon suggests the Government 'ought to
tell us frankly whether these prisoners are really legally detained at
all.' It is a question that will resurface at regular intervals over the
next five years. Asquith is asked to explain why the Irish prisoners
are denied the right to due process. He replies:

> You would only have a crop of trials, a crop of verdicts,
> and a crop of sentences which would do more to embit-
> ter that state of feeling to which my Honourable Friend
> has referred than any amount of internment of these
> men. I am satisfied that that would not be the right
> course. I should be very sorry to impose on our English
> judges and courts the duty of hearing these trials. That
> again, would be regarded in Ireland as a new source of
> grievance . . .
>
> I believe the wise and humane course is the one we are
> taking – that is to say, to take advantage of the no doubt
> very drastic and arbitrary powers which are vested in

the Home Secretary under the Defence of the Realm Act and keep these people for the time being in detention, but at the same time to give them the power of appeal to the Judicial Committee specially appointed for the purpose.[137]

Initially, appealing one's case is a matter of individual choice. However when the prisoners ignore the Sankey Committee it is decided that each case must be appealed, whether the prisoner wants to or not. At exorbitant cost during wartime each and every prisoner will be transported under escort by train from North Wales to London, transferred to Wandsworth or Wormwood Scrubs for a few days, so that they can go through the motions with a review body they don't recognise.

To the outside world the appeal process looks fair. Even the composition of the committee is intended to make the right impression overseas. The Home Secretary emphasises the importance of optics in a handwritten letter to Sankey.

> It would be advisable to add to the Committee an Irish Judge, so that it should not be said that Irishmen were being tried by an almost wholly English tribunal.[138]

Asquith then informs the House of Commons that the six-man Advisory Committee will include one Irishman, Newry MP John Mooney of the Irish Parliamentary Party.

Of greater relevance to Grandpa, Samuel also marks Sankey's card regarding cases involving civil servants.

> A certain number of civil servants in Ireland are suspected, presumably on good ground, of connection with the Sinn Féin movement, although there is not such definite evidence of participation in the rebellion as to warrant immediate dismissal from the public service. It is felt that these men ought not to be left as officers of the various departments if they are in fact actively disloyal.[139]

Justice Jonathan Pim of Dublin is added to the judicial side. While it may allay Nationalist concerns, the announcement perturbs a senior Home Office official named Broderick who communicates directly with Sankey.

> I must confess to feeling very nervous about the Irish representatives. If you put new wood into a seasoned house, in which the timbers are old, you very often start dry rot.[140]

Sankey writes to Pim about how the Committee might operate.

> The persons detained are at present at many centres – London, Stafford, Knutsford, Wakefield and Lewes but there is an idea of transferring them to an internment camp at Bala in North Wales and it maybe be necessary for us to sit there, as well as in London and Dublin.[141]

Pressured into an urgent reappraisal of prisoner distribution, the Home Office sees Frongoch as the best option to cater to the sudden influx. Officials see no danger in putting large numbers of Irish prisoners together in one place. There is always hope that the resolve of the rank-and-file will weaken after an indefinite spell in dreary conditions.

As far as the Home Office is concerned, finding such a sizeable, faraway but accessible facility makes Frongoch fit for purpose. Home Secretary Herbert Samuel goes as far as to say:

> The sanitary conditions at Frongoch are reported to me to be excellent . . . there is a warm pipe in one of the dormitories, but the beds are well removed from it, and this dormitory is neither overheated nor ill-ventilated I may add that this camp was previously used for German prisoners, and was then visited on several occasions by representatives of the American Embassy, who not only found no ground for criticism but considered it an ideal camp and one of the best in the United Kingdom.[142]

German POWs at Frongoch (Courtesy S4C Cymru)

There is no evidence that Frongoch ever received such a ring-ing endorsement. An inspection committee led by special attaché Boylston A. Beal from the U.S. embassy did visit Frongoch at the end of March, 1916. He found:

> There was no ground for criticism of this camp. It is situated in a very healthy mountain country, and there has been little illness.[143]

At that time the camp held just 990 German POWs, half the Irish complement. Regular route marches were provided for pris-oners and, more pointedly, the camp was run by a different Com-mandant – Major K.C. Wright.

The use of a euphemistically described 'open' camp serves a useful counterpoint to anti-British publicity being generated by Irish-Americans. It is vital to the War Office that nothing will jeop-ardise diplomatic efforts to win U.S. support for Britain against Germany – the U.S. finally enters the war alongside Britain on April 4, 1917.

General Maxwell has hundreds more arrested in Ireland, rounded up on suspicion of republican sympathies or arbitrarily fingered by military and police authorities. Going far outside Dub-lin for suspects Maxwell's hit list now includes 'those who have taken an active part in the movement although not in the present rebellion'. Among them is Frank and Jack's younger brother, Bertie, a shop assistant, arrested with ten others in Ballaghaderreen and sent to Wandsworth Prison in London. In the high-handed authority of the day it is deemed irrelevant that Bertie was not even in Dublin during The Rising. His Sinn Féin sympathies are sufficient to warrant arrest. It also means that three of Christina Shouldice's sons are now imprisoned in Britain.

The steady percussion of repressive measures are also re-shaping Ena's political views. She writes to Frank:

> Have lost interest in Home Rule – the 'Party' have agreed to Partition, their followers mostly declare they won't have it. In any case it's not worth fighting for such a rotten Bill.
>
> Regdg Bob there appeared a few notices in the paper saying some of the Wandsworth fellows were sent to something like Fronloch (sic) Camp and also to Bally Camp* but gives no names. Can you write to Bob. Do so if poss and cheer him up. Had a few lines from him – said he was ok but I think he's a bit homesick – not being away much before. I do hope you are lucky enough to get together.[144]
>
> *Ballykinlar Camp, County Down

Weeks before the transfer of Irish prisoners takes place four German prisoners – Julius Barnard Koch, 22; Heinrick Brinkmann, 24, Hans Schaenheir, 21 and Wilhelm Arenken, 23 – make an escape. They get as far as the moors between Flintshire and Denbighshire but are recaptured within 48 hours. Arrangements are hastily made for extra trains to transfer the German POWs elsewhere – reportedly 'to France and Belgium for reconstruction work' – and vacate Frongoch.

The location of the camp makes it easy to channel prisoners from Ireland in numbers. Deportees can be shipped from Dublin to Holyhead or Liverpool and put on a train to Crewe or Chester before switching for Bala. Under heavy escort, the first Irish prisoners arrive at Frongoch by rail on June 9, 1916.

From a sodden but picturesque small train station they are marched in pouring rain just 50 yards along a roadway fenced in by barbed wire to the old distillery. The three-storey building by the River Tryweryn has been sub-divided into five large dormitories. It also houses the kitchen, a canteen, a rudimentary hospital and the censor's office.

Signs around the camp are written in the German language. The new prisoners are prohibited from replacing the signs with anything written in Irish. Many of the prisoners find breathing difficult owing to air inside being extremely dusty and stuffy. The living quarters in the old granary are rat-infested – a special request for six bottles of liquefied Daney's Virus for Rats is itemised on the Irish National Relief Fund shopping list.[145]

Back in Stafford Frank duly receives an Internment Order under Regulation 14B of the Defence of the Realm Act (DORA). 'The Order is made on the ground that he is of hostile association and is reasonable suspected of having favoured, promoted or associated an armed insurrection against His Majesty,' says the document. It is issued on June 5 by Col. F.A. Heygate-Lambert, Commanding Officer, Prisoner of War Camp, Frongoch. Significantly, the document makes several references to house rules for 'Prisoners of War.'

The Order seems a little redundant seeing as Frank has already been captive at Stafford for two months. However it extends his stay indefinitely at His Majesty's pleasure even though the charge is vague and there is no prospect of a trial. A similar order is issued to 1,862 Irish prisoners.

Not all Stafford's Irish inmates are sent in the same direction. Some, like Arthur Griffith, are bound for Reading Jail. Prior to the Order each prisoner has little idea where he will be taken. After weeks of rumours and speculation about their next place of detention, the name 'Frongoch' becomes a reality for the first time. And now Frank knows his younger brother Bertie is already there.

News reaches camp that Herbert Kitchener has drowned. The British Secretary of State for War was aboard *HMS Hampshire* for high level talks with Russia when the ship strikes a German mine and sinks off the Orkney Islands. Kitchener is the face that adorns 'Your Country Needs You!' posters, his admonishing finger pointed directly outwards to summon the reader for military duty. It is a recruitment campaign vigorously opposed by Irish Volunteers – and later by Sinn Féin – who see peculiar irony in such a patriotically British appeal being made by a native of Ballylongford, County Kerry.

It was Kitchener who sent General Maxwell to Dublin to suppress The Rising. He may have been a Kerryman but there is no lamenting his misfortune among Irish internees at Frongoch. Among his many competing exploits overseas – Egypt, Sudan, India – Kitchener was commander-in-chief of British forces in the Second Boer War in South Africa. It marked one of the first known uses of internment camps for civilians in a military conflict. An estimated 26,000 Boer women and children died in the camps.

No women or children are interned in Frongoch and although malnourished by rancid prison fare no Irish prisoners die from starvation. To the naked eye however it looks every inch a prison camp. As Prisoner #352 Joe Stanley observed:

> The day started for the men at 5.30 a.m. when the calm of the valley was shattered by the piercing echo of a shrill steam horn – reveille.[146]

The South and North Camps are separated by barbed wire 12-feet high, eight lookout towers and a patrolled roadway. Sentries are under orders to shoot any prisoner who approaches the outer fence. And while many prisoners will be released over the course of a very wet summer others have no idea for how long they will be detained.

According to a prisoners' statement the rules and regulations appear excessive for men interned without charge.

> At 6.15 a.m. the men are paraded in the open air with bare heads for the purpose of being counted and are kept stationary for about half an hour. The effect of this after 12 hours in a suffocating atmosphere is extremely serious and many case of fainting occur in the morn-

ing. In wet weather the men have to remain in the dormitories during the day and as there is no covered exercise accommodation this adds to the foulness of the air in the dormitories.[147]

Bertie is housed in South Camp. He writes to his brother in North Camp, unaware that Frank has yet to leave Stafford.

My Dear Frank,

I hope and trust this note will find you near at hand. I heard this evg your crowd from Stafford arrived. If such is the case I hope to see you at a not far distant date. Now if you are here you'll get a slip of paper to write home so write to Mama and it will save me the trouble. Say to her I recvd the pcls ok and some eggs for you. Am delighted you came safe out of the scrap. Also Jack . . . I am in the pink and hope you are the same. Several were asking for you. In fact every side I turn you were mentioned . . . bye now and hoping to see you shortly.

Bertie Shouldice: Not involved in Rising but arrested in Ballaghaderreen

Your fond affect Bro, Bertie.[148]

With the numbers of incoming prisoners soon exceeding capacity Frongoch has to expand. Extra wooden cabins are brought in and sited in an elevated field just north of the distillery. The North Camp comprises 35 wooden huts that can accommodate a total of almost 900 men. Built on higher ground the huts are notoriously cold when temperatures fall. Passageways between them – dubbed Pearse Street and Connolly Street – are unpaved and the whole area washes into a quagmire during unseasonably heavy rainfall through June.

Initially there is some freedom of movement between the South Camp and the North Camp but this practice ends when the numbers became cumbersome. Frongoch effectively becomes two camps – South Camp in the old distillery and the North Camp made up of timber cabins – all under the auspices of Camp Commandant Colonel F.A. Heygate-Lambert – unflatteringly nicknamed 'Buckshot' by the prisoners.

Bertie's South Camp home, also known as Camp One, holds 936 prisoners by June. After that, new arrivals are filtered into the North Camp, labelled Camp Two. The prison guard numbers several hundred but the daily needs of catering to nearly 2,000 men – twice the population of Bala – also creates employment for local civilians.

The prisoners organise themselves very quickly, electing a General Council on June 11 'to look after the welfare and attend to the wants and comforts of the Irish Prisoners of War at Frongoch' and forming an Executive 'for the general management of the camp.' The Council divides up its civil and military concerns and is soon functioning like a mini-government.

An emergency general meeting is called at the main dining hall – dubbed Tara Hall – on June 27 when two internees are put into detention for failing to salute Col. Heygate-Lambert. According to minutes of the meeting, the discussion gets heated with prisoners seeking clarification on whether they are Prisoners-of-War or not. Some say they must be POWs because any postal envelopes they use are stamped accordingly. The Executive resolves to take up the matter with the Camp Commandant.

Numerous other committees are established for a variety of purposes. The Wants Committee meets with Heygate-Lambert on June 20 'to ask facilities for business men to conduct their business correspondence. The Commandant was unable to say what were the regulations governing the writing of business letters as the code containing them had been mislaid . . . the Committee could have a typewriter and duplicator by paying for it but <u>black</u> ink must be used . . the Commandant then closed the interview by assuring the Committee that if they played the game with him he would play the game with them.'[149]

The prisoners' Amusements Committee oversees the 'conduct of concerts on two nights per week until nine o'clock p.m. (two

Sketch of Frongoch North Camp by prisoner N.T. Murray

days notice to be given to Heygate-Lambert), sing-songs, dancing, aeridheachts, singing classes, choirs – church and secular.'

Reflecting the broad spectrum of the prison population, the internees include a number of primary and secondary teachers. The Educational Committee sets up classes for letter writing, commercial class, shorthand and bookkeeping, manual instruction, Irish language, Welsh language, modern languages, a lecture and debating society, mathematics, science and singing.

The prisoners are gearing up for a long haul yet when Bertie receives his first letter from home it sounds less like the anxiety of political persecution than a mother preparing her son for summer camp.

> I got your letter. I was glad to hear you like that place. Lillie is sending your football boots and shoes also knickers, 1 pair socks, shirts and your light and heavy undershirts. Let me know if you want drawers.

> Tell me also if you want some food. I can send some to yourself and Frank. Is he there now? I am sending over some eggs. They will do both of you for the present. I can send over some next week.[150]

Ena adds a note. Knowing prison-bound letters are examined, she is happy to give the censor something to think about.

> You may have Frank there anyday. He'll be happier than ever at meeting all the 'boys' again. His letters are the biz. Heard from Jack recently. He's very well and quite content, not badly treated. Food better than he was led to believe. He's not hard worked and gets reading to do. Can have baths too. I see the Advisory Committee are sitting next week. You will have another trip to Wandsworth soon. They are not allowing any legal assistance but in any case you should get off DV as you are absolutely innocent. It's a queer sort of 'justice' if innocent folk can be kept in prison.

General supplies for prisoners procured with the help of the National Aid & Dependents' Fund[151] include educational books ordered from MH Gill & Son in Dublin, Irish grammar books, chalk and pencils.

On June 22 the Executive meets to discuss prices to be charged at the prison's barber shop. They set the barber's pay at seven shillings a week and the list prices at 1d for shaving, 2d for haircuts, 3d for a shampoo and haircut or special baths. Timothy Finn is appointed master tailor for the camp and Thomas Traynor master shoemaker.

Proceeds from the barber shop will go towards various expenses covered by the Council, such as daily newspapers ordered from W.H. Smith in London. The camp will receive 18 copies of the *Daily Mail*, 12 *Daily News*, 6 *Daily Sketch*, three copies of the *Times*, *Daily Chronicle*, *Yorkshire Post* and *Manchester Guardian* and one edition of the *Morning Post*. A request is put to Heygate-Lambert to include Irish newspapers in the order. According to the minutes, 'The Commandant stated that regulation was English papers only. He did not know if English meant 'Irish' also but would make enquiries.'[152]

The camp will also have its own Dramatic Society. It is set up by Arthur Shields, an Abbey Theatre actor whose brother Barry Fitzgerald will achieve screen stardom in Hollywood. Shields was part of the Abbey company but took up position with the rebels at the GPO on Easter Monday when he was due to appear in the premiere of *The Spancell of Death* by T.H. Nally. Production of the play was cancelled and it never saw the light of day until a partial reading on the Abbey stage in 2015 as part of 'Road to The Rising' commemorations. Another member of the Abbey troupe, 33-year-old actor Seán Connolly, was killed in action on Easter Monday. Captain Connolly was fatally wounded in the domed roof of City Hall during a firefight with military forces at Dublin Castle.

Ena writes to Frank in Frongoch, presuming his transfer has already taken place. She asks about Bertie (Bob).

> Meant to have written sooner but haven't had much time and been a little bit off form besides. So I felt lazy. Have you seen Bob? How is he? Tell me all you can when you write. . . am going to Bolands this evg to collect your togs. You can expect them during week. Had a short note from Bob. He says he's okay but his letters don't sound as jolly as yours. I hope he'll be happier now that you're near him. There's talk of an amnesty but not a general one – tho' some think you will all be out soon as The Question is settled.[153]

Michael Collins is also anticipating the move from Stafford. He writes to Mollie Woods of Cumann na mBan:

> I think we shall be off to the old camp sometime in the coming week. By all accounts it will hardly be a change for the better, but at any rate we shall have some beautiful scenery, also a dismantled brewery or distillery. This latter will recall happy memories at any rate.[154]

There is a delay of several weeks because of a case of measles in Stafford. Frank writes to his mother.

> Dear Mama,
>
> Still here! But it won't be for very long now. We expect this week to finish our term here! I had visitors from Dublin (Mrs Cotter and her daughter) a few days ago

and they told me B. was in the camp. Paddy R. also is – so we have great hopes of meeting all the boys when there will be <u>some</u> jollification!!

There are visitors often here. Irish girls – teachers etc – from B'ham and all round come in bunches and ask for a lot of the boys. They might have known one of the lads first you see and then he gives them a list of names which they ask for on their next visit. I haven't got on the list yet. It's very handy if we can slip out a lr by them as it saves a lot of time – but we are watched closely and have to talk thro' a barred gate. I am getting this out by two Dublin girls (Cumann na mBan) who are visiting today. You said my lrs weren't well closed – but I have to send them open, so that the censor may get a peep.[155]

Grandpa is told to gather his belongings on July 6. With other prisoners he is marched to the train station and they leave Stafford behind. The group includes Patrick O'Hanlon, who accompanied Grandpa up Jameson's malthouse in Easter Week. Unknown to them, Stafford is soon to close its gates for 23 years before reopening at the outset of World War Two.

Volunteer Patrick Rankin recalls waiting on the platform at Stafford station.

We were told to first give a cheer for the Camp O/C, next in order each good sergeant and last of all the sergeant who ill-treated us. Michael Collins gave the signal by whistle and you should have heard the salvo for the former men and the appropriate one for the latter who was present.[156]

There is some irony about a Ballagh man transported to a town called Bala. Taken from there to Frongoch, Grandpa is escorted under armed guard from the train station, through a channel of barbed wire into the camp. On arrival, he uses a school jotter to start a diary.

Left Stafford with a crowd of about 50 at 2 o'clock . . landed in Frongoch at about 6.30.

As ever, relatives and friends will be first to hear the rumour and last to be properly informed. A letter from Sheila O'Regan arrives in Stafford Jail long after Grandpa has been moved out. It is forwarded to North Wales.

> I have attended Masses for our heroes who were shot and Frank it would be rather hard to describe my feelings . . . I had a most extraordinary dream about you a few nights ago, Frank, you were sentenced to a long term of imprisonment and the weary years you were doomed to spend in the far end of Asia Minor . . .[157]

She signs off, wondering, like so many others, what is yet to come.

Good night E-29.

But he is no longer Prisoner E-29.
His new identity is Prisoner #1676.

14.

'That may terrify you, but I declare most solemnly,
and I am not ashamed to say it in the House of
Commons, that I am proud of these men'
– John Dillon, Irish Parliamentary Party, 11 May 1916

With Frank leaving Stafford, Jack in Dartmoor and Bertie in Frongoch the rest of the Shouldice family – Christina and her daughters Ena and Lily – try to get on as best they can. The National Aid Fund gives Christina a real boost with assistance of 15 shillings a week. There's no indication of how long it will last but the Fund helps out hugely with a bonus lump sum of £25 to tide her over.

Ena, named after her mother, is employed as a telegraphist at the GPO in Dublin. On leave for Easter she is not at work when the Rising breaks out. Ena is close enough to Frank, Jack and the Bolands to know that if anything was afoot her brothers would be involved. In fact, it would not have been in the least bit surprising had Ena joined them at the barricades – her political sympathies are republican through and through but for whatever reason, possibly discouraged by Jack and Frank, she does not take part directly in the insurrection. Months afterwards, she writes to Frank to relate a dream she had just prior to The Rising.

> Of course I never had an opportunity of telling you I dreamt of a revolution a week before Easter. Was in Spelman's near Gurteen for the weekend. Was blowing very hard – the weather, not me – I thought I heard the guns and shouts etc and saw women picking their steps in blood round by the Bank of Ireland!! I woke up with a terrific shriek and nearly paralysed Baby Spelman and Mary Morley who were in same room with me!![158]

Postal operations move to Amiens Street while the GPO is being rebuilt – the main post office will not reopen fully for business until 1929. Martial law remains in force in Ireland so Ena stays with the Bolands in Fairview. She writes from there to Frank at Stafford on May 25.

> Your things are all OK in Boland's where I'm staying this last few weeks on account of martial law . . . Am working away at Amiens St. (temporary office), kept fairly busy since I came back.[159]

The key relationship between Ireland's military authorities and the civil communications network makes Andrew Hamilton-Norway a vital, if unwitting, figure in the British administration. Hamilton-Norway is Secretary of the Irish Postal Service as well as manager of the GPO. His son Frederick was killed on the battle-field in France; another son acquitted himself as a stretcher-bearer during the Rising and would later emerge as a renowned author under the *nom de plume*, Nevil Shute.

Ena does not return to work immediately. The absence of a telegraphist may have attracted attention at Dublin Castle but with two brothers in custody immediately after The Rising her family connections are already catching the interest of detectives at 'G' Division.

In the early chapters of what will become an 83-page dossier on the Shouldice family,[160] members of the RIC in Ballaghaderreen have their pencils sharpened and notebooks at the ready. The lengthy report, characteristic of many intelligence reports, is a mixture of observation, fact, guesswork and hearsay. Alarmingly, it is on the basis of these documents that military and civil authorities make far-reaching decisions that affect the lives of the individuals concerned.

With the ink barely dry on Padraig Pearse's surrender in Dublin, the RIC has Ena Shouldice under observation in Roscommon.

Ballaghaderreen 29:4:16

I beg to submit Decipher of Telegram handed in at 11.15 am today to DI Boyle: - 'Miss Shouldice GPO staff gone to Dublin today first train. In close touch with Sinn Féiners here. Booked Mullingar.'

> Miss Shouldice was here on leave from the Post Office Department Dublin which expired 22nd Apr 16, she went to Dr John A Coen of Ballaghaderreen and he gave her a medical certificate for a week. He told me on Tuesday last that there was no real necessity for her to seek an extension of leave and that he suspected she was evading the Rebel outbreak in Dublin.

> She has 3 brothers Bertie, John and Frank, all of mature years: – John and Frank are in Government offices in Dublin and are said to be Generals with the Rebel Forces in Dublin. Bertie and the mother are living here and Bertie is in Flannery's Bar and founded the Irish Volunteer Branch here with PJ Ryan & Co.

> The girl was seen away this morning at the station by Mrs Mary Morley and her daughter (Mary). Mrs Morley's son is absent from here and is said to be with the Rebel Forces.[161]

At which point a Special Branch detective inserts into the file 'no evidence from Dublin of this.'

> Miss Merriman was also at the station to see this lady away. She is manageress for P.J. Ryan who is also absent with the Rebel Forces having left here on Saturday the 22nd inst for Dublin.

Again the report is marked 'no evidence from Dublin.'

> Frank Shouldice was here on holidays from Dublin and went to Dublin in company with Ryan. Miss Shouldice has talked freely of the part herself and her brothers have taken in the movement but I can't get evidence of this beyond the circumstances stated. Mrs Morley's daughter who was seeing away Miss Shouldice is engaged to Alexander McCabe of Keash Co Sligo and

> Miss Merriman is keeping constant company with Joseph Kelly who is awaiting trial for Larceny of a motor car presumably to join the Rebel Forces at some point on Monday night last the 24th Apr 16.
>
> I think Miss Shouldice should be closely observed as she is likely to be spying for the enemy.[162]

This information is ciphered to RIC stations in Sligo and Mullingar. Intrigued, the RIC Inspector in Roscommon writes back.

> It is not stated who Miss Shoredice (sic) is. I understand she may be the daughter of a Police Pensioner of that name. Is it known what Government offices in Dublin John & Frank Shoredice are employed? Who is Mrs Morley?

Despite many inaccuracies there are sufficient grounds to stoke further interest. A decision is taken to monitor Ena. On her next visit home Constable John O'Toole approaches her before filing his next report to 'G' Division:

> Ballaghaderreen, 3.5.16.
>
> I beg to report that Miss Shouldice returned by rail to Ballaghaderreen today. I asked her if she had any objection to giving her address while absent and she told me she stayed at 29 Shandon Road, Dublin. She said she did not report herself to any of the Post Office officials as they are disorganised. She travelled with John F. Morley, assistant drill instructor to Irish Volunteers here.
>
> Miss Shouldice's father was in the RIC but is dead. John and Frank are in the Civil Service. It is said John is a clerk in the Dept of Agriculture and Frank is in the Irish Land Commission offices.
>
> They spell their name 'Shouldice'.[163]

The wheels are in motion. From being a 'person of interest' Ena is now under an active suspect. Her movements are under surveillance through an intelligence network that connects Special

Branch at 'G' Division in Dublin Castle, the Dublin Metropolitan Police (DMP), Royal Irish Constabulary (RIC), British Army Command in Ireland at Parkgate and MI5 in London. The Chief Secretary's office is regularly updated although in practice it is usually the Under-Secretary who is hands-on with the case.

A police order is issued publicly on May 5 to state 'employees and workers in all occupations, particularly those in the Food, Munitions and Coal Trades, should return to work today.' All pubs are to remain shut for three days.[164]

Ena ignores the order and stays at home. She does not know her every move is now under observation. Unsubstantiated speculation about Morley and Ryan, previously questioned at Dublin Castle, is repeated without query this time, effectively turning it into fact. Each report is countersigned by W.J. Edgeworth-Johnstone, Chief-Commissioner of the DMP. On May 8 Roscommon RIC notifies Special Branch that:

> Miss Christina Shouldice who is an employee in the General Post Dublin and has two brothers there in civil positions and reputed Sinn Féiners, left here this morning by 9.30a.m. train for Dublin. Her baggage was addressed to 60 Cadogan Road. She was seen off by Mary Morley whose brother John F. Morley was up at the fighting in Dublin and Lizzie Merriman manageress to P.J. Ryan who was also at the rebellion in Dublin, Joseph Kelly a prominent Sinn Féiner here and her brother Bertie who is also a leading Sinn Féiner in Ballaghaderreen and an assistant in Flannery's & Co.

After 'confidential enquiries':

> I am informed that they are the children of an ex-member of the RIC, Henry Shouldice No. 11918 pensioned on 1 Nov. 99 but date of death is not recorded here. They resided in Dublin for some years and came here about 12 months ago.

> Miss Shouldice has stated that she could not find her brothers when last in Dublin and that she heard they surrendered at the Four Courts. We cannot get evi-

dence of this statement, and it is only hearsay. Henry Shouldice, ex-R.I.C., is said to be the child of <u>a German</u> who was employed at Rockingham, Boyle, or that vicinity.

The provenance to a German national – even a long dead one – adds intrigue to the military/police wartime investigation. On the back of Casement's capture in Kerry and the sinking of the *Aud* it offers a plausible, if convenient, rationale why the sons and daughter of a deceased RIC sergeant might conspire against the British administration in Ireland.

In actual fact Henry's father Henrik was born in County Clare and the German connections trace back to the early 1700s when thousands of Palatine families fled religious persecution in southern Germany. A few hundred of them who made it to Ireland landed in Limerick and, from there, spread inland. The convenient untruth about Henrik as a German national is allowed sit however and can be repeated and referred to whenever the Shouldice file is opened by police or military authorities. Simple repetition, in effect, turns it into fact.

As far as the RIC is aware, Frank was killed in action during the Rising. The RIC Inspector General in Roscommon asks the DMP to verify that 'one of her brothers was a rebel and killed in Dublin.' Nine days later, Roscommon RIC report 'Miss Shouldice leaves Ballaghaderreen for GPO Dublin.'

> This girl's brothers are said to be active Sinn Féiners and one is believed to have been shot as a rebel in Dublin. The other sentenced to death but the sentence was commuted to 5 years penal servitude. Another brother Bertie was arrested at Ballaghaderreen on 11th inst. And sent to Dublin.[166]

There is no mention of Frank in the DMP reply.

> It's understood that John Shouldice is under arrest as a leader.[167]

What's more, the DMP is convinced that:

Miss Shouldice is evidently a dangerous person.

Thus advised, the Chief Secretary's office at Dublin Castle orders that Ena's employer, the Irish Postal Service, is notified of 'this girl's associates in Ballaghaderreen.' Two days later the Secretary at the GPO receives a letter from Dublin Castle.

> Sir,
>
> I am directed by the Lord Lieutenant to inform you that from reports received by the Police it appears that Miss Christina Shouldice, who is stated to be employed at the General Post Office, Dublin, associated with well known Sinn Féiners when stopping recently at Ballaghaderreen. She left Ballaghaderreen on the 9th instant for Dublin.[168]

The GPO acknowledges the Under-Secretary's letter with a promise that it 'shall receive attention.' A Special Branch 'G' Division file marked SECRET on 'Miss Shouldice, Telegraphist, GPO, Amiens Street (May 31, 1916) reports that Ena is now living in Sutton. Given the close collaboration between the Chief Secretary's office and Hamilton-Norway it might be presumed that Ena will soon find herself out of a job.

> She was afraid to remain in the city, owing to the trouble. She was never observed to associate with the extreme section in Dublin or to be a member of any extreme organisation.[169]

This information is passed onto Neville Chamberlain, Inspector-General of the RIC – and namesake of a future British Prime Minister. Raising the stakes, Special Branch 'G' Division then informs Under-Secretary Robert Chalmers.

This girl must be regarded with great suspicion.

The surveillance continues. Major Price's Intelligence service intercepts a letter from Ena to her older brother Jim in the United States. When writing to her incarcerated brothers – Frank, Jack

and Bertie – she makes little secret of her political leanings even
though she knows those letters are
first read by a prison censor. She
might feel a lot freer writing to New
York, never once thinking that a
private letter crossing the Atlantic
would be pored over by operatives
at MI5. She speaks openly with Jim;
little does she know who is listening.

*Ena – 'must be regarded
with great suspicion'*

We don't know what Ena wrote
– it's not on file with Dublin Castle
although MI5 retains the letter –
but it pricks a stiff response from
Irish Army Command HQ at Parkgate. The military authorities want
her fired. They are unhappy with
the slow response from the GPO
in Dublin so Major-General Friend
sends a request, on behalf of General Maxwell, to the Postmaster
General in London, which oversees
the Irish Postal Service.

Sir,

I am directed by the General Officer Commanding-
in-Chief the Forces in Ireland to forward herewith
the attached letter which has been intercepted by the
Censor, addressed to J.B. SHOULDICE, Esq., 142 East
52nd Street, New York, from 'ENA', 15 Marino Crescent,
Clontarf, Dublin.

The writer would appear to be MISS SHOULDICE, a
Post Office Servant, now employed at Amiens Street
Railway Station, Dublin. In view of her apparent con-
nection with the Sinn Féin Volunteer Organisation, the

question of permitting her to remain in the Postal Service appears worthy of your consideration.[170]

There are no records available of correspondence between London and Dublin but the Irish Postal Service appears to object to the military's interference. The GPO does not, as might be expected, abandon its telegraphist. We don't know whether Hamilton-Norway is involved but it's highly unlikely he is unaware of the matter. Either way, the request to remove her from employ is rebuffed.

Ena has no idea of the drama being played out behind the scenes. She continues to write to her brothers and tells Frank that Jim might get to visit later in the summer.

The constabulary appears quite assiduous in its pursuit of Ena Shouldice but the rank and file are far from content. 'There is much unrest and dissatisfaction,'[171] DMP Chief Commissioner Edgeworth-Johnstone reports to Under-Secretary Chalmers. Constables are demanding a 3/6 rise per week as a 'war bonus' in line with their colleagues in England and Wales. Following busy correspondence between Dublin Castle and the Home Office, Chalmers is told by telegram:

> Govt has decided that war bonus shall be granted to RIC & DMP – you can let this be known if you consider advisable.[172]

Although details are vague the concession appears to placate a disgruntled force. The authorities' desire to break into Sinn Féin circles leaves the door open to all comers, including anybody with personal enmity or a grudge towards intended targets. Dublin Castle and local police stations are frequently provided with anonymous notes, singling out individuals for attention. Such as the handwritten note dropped namelessly into 'G' Division at Dublin Castle on May 15, 1916.

Sir,

Sitting at the silk department in Forrists Grafton Street
you will find a Sinn Féiner. He should join his comrades
in England.[173]

But the informer process is two-way. Information may be
obtained by threat. Alternatively, incentives may be offered,
including cash. Providing an insight into its *modus operandi*,
Edgeworth-Johnstone writes to Under-Secretary Chalmers on
June 26, advising:

My secret service fund is almost used up. Hitherto it
has been replenished by The Chief Secretary upon my
application – by private letter. A cheque for £100 is the
usual response and I'll be glad if you would kindly provide this amount for me from the proper quarters! [174]

The request is passed on to Home Secretary Herbert Samuel in
London and payment is swiftly made.

Despite a concerted effort the RIC in Ballaghaderreen makes
little progress producing any further evidence against Ena. She
carries on her work as telegraphist unaware that her position at
the GPO hangs by a thread. Close surveillance will continue for at
least twelve months. Next time round, however, correspondence
gathered by an ever-diligent censor will make it a lot more difficult
for the GPO to save her.

15.

*'I think I can be forgiven for saying that the
men in Frongoch were a band of brothers'*
– Joseph Good, Irish Volunteers, Kimmage Garrison

I follow Grandpa's footsteps 99 years later and arrive in Frongoch on a warm April evening. Even today Frongoch would more call itself a hamlet rather than a village. A café and a couple of houses line the side of the main Bala road.

Almost a century later the eye strains for traces of almost two thousand Irishmen who passed through here. Turn left for the site of the old distillery where a primary school now stands. A cul-de-sac with a row of houses forks left and right. The railway that served Frongoch was discontinued in 1961 but through the treeline it is possible to pick out an embankment. The former single-track is now a laneway which leads across a rusted metal bridge to the rear garden of a modern bungalow. Further examination reveals the bungalow to be the former train station. The signal box stands intact. The shape of a platform is visible with an ornate canopy trellis that sheltered the station's waiting area. Virtually nothing else remains.

North Camp, where the wooden huts were arrayed, is now a grassy field inclined towards higher ground. Local man Alwyn Jones, a retired farmer, has built a new family house where the old distillery once served as South Camp. The stump of an old foot-bridge suggests interrupted passage across the River Treweryn to an open acre now overgrown and clumped. It takes a stretch to imagine prisoners holding a riotous sports day here when Grandpa threw the shot-put 28 feet, 11 inches to pip Michael Collins by nearly three feet.

By night Frongoch presents a silhouette of low lying hills to the east and the brighter horizon of higher peaks to the west. It's wooded and grassy and the only sound is the rush of the Tryweryn themed by gentle birdsong. The river skirted South Camp when the men were interned here. In summer a stream, gurgling and pleasant but in winter a torrent, urgently seeking its course.

The Irish prisoners were told 1916 was the wettest June for years. Under weeks of constant rain it is easy to imagine this lush, green valley moist and mildewed. In the shade of undulating forest there remains a feeling of incipient damp. Occasionally, the spectre of dotted headlights pinpoint the main road that leads into Bala. It's not so busy now and was hardly busy then. Car beams spot the fields like searchlights, dipping, rising, cresting the hilly pass and disappearing, inking the valley once more into blackness.

The distillery's tall brick chimney was toppled in 1934, eradicating the area's focal point and restoring an unobstructed panorama of the valley. Alwyn Jones is keen to rediscover the history of this townland and place it on the map for generations of Irish visitors following those who were interned there.

In the darkness of a still night I hear a dog barking in the distance. A cow lowing. Then silence once more, filtered only by the constant pull of Tryweryn waters hurtling into Lake Bala. The clear outline of the surrounding hills offers a strange beauty, captured in pencil by some prisoners who etched the image into the autograph books of their comrades. Others drew sketches of their billeted quarters, the temporary huts that for an indefinite time they called home. Those of a less artistic hand instead summoned lines of rhyming verse for the open page, usually a nostalgia-filled rhapsody to the land they left behind.

I am reminded of Joe Lawless' vivid recollection of the camp.

> After the evening roll call when we were locked within our dormitories small groups sat around here and there on the beds talking or playing cards, while others read or lay wrapped in thought. Tattoo brought the garrison bugler out on the road between the two camps to sound the last post, and always, as with one accord, there was complete silence in the dormitories until

the call had ended. I do not know why this should be, but that particular musical combination sounded on a bugle always seemed charged with a special solemnity and significance.

Former train station at Frongoch (photo by the author)

It's as though Frongoch was plucked from obscurity and then sent back. Yet its designation as an internment camp after the Rising made this dot on the map a household name for two thousand Irish families in 1916 and for generations afterwards. Today, a small bronze roadside plaque, inscribed in Irish, Welsh and English, marks the location of the camp.

Since his deportation in April Frank has already been away from home for 67 days. He is glad to get out of the brick and concrete of Stafford and prefers the rural suggestion of Frongoch. He jots a few thoughts in a makeshift diary – despite various hardships, his rail transfer under armed guard reads like a day out.

> 6.7.16 – Had a very pleasant journey, up and down thro' the centre of England and Wales via Shrewsbury. Wales is a very nice country – scenery beautiful. Landed in Frongoch at about 6.30. There are two camps here – a public road running between. One where B + McC etc are is an old distillery and ours is comprised of wooden

huts – 32 men to each. The position is grand but the place is very mucky owing to almost continual rain. After passing all our goods and chattels thro censor and being searched we got thro – and after a welcome cup of tay we adjourned to our hut. The huts are about 20 yards long – 6 windows each side – very bright and airy. Straw mattresses on the usual wooden pallet are an improvement on Stafford.

Prisoners' representatives in South Camp are elected from each dormitory in the old distillery while in North Camp each hut elects a Hut Leader. In this way prisoners' issues and grievances can be dealt with more efficiently. The re-structuring will have a significant bearing on how Frongoch becomes a future model for Irish political prisoners.

On arrival, Frank is billeted at Hut 14 in North Camp. The only Mayoman, he is elected Hut Leader to represent the 32 men housed there. Twenty-two of the men are from Dublin with five from County Galway, two from County Wexford and one each from County Kerry and County Cork.

Many of the men at Frongoch – including Grandpa, George Geraghty, Dick McKee, Michael Collins, Richard Mulcahy, Sean T. O'Kelly, Joe Clarke, Barney Mellowes, Patrick Rankin, Tom Byrne, Mark Wilson and scores of others took up arms in the Rising but many others did not. Inevitably, hundreds of men rounded up under DORA's wide-ranging maw are completely innocent.

The political question of how to handle them is blithely dumped on the Prison Commission unclear on how to categorise the prisoners put in their care. Are they criminals or are they POWs? Or are they something in between?

The Home Office is suitably ambiguous. The Irish prisoners are not to be regarded as criminals. They are political prisoners but not Prisoners-of-War. In a strange contradiction, Grandpa's internment order under DORA Section 14B refers to the 'Prisoner of War Camp'; his early letters are also stamped 'Prisoner of War' but this appellation is discontinued when status becomes a serious point of contention.

Prisoners have no doubts about how they should be considered. In a direct precursor to events in Long Kesh 65 years later they want to wear their own clothes – some are still dressed in Irish Volunteer or Citizen Army uniforms – in addition to free association and a relaxation of camp rules on visits and mail. The longer they are held captive the harder they will fight for these concessions.

Given the broad sweep of deportation orders against them, 'C' Company veteran Sean Prendergast sees a subtle distinction among the Camp population.

> Among the mixum-gathering of men incarcerated in Frongoch Internment Camp, were a large number who felt sore and downcast for being denied the chance to fight (in the Rising) . . . that men who did not participate in the Rising were sharing the rigours of internment with men who did participate added a certain spice of piquancy to the proceedings of mingling the might-have-beens with the has-beens. So it was, however, that men who had fought in the Rising, and those who did not fight, held in a way common ground – as prisoners . . .[175]

View from the door of Hut 14, handpainted
by prisoner Cathal MacDubhghaill

Prior to the Stafford contingent arriving, there is growing impatience that the prisoner representative body is unable to get grievances resolved. A groundswell of bother leads to a vote of no-confidence in the Council Executive articulated in a general letter of complaint.

The Executive resigns on July 3, fully aware that the character of the camp is about to change. Many of the early internees completely unconnected with the Rising are on their way home. Some of them will have been politicised by the experience. However the arrival of active republicans from jails around Britain is set to transform the dynamic at the camp. In its resignation notice the outgoing Executive concedes,

> As practically the entire body of officers of the Volunteer and Citizen Army are now in camp we think it proper to suggest to you to call a <u>full</u> meeting of their officers with a view to considering the military reorganisation of the camp.

The prisoners overhaul their own system, replacing the General Council with a military-style council. The Irish Volunteers – already rebranding as the Irish Republican Army – take control of the prisoner agenda. J.J. O'Connell acts as Camp Commandant with W.J. Whitmore-Brennan as his adjutant at South Camp. Michael O'Reilly, active in the Imperial Hotel during Easter Week, commands the North Camp.

Not all new measures go down so well among the prisoners. For some, it's enough having to put up with a fussy colonel running the camp without having to deal with even more rules and regulations imposed by the prisoners themselves. Two prisoners caught playing cards for money are banished to solitary confinement for a week. Joseph Good, a London-born Volunteer of the Kimmage Garrison, takes exception.

> However well-intentioned this was, it had a most depressing effect on the Volunteers occupying that portion of the camp. Fortunately, Whitmore- Brennan was

released early and the rules he had drawn up were completely ignored.[176]

The camp's evolution is not lost on historian Sean O'Mahony, whose seminal account *Frongoch: University of Revolution* is the most detailed study of life there. 'I believe that this internment camp made a major impact on the course of Irish history', he proposes with some justification.

Prisoner #1652 Patrick J. Kelly in Hut 15 explains further:

> The camp was run on military lines by our own staff. Each hut elected its own officer, and they in turn elected a Camp Commandant, Quartermaster and Adjutant . . . Each day the Military Governor paid us a visit. We would line up in Companies under our own Commandant. The Governor would enter with his staff and call us to attention. We did not obey his orders but immediately we would be called up by our Commandant, Capt. Morkham. Salutes would be given and returned and the Governor and his staff would retire. Each company would now carry out a period of foot drill, and it was here I drilled my first squad of men. Frongoch was really the training ground for the Irish Volunteers.

Stranded either side of the camp, Frank and Bertie are aware of each other's presence. On Frank's second day they spot each other by chance for a very brief exchange. It is the first time they have seen each other since before The Rising. Unable to talk freely Prisoner #232 writes Prisoner #1676 a letter, from South Camp to Hut 14, North Camp.

> My Dear Frank,
>
> Was very sorry I couldn't delay a bit longer with you to day, however I hope to see you oftener as you're near. Twould be well for you write Mama and say you arrived here also you saw me. I just got up by chance to day and may not again for a good while. You try and be on any fatigue party that may come our way . . . Am sending cake. Hope you get it safe. Have you been tried yet in London? I haven't but expect to be in the

near future say next week. I shouldn't like this camp of yours although it's much more healthy than ours. The only objection I have is the grounds. Our place is quite the contrary, good grounds, bad rooms. Anyway I take plenty of baths. We go to the field often and have a football. I have my football boots and say if you require them. I don't believe we'll be here for the winter, as is the general opinion of our camp. They say after this inquiry business, releases will start. No need to tell you I'm expecting my release a good while back. This Home Rule question is almost at an end and temporarily settled.

Anyway you are looking in the pink . . . I'm sorry you are in that camp it's so mucky. Otherwise ok. A few of ye should apply for a transfer. Anyway, whatever you say yourself. I'd like to get an account of your experiences, as I may be released after interview in London at least I expect to. Several have been asking for you, both in the camp and outside. . . . I wrote Jack when leaving Wandsworth and it was returned to-day saying I couldn't write him until he wrote me. Anyway he wrote home, that's enough . . . we are having a strike owing to not getting enough note paper and also having to stamp that prisoner of war envelope which formerly was sent free. Am here since June 16th. Three weeks in camp and like it alright . . . We got a great send off from Ballagh. All the people around that locality are completely changed in sympathy with us. It's the best thing ever happened.[177]

Frank and Bertie's experience is not unusual – Frongoch's population includes more than 100 sets of brothers. Besides family connections, many of the prisoners know each other from involvement in the Volunteers, Gaelic League, GAA or simply as neighbours. Despite their many discomforts the prisoners' morale appears to remain high and relations relatively harmonious. They keep themselves busy, which helps.

Liverpool is only 70 miles north of Frongoch but poor roads magnify the distance. Getting there by train is the best option.

Even though the journey is long and expensive, visitors are not so easily deterred. Some relatives travel from Ireland or friends might come from the Irish communities in Liverpool and Manchester. Made possible only two days of the week, visits run for a maximum of 15 minutes in the presence of a guard. It is not unusual for relatives and friends to make the journey only to be refused access because they arrive at the wrong hour.

In the absence of visits, newsy letters from home are a comfort. Frank's most regular correspondent, Ena drops him a line.

> S'pose you see in the papers we've got Home Rule! What's in a name anyway. I don't think the Partition business will work . . . Heard nothing further from Jim. He may not come for a bit. I explained how things were exactly.[178]

The camp settles into routine and prisoners are allowed write two letters each week. Strict conditions apply. The letters must be no longer than two short pages but prisoners may write on both sides of the page. Outgoing post is first sent to London for the censor's attention. No references are allowed to conditions at the camp and political comment is also prohibited. The result is that much of the correspondence is anodyne chat about the weather or hopes of release. The prisoners feel suitably restricted, complaining in rather plaintive terms to the Irish National Relief Fund, a key support group.

> Anyone writing the truth has his letter stopped, the envelope is returned. Those over us are acting the tyrant.[179]

At first, postage is paid by the Home Office but this privilege is soon withdrawn and prisoners have to pay for their own stamps. Incoming letters are also examined by the chief postal censor in London. At Frongoch the monitoring process is repeated at a special room in the old distillery by the camp censor who, by strange arrangement, employs the assistance of several prisoners. The advantages of placing internees in the censorship process clearly outweighs any objection to prisoners being used as cheap labour, particularly when one of the assistants, Tom Pugh, is a close associate of Michael Collins.

For many, the move from prison-style incarceration to an internment camp clearly takes some adjustment. Prisoner #1365 Barney Mellowes is placed in Hut 19; Prisoner #1320 Michael Collins is in Hut 7; Prisoner#1051 Gerry Boland is in Hut #4.

Just months previously Frank was playing inter-county football for Dublin. He is extremely fit and in his prime but weeks of confinement have made him restless. After the grey concrete of Stafford, the grassy field on the other side of the River Tryweryn stretches like a long-awaited invitation.

The field can be reached by a footbridge across the river. It becomes the camp's sporting arena where full-on Gaelic football – hurling is banned – is played for pent-up pride. Teams are formed with names like Casements, O'Rahilly's, McDermotts, Fianna Fáil, MacBride's and Markievicz. Other top inter-county GAA players – All-Ireland winning captain Dick Fitzgerald and Paddy Cahill from Kerry, Dublin's Brian Joyce and Frank Burke, Antrim's Seamus Dobbyn – all take part. Hand drawn posters advertise the games advising that 'wives and sweethearts should be left at home.'

The prisoners refer to the field as Croke Park. Intern them and they will come.

On his second day at the camp Grandpa notes in his diary.

> 7.7 – This was a glorious day and in the evg we got out to our own football ground, a fairly large ground but hilly, and I had my first game (with a real ball) since the Croke Cup Final.

The good weather ends overnight.

> 8.7 – Rain. Rain. Rain. All day. I believe there are about 5 good days in the year up in these mountainy parts. Talk about BD and the west of Ireland! And then the slush and mud. There is no space worth speaking of – except the field and we only get out there when it's

fine – it's a continual matter of digging yourself out of mudholes and washing your boots.

But it has its consolations.

> What a pleasure it was to sit down to a good dinner yest – the first since Easter – and knives and forks too!! Felt a bit awkward using 'em at first !!

His spirits lifted somewhat, he drops a line to his mother in Ballaghaderreen.

> It's a grand country around here – but rains a desperate lot – worse in fact that our own wild west. . . . I met Bob one day. He is in the South Camp with the other BD lads except McCormack and O'Hara who are on my side. A public road runs between and we can't mix – as yet. It's a pity our only chance of meeting is when either of us is on some job in the other camp. There are 800 here and over a 1,000 on B's side. He's looking good. About 30 men in a hut – plenty of light and air – better food than in Stafford.

> We are running the whole show here ourselves under a captain of the I.V. and a man in charge of each hut. I'm the hut leader of this one. Have to arrange about getting it cleaned every morning and generally looking after everything – so as to have it ready for inspection daily. Our own men cook and serve at table and do all that's required.

> So you can see we have quite a small colony here; there's a football field also for fine days and when we had a match the other evg the f'ball was very big and strange after our small rag ones in Stafford.

> All the men are going down to London in batches to be examined before the 'Advisory Ctee' but neither B. nor I have had the pleasure of that trip yet.[180]

By July 12 things are beginning to look a little brighter. The first parcel arrives from home. A package from his mother Christina.

Miraculously, Christina and Frank's youngest sister, Lily, have devised a way to send fresh eggs.

> Dear Mama,
>
> Many thanks for the eggs and cakes and butter – all of which arrived ok. There was only one egg broken – so you can fairly well congratulate yourself this time! They were all grand and fresh too, and took the cobwebs of Stafford off my throat in great style.
>
> I saw B. in the distance – once or twice since, also Paddy, Joe F, Jim C & Co. and various others in the South Camp. It's a bit awkward that we are separate, but so long as we know things are ok it is sufficient. There have been a few batches released this week including Maurice Collins and I believe there are more to follow. I haven't been to London yet but expect to any day. It's possible most of the BD boys will be getting home shortly and maybe as such will be out before it's too late to give a hand at the hay![181]

But tensions are already brewing. The prisoners are irritated by ongoing delays over deliveries. Given there are almost 2,000 prisoners at the camp the sheer volume of post in and out of Frongoch brings about regular hold-ups. As in Stafford, many items also go missing, such as indicated by a letter from Prisoner #1454 to his mother.

> Dear Mother,
>
> I received your letter today. I am glad to see you are all well at home. I came to camp out here on June 30th. I got 2/6 all right but I did not get the socks you mention.[182]

The prisoners are getting tired of damp conditions, the infestation of rats and sub-standard food served up in South Camp. They find the Camp Commandant's haughty manner another provocation – Mort Ó Conaill describes Col. Heygate-Lambert as 'an incompetent of the Yeomanry, who must have had big a pull in military circles to get such an appointment as Camp Commandant.'[183] For 'B' Company's Michael Lynch he was 'completely without imagination, and kept the camp in constant turmoil by his bungling of every delicate situation which arose.'[184]

General antipathy towards Heygate-Lambert later finds voice at the House of Commons with Dublin MP Alfie Byrne acerbically asking if 'in the public interest' the Commandant be transferred 'to some more suitable office in France where he will not have unarmed men to deal with.'[185]

16.

*'It is now 11.15 am. All are out but Hut Leaders. I like this
time best as I get tired of continual company and it's very
hard to have a quiet 'think' or read with 800 knocking
round in such a small campus. It's nice and peaceful now
and as I listen to the hum of a mowing machine wafted
up from some valley below and hear the birds chirp in
the trees around I find it hard to imagine that I'm still
imprisoned. But the barbed wire fences and the heavy
looking sentry perched up in his box soon dispel all doubts.'*
– Frank Shouldice, Hut 14, Frongoch, 15 July 1916

For all its shortcomings there is no comparison between conditions at Frongoch and the Stygian bleakness of Dartmoor
where prisoners are not even allowed to speak to each other. Jack
is only allowed write a letter home every four months. He spends
six months operating a sewing machine, working from 9.00 a.m.
to about 4.00 p.m. Poor light and attention to detail does nothing
to help his eyesight and by his next birthday, aged 35, he needs to
wear spectacles all the time.

The last Irish prisoner admitted to Dartmoor is Eoin MacNeill,
Chief of Staff of the Irish Volunteers. Any resentment over his
countermanding order at Easter is swiftly nipped in the bud, as
Jack tells the Bureau of Military History:

> When he came down from his cell to join us in the
> morning prison parade, Dev – to the consternation of
> the chief warder and his assistants – stepped out from
> our ranks and gave the order 'Irish Volunteers – At-
> tention – Eyes Left' and he and we saluted MacNeill. It
> was a thrilling moment for us and any ill- feeling that
> might have been against MacNeill vanished from that

143

moment. He was a brother Irishman and that was good enough for us.

Harry Boland refuses to be cowed by the prison regime. Despite his upbeat demeanour he leaves much behind, including a partly requited fancy for Jack and Frank's younger sister, Ena. It is evident to those around them that he is somewhat besotted by her and although she sees appeal in him she is not fully convinced. David Fitzpatrick charts their paths in his forensically thorough work *Harry Boland's Irish Revolution*.[186]

Ena has no shortage of suitors but Harry's affections for her will be a little less unrequited upon his release. When Ned Boland visits Harry at Dartmoor he brings some photographs from home, including family pictures of their sister Kathleen and Ena Shouldice. Writing to Ned, Harry says the pictures 'caused a sensation in Dartmoor' with many enquiries about Kathleen.

> As for Ena, tell her I had to hide her photo as I was afraid it would be stolen, so many admirers had she, both Warders and Convicts. You have no idea how they brighten up a cell. I have built a shrine and workshop and commune with ye all . . .[187]

Ena may have survived the rigours of close surveillance but because of her relationship with Harry the military will redouble its effort to have her removed from the Post Office.

Jack and Frank already know they are sure to lose their jobs.[188] Jack's imprisonment has put paid to his position at the Department of Agriculture. Frank's employability has been on his mind for some time and he puts pen to paper in his Frongoch diary (which unfortunately goes no further than July 24).

> Have been talking seriously to E. re mise and my castle-building while in dungeon deep! Prospects are none too bright for an outcast on the world . . . still 'I'm strong + hale + hearty' as the song says; and will probably try what I can do in the New World – for the present I must lie low – like Brer Rabbit!

(L-R) Harry and Kathleen Boland, an unidentified friend, Ena and Jack

He is aware that a full-time position in the Civil Service virtually precludes participation in the Irish Volunteers. In the months prior to the Rising 'F' Company Capt. Fionnán Lynch was warned by his school manager that holding a rank with the Volunteers would cost him his teaching job. Lynch stepped down as Captain and Jack was offered the position. Jack passed up promotion for the same reason but now it's payback time.

At the behest of Home Secretary Herbert Samuel a Royal Commission is set up in May 'to inquire into the causes of the recent outbreak of rebellion in Ireland, and into the conduct and degree of responsibility of the civil and military executive in Ireland in connection therewith.' Three months later the Right Honourable Sir Guy Fleetwood Wilson and Sir William P. Byrne publish a 15-page report on the 'Cases of Irish Civil Servants Suspended in Connection with the Recent Rebellion.' The authors visit Dublin to interview 14 Heads of Department and 42 civil servants.

The Attorney-General for Ireland advises that 'it is most desirable that an expression of His Majesty's pleasure should be obtained that the civil servants in question should be removed from the offices now held by them in Ireland.'

Every civil servant involved in the Rising is evaluated individually but the rule of thumb is to get rid of them. They note that two assistant clerks at the National Health Insurance Commission – case # 1184 F.J. Shouldice and Case # 1545 T. Cotter – are 'arrested and deported' before arriving at a tidy conclusion for each man: 'Interned. Dismissed.'

Ever since arrest and deportation, strenuous efforts are made by Ena and Tom McKenna on Frank's behalf to get a decent lump sum payment. It finally comes through and is forwarded to #1676, Prisoner of War Camp in Frongoch to the tune of £40-15/-3d. It is as good as could be hoped for – Frank happily tells his mother 'my dismissal is nothing unexpected . . . but I didn't expect that cheque.'[189] The NHIC letter accompanying it says:

> Sir,
>
> I am directed by the National Health Insurance Commission (Ireland) to inform you that His Majesty's Government have had under consideration the question of your complicity in the recent rebellion in Dublin, and it has been decided that there is no further need for your services in this Department.[190]

The edict to dismiss activists brings a wide-ranging casualty list, including Patrick Joseph O'Connor, an attendant at the National Library. Enniscorthy postman Thomas Meagher also gets his dismissal notice whilst interned in Frongoch.

Various Irish MPs warn that the cumulative effect of executing the Rebel leaders and imprisoning innocent men under DORA will only galvanise resistance to British rule. At Frongoch there are growing signs of organised opposition when the vast majority of internees decline the offer of a case-by-case review under the Sankey Committee. Faced with the possible accusation of jailing suspects without charge and then denying them a day in court, the Home Office makes the review compulsory.

Gearing up to process over 1,800 cases, police files on internees are sent over from Ireland. Each case will be reviewed individually even though General Childs predicts Sankey will not find
'a single case for release.'[191] Broderick, a senior official at the Home
Office is initially enthusiastic about the quality of the prosecution.
He writes to Sankey:

> The cases are much better prepared than the MI5 stuff;
> they constitute merely of Police Report in concise lan-
> guage and the accused's own statement. [192]

On further reading, Broderick is a little less sure and writes
again to Sankey.

> It is clear from the papers sent over from Dublin that
> there are a number of very thin cases.[193]

By way of postscript, he adds chirpily:

> In the meantime a plot has been discovered in Egypt,
> and 18 people have been deported to Brixton Gaol and
> will appear before you under 14B. So that there will be
> plenty to go on with.

Barrister George Gavan Duffy is completely immersed in the
trial of Roger Casement so he gets an Irish solicitor named Mc-
Donnell to stand in as prisoners' representative. Their refusal to
recognise the Committee renders legal assistance largely academic. Not that the prisoners expect too much from what appears to
be an elaborate charade. Prisoner #1459 writes to his mother from
Hut 10:

> I expect to be going up to London for trial any day now.
> They are all going up in batches but it is only a matter
> of form they are all sent back to camp again . . . well we
> are all having a very good time here up the mountains.
> Nothing to do only playing football. All we want is fine
> weather – it is a wretched place when raining. I will say
> goodbye with best love from your fond son, Pat. (send
> me a shirt) [194]

Michael O'Flanagan's arrival at Paddington illustrates exactly where the Irish Volunteers fit in the minds of the British public. En route to the Sankey Committee at Wandsworth Prison he is escorted through a milling crowd at Paddington station.

> This crowd was made up of two groups, one awaiting the arrival of prisoners from Frongoch, the other awaiting the arrival of an ambulance train bringing wounded from the western front. As soon as the train stopped and we got out on the platform, the attitude of the people awaiting the arrival of the ambulance train, and who had learned who we were, became very hostile, and the attitude of the crowd who were waiting on us became boisterously friendly. The guard, which was small . . . succeeded in separating the two crowds and got us on to the buses without incident.

Curiously, once he was seated before Sankey, O'Flanagan found the questions very specific.

> I had the impression that the Committee were anxious to find out if I was one of the Members of the garrison of Riley's Fort where the British forces suffered heavy casualties.

For Joe Lawless and every other prisoner who refuses to play along, it's a pointless exercise. 'Most of us took a cynical view of the whole thing,' says Lawless, who was also taken to Wandsworth.

> Behind the table, extending practically the entire width of the room, sat a number (I think there were six or eight) of prosperous-looking, well-dressed gentlemen, in the centre of which sat the one I took to be Sankey. The others wore either a very serious or a bored expression but Sankey was smilingly affable, suave, and even friendly as he motioned me to be at ease.

The courtesies, however, conceal a less benign purpose.

> My name, age and activities during Easter Week he read out to me from a sheet he held in his hand, now

and then requesting my confirmation or denial of these facts. And as he came to the end of the recital he suggested in a sort of sympathetically confidential way, 'But of course you could not know what you were being led into when you took up arms.' This was it, I thought. We were right in our surmises as to the purpose of this committee, so I left him and the assembled committee in no doubt as to my past, present and future views of the British occupation of my native land.[195]

Joseph McCarthy, a Volunteer from New Ross, appeared before the Committee at Wormwood Scrubs. His account would be comical except for what is at stake is his liberty.

Seated at a spacious table were Judge Sankey and Mr Mooney. It was easy to know Sankey with his precise, imperious manner. Mooney, a member of John Redmond's Irish Party, sitting at his side, had a condescending, futile appearance . . . a lackey in bowing servility brought forth a file from the shelf in answer to Sankey calling for the file dealing with me. Sankey opened it and looked at some sheets of records therein, of which there were many, and put the question: 'Are you Joseph McCarthy?' in answer to which I said, 'Yes.' In the meantime, Mooney pulled the file over and had a peep. He could not have read two lines when Sankey pulled it back. Sankey asked me a few silly questions such as where and when was I arrested, where was my uniform. I told him the RIC took it in a raid on my house on Easter Monday of which he knew already. He closed the file and wrote a few words. Mooney urgently pulled the file to him but Sankey reached for it and handed it to the lackey and said, 'Next!' [196]

Frank Shouldice and a few others from South Camp are called at 6.00 a.m. on July 19. He's glad for a change of scene and packs 'some butter from Ballagh, homemade scones, sugar and a few books' before they walk to the camp's train station flanked by Royal Welsh Fusiliers.

> 19.7 – Our guard was a decent sort too (RWF). Those
> Welsh soldiers speak only their own tongue between
> themselves – would probably be dubbed Sinn Féiners
> if they had the misfortune to be from the Green Isle.
> Weight 12½ st at Frongoch Stn. Put on 6 or 7 lbs since
> arriving here.

The men play cards on the train, passing through Shrewsbury, the Midlands and High Wycombe before arriving at Paddington Station. It is Frank's first return to London and he finds the summer air clammy, the bustle of crowds and traffic 'making living so uncomfortable. Glad am I that I was lucky enough to get out of it!' Still under escort, a bus ride through the city drops them at the gates of Wandsworth Prison.

> The air (after the Welsh mountains) is dull + heavy and
> the heat very great. It was a relief to land in the wel-
> come shade of Wandsworth Gaol. The boys on top (of
> the bus) sang nearly all the way and it was really amus-
> ing to listen to all their rebelly tunes floating out over
> the bustle and din of the street traffic . .

> Got a nice drop of tea and chunk of brown bread. The
> cells are not too bad – and we have two sheets on the
> bed. There are two window panes for ventilation also
> – an improvement on the sealed windows of Stafford.

> The quietness and solitude here in the evening is like that
> of a churchyard – what a change from the bustle, banter
> and pillow-fights of camp! The silence is only occasion-
> ally broken by the distant rumble from that mighty in-
> ferno called London and we might as well be exiled away
> in Siberia – as far as proximity to London life counts!!
> Little did I think when leaving London in March 1910
> that I would enter it again as the result of such a glorious
> episode in the history of our own wee isle.

He's put into cell C2-61, six doors from where Bertie was first imprisoned. The following day – after dinner – he is called for his case to be heard.

20.7 – In with solicitor first who was most anxious to know what I'd answer if asked did I know about the 'biz' coming off on Easter Mon. I told him I wouldn't reply to such a question – and further that on all mobilizations we went out prepared for anything that might occur. His belief, he says, was that I went out on an ordinary mobilization or as his 'tout' put it expecting only a 'scrap'!

It doesn't matter what your belief is ses I and I don't mind what may come of it! I believe they were in communication with the old ctee thro' a side door and I'm nearly sure now – as the latter never touched on the above point at all. That's what they are there for, to inveigle fellows into saying they were <u>led</u> into it with their eyes closed – so to speak!! Even if the rank and file <u>didn't </u>know what was on – they went out fully equipped and ready – and it's ridiculous to suggest that <u>every</u> <u>one</u> should have been in the plans. It's the only opportunity the Brit. Govt have of trying to justify their murders and savage sentences and to say to the world 'well these unfortunates were only dupes; led by a few hair-brained revolutionists' . . .

He recalls being finally brought before the Sankey Committee.

Well – at the Ctee some small fat-headed old John Bull questioned me as to name, age, address, occupation, if married, whether people live in *Dn

*Dublin

Afterwards, Frank sets out in the jotter-diary what he remembers of the entire interview.

Q: How long an I.V.

A: Since shortly after start.

Q: Rifle + uniform.

A: Rifle

Q: Were you a private

A: No. Sort of clerk over the bks

Q: Did you look after the bks

A: No. I helped the Sec.

Q: You weren't a Captain.

A: No.

Q: On Easter Mon where did you go to?

A: Mobilised as usual at Blackhall St.

Q: Where did you go then?

A: The district around.

Q: Were you doing Sec work in fighting?

A: Oh! Anything that was required.

Q: Were you in a house?

A: Yes.

Q: What house?

A: Various houses.

Q: In what St?

A: Won't say.

Q: Well on Tues where were you?

A: I was in same place all week.

Q: In Brunswick St.

A: No.

Q: Around Church St perhaps.

A: Won't say.

Q: Well then I don't think we'll press you any further. Good day!!

That, roughly the gist of my exam! Goodnight!

17.

*'A Corwen Railway Guard was waving a green flag in
order to give a signal to an engine driver on a train
at Bala Junction on Saturday and suddenly he was
loudly cheered by the crowd of Sinn Féiners who were
being conveyed to Frongoch, but when he realised
what they were shouting about he dropped that flag
like a hot potato. Didn't you Guard. Right away.'*
– Yr Adsain, 27 June 1916

The apparent laxity of life at Frongoch masks a punitive and rule-laden regime. The men hold the Commandant responsible for two prisoners suffering serious breakdowns. Growing depressed at the camp Dubliner William Thomas Halpin tries to cut his own throat and is moved to the North Wales Lunatic Asylum in Denbigh. He is eventually transferred to Grangegorman Mental Hospital in Dublin where he dies a year later.

Another prisoner, Eamonn Tierney, is given seven days solitary confinement for writing the word 'blast' in a letter. Originally from County Antrim, Tierney distinguished himself with 'F' Company at North King Street when, under heavy fire, he retrieved the Company flag from the barricades at Reilly's Fort on Easter Saturday.

Tierney emerges from solitary confinement in an agitated state. Having spent years in England prior to the Rising he is extremely anxious about conscription. His fellow prisoners take care of him but he shows no signs of recovery, even after a visit by his wife and family. He is also moved to Denbigh 'continually saying he was a disgrace to his friends'. With kind intercession from a Miss Richards of the INAAVDF in London, Tierney is moved to the Longwood Asylum in Epsom where it is easier to visit him. It

Inside signal box, now disused, at Frongoch station
(photo by the author)

is reported that he subsequently relocates to Cork where he passes
away in 1921.[197]

Tierney's initial fears were not entirely groundless. The Military Service Act has been introduced in Britain but does not apply
to Ireland. However any British-born or UK-resident males aged
19-41 years can be conscripted and several prisoners at Frongoch
qualify in this way.

Col. Heygate-Lambert makes it a personal crusade to unearth
these men – dubbed 'refugees' by their fellow-prisoners – and
hand them over to the British Army. The main difficulty for the
Colonel is finding out who they are. Although each prisoner has a
unique number and the names of some prisoners are known, many
others are anonymous figures. The prisoners frustrate his efforts
by keeping it this way.

His first targets are the London-Irish Nunan brothers, Sean,
26, and Ernest, 19. Sean recalled it many years later to the Bureau
for Military History.

> It would appear that my brother and I were the test
> cases – or guinea pigs – for the others in this operation.

It struck me as rather naïve for the British to expect us to join their forces after having taken up arms against them only a few weeks previously – but that's the way the official mind works![198]

When they are finally identified they are sent to recruiting officers in London. Both refuse to sign up and are treated as deserters. Gavan Duffy defends the Nunans at court-martial but the best he can do is limit their respective sentences to six months and four months hard labour. It is not the end of the conscription issue.

Late summer brings some welcome sunshine. Writing 'Notes from Aberayron' for the *Cambrian News*, a journalist initialled J.M.H. paints a sort of rural idyll when visiting the outskirts of Bala late July.

As we passed Talyllyn Lake on Sunday morning the atmospheric conditions that perfect day made the lake a mosaic in ebony and grey, of hill and glen. It was ten o'clock when we came to Llanyedl Churchyard. In the shadows of the great yew trees the dew had not left. The grass was clipped and the sod was silken and springy. The consecrated acre bears the sign of being well and constantly looked after.[199]

And then, it's as if he suddenly happens upon the camp.

Frongoch Camp, the old whiskey distillery in which a thousand Germans were interned (whom I saw there twelve months ago) was now occupied by 1,700 Irish rebels. To look at 1,700 civilians – men and boys from the villages and hillsides of Ireland dubbed and treated as rebels and caged within barbed wire entanglements, would be calculated to embitter one's thoughts. It should not be *possible*.

Perhaps the incongruity of such a quiet and remote place is a balm to many men who arrive here after witnessing scenes of great violence – first the scores of German POWs captured at the Western Front, then the Irish Volunteers who saw action for the first time in The Rising. Little wonder that it reminds Grandpa of home.

> This would be a beautiful spot in good weather – mountains and wooded hills all round – through which I'd love to have a ramble . . .

> There was great sport here over the releases – processions and funerals accompanied by tin can brigades paraded in all the glory of crimson, black, yellow and multicoloured blankets . . . such is life in Frongoch with a lot of cheery rebels who <u>won't</u> be downhearted. Our football field is pretty large but too much of the hill and valley type for comfort in football matches. We're not out for comforts though, and therefore can enjoy it as well as Croke Park.[200]

The camp is unsettled by comings and goings, traffic generated by releases and visits to Advisory Committee in London. Bertie is called before Sankey but has nothing to say. Frank writes to his mother, clearly feeling restless.

> We are leading a real simple life, going about in shirt and trouser style, some in their feet! The camp has much improved with the dry spell and the grub is ok – of course little extras are welcome always but you needn't send on any more parcels as I've great hopes of getting out shortly! Batches still continue to be sent home every day and Ger F. is the latest!! So unless there's anything special I should be off any day.

> I was in London last week and enjoyed my trip and the return to the quiet cell life for a few days in Wandsworth! I was only 5 doors away from where B. was originally. The bus ride – for an hour – thro mighty London (we never had such sightseeing in our lives) was very enjoyable and the examination of conscience before the Advisory Ctee I'll tell you of later!

> B. is fine. Saw him a few times recently. He's just after his London trip . . .

> I'm feeling in the pink – put on ½ stone since coming
> here and brown as a hindoo! Will be lonely quitting this
> open air convalescent life!! [201]

The prisoners are asked to fill out an identification form, os-
tensibly a bureaucratic pre-requisite to establish Prisoner of War
status. Prisoners suspect if they identify themselves, the authorities will use the information to single out 'refugees'. They refuse
to comply, even when lured by promises of parole in return for
naming names.

All prisoners are called for special assembly in the yard. Another candidate for conscription, Prisoner #1454 Hugh Thornton,
is called forth. Arrangements are already in place between prisoners to swap names and numbers, if necessary. When the roll is
called no reply returns from the body of men.

Observed stonily by the Colonel the guards assemble the prisoners a second time with guns loaded and bayonets fixed. The roll-
call begins again. Although he has a means of avoiding identification Thornton, aged 19, steps forward to spare his fellow prisoners
unnecessary hardship. He is duly arrested, court-martialled and
sentenced to two years' hard labour. Heygate-Lambert then pun-
ishes the entire camp for insubordination by cancelling all visits
and post for one week.

The 14 Hut Leaders in North Camp complain in writing to
Herbert Samuel, Secretary of State at the Home Office.

> We beg to submit that the responsibility to identify any
> prisoner rests solely with the military authorities and
> that it is utterly illegal on the part of these authorities
> to punish any prisoner for failure to identify another or
> even for being unwilling to do so. We ask that the pun-
> ishment inflicted be <u>immediately</u> withdrawn and that
> the necessary steps be taken without delay to secure for
> the general body of prisoners immunity from such il-
> legal punishments and to secure them against the dan-
> ger of being driven to insubordination by the adoption
> towards them on the part of the Camp Commandant
> of an attitude similar to that adopted towards them in
> the present instant.

We are, Sir, on behalf of the general body of the prisoners,

Your obedient servants.[202]

The Secretary of State does not reply.

British Army officers at Frongoch Prisoner of War Camp

Prisoner #744 Joe Lawless observes how camp authorities swoop for particular prisoners – usually those eligible for conscription – and line them up for punishment, often to be meted out in prisons elsewhere. He writes:

> Somehow we felt that from henceforth life was not going to be so easy. Perhaps the enemy had awakened to his mistakes, and believed he could be more harsh and peremptory with the number of prisoners now held. For our part we had learned many a lesson since we first became prisoners, and were less than ever inclined to be docile.[203]

Separately, and secretly, the Irish Republican Brotherhood (IRB) also begins to reorganise at Frongoch. Grandpa is an active IRB member. Collins and Dublin solicitor Henry Dixon, one of the oldest prisoners at the camp, are behind the overhaul. In a mirror image of arguments within the Provisional IRA over political strategy in the 1990s Eamonn Dore is strongly opposed to the IRB entering the electoral limelight. He recalls clashing with Collins.

> I was not invited to attend another meeting in Frongoch at which Collins, Dick Mulcahy and Frank Shouldice were present amongst others. Shouldice told me about this meeting afterwards, and that one of the things proposed and agreed to at this meeting, was that a policy of political action should be adopted by us on our release. This meant taking over the reins from the Irish Parliamentary Party, as advice from home indicated that the latter party was in rapid decline while our popularity was high in the ascendant.[204]

General relations between camp authorities and prisoners deteriorate steadily and the conscription issue will come to a head in November. But the question of prisoners' status overrides everything. It is never dealt with satisfactorily so it resurfaces in different forms, mainly disputes over work and military service. It is addressed in what amounts to a policy statement by prisoners.

> The men want it to be established that they are only to do work connected with their own camp and they want it clearly stated what regulation they come under and what their status is. The Commandant told them they were not Prisoners-of-War but they were treated as such by the courts of the Government.[205]

As POWs they would not be expected to work for their captors. However the camp needs upgrading and staff officers feel they have ready access to an available workforce. It is advertised as paid work at an hourly rate of 1½ d but as the Colonel discovers, those who are available are not necessarily willing.

North Camp Commandant, M.W. O'Reilly, favours accepting paid work but the mood has changed and the men will not accept being treated as cheap labour. Capt. O'Reilly defers to their wishes.

I was informed that they were dissatisfied with the conditions under which they were operating, and they proposed not to report for duty the following morning. While I was disappointed that the work was going to be stopped, I nevertheless realised I could not order them to carry on.[206]

Grandpa is not convinced about the value of the 'strike' and is called to a Hut Leaders' meeting.

15.7 – At a meeting of hut leaders ar maidin seo it was decided to continue work – there were 3 or 4 dissenters but as in the 'UIL' they weren't chucked out or dropped from the roof so that a unanimous result could be supported! A memorial drawn up by Mick Collins referring to the fine state of muck prevailing here, the stamping of lrs, the ridiculous rule regarding visitors (some have been turned away because they arrived after the stipulated ¾ hr from Cork and Liverpool) and the general matter of outdoor work – was read.

In a standoff that will be replicated by Irish prisoners throughout Britain, men at North Camp refuse to obey when the authorities order them to work. They are despatched to South Camp to face disciplinary measures.

The dispute escalates when prisoners, who clean out their own quarters, are ordered to clean out the guards' huts as well. They refuse point blank. The Camp Commandant sees this as a direct challenge to his authority and disciplines the prisoners by withdrawing privileges. Successive teams of eight prisoners are drawn up, each refusing to carry out the order. This stand-off runs for weeks until 107 prisoners under sanction are on bread and water, all of which causes deep resentment throughout the camp.

The so-called 'ash pit' dispute is resolved by intervention from an unlikely source. The Secretary of State orders Heygate-Lambert to back down and instructs M.L. Waller, a senior official from the Home Office, to convey the position.

> It appears to him that they (the prisoners) have now been sufficiently punished for this offence. He has, therefore, decided to remit the remainder of the punishment and also for the future to relieve them from this particular duty, which he understands from you can be properly performed by the guard.[207]

In the dreary regimen of day-to-day prison life it's a huge moral victory for the prisoners and a serious embarrassment for the Colonel. Samuel asks that the notice be posted at the camp for all to see. Significantly, the Home Office's letter is addressed to The Commandant, Prisoner of War Camp, Frongoch, even though the prison authorities continue to quibble with the internees over status.

There is no hint in Grandpa's letters home that life in Frongoch is an ongoing confrontation between ruler and ruled. However his censor-free diary suggests a different perspective.

> 14.7 – A further batch of strikers have gone before The Comm this morning and he has summoned a meeting of hut leaders after inspection to read out rules of Hague Convention. Are we Prisoners of War or are we not?

The novelty of camp life appears to have worn off. Michael Collins, a rapidly emerging figure at the camp, begins a letter to former internee James Ryan.

> Same Kip, Monday 2nd.[208]

Col Heygate-Lambert and his adjutant Lieut. J.T. Burns are aware the prisoners are reorganising themselves with a more hardline, military-based structure. Thirty Volunteers, including many in leadership positions, are transferred to Reading jail in an attempt to scupper the new organisation. But the attempted emasculation has little effect. Michael Staines replaces Reading-bound J.J. O'Connell and the structure remains intact. Like the Shouldice brothers, Staines is the son of a former RIC officer.

Still licking his wounds, Heygate-Lambert regards the prisoners as lazy and useless. He orders that they are taken on fast-paced six-mile route marches through the Welsh countryside. It is a struggle for the elderly prisoners who are also forced out on the road. For younger, fitter prisoners however route marches are a welcome diversion. Instead of finding it a punishment, they enjoy the exercise. The hills and valleys around Bala soon echo to the passing chant of Irish rebel songs.

Frank Hardiman, a Galway IRB man, recalls:

> During one of the early marches we noticed a woman standing at the door of her house and shaking her fist at us. We were rather surprised at this sign of hostility, and to show there was no ill-feeling between the Welsh people and ourselves, I suggested to a few of those near to me to strike up the Welsh national anthem. Soon we were all whistling it, and in our marches afterwards we included it with our own patriotic tunes.[209]

Unidentified Irish prisoners at Frongoch (Courtesy S4C Cymru)

Grandpa writes in his diary:

> Great consternation at being called before half-five an
> maidin seo – no Mass today (every second day; upper
> and lower camps). It's ridiculous sure enough for us to
> be getting up at 5.30 with nothing to do and breakfast
> time only about 8 o'c!![210]

He tells his mother about the neighbouring area, at least what
they get to see of it.

> I suppose B. has told you all about Frongoch. I don't
> fancy it much for winter but one can get accustomed to
> anything, it strikes me. We do have an occasional route
> march a few miles up the country – and it's very fine
> scenery around. Hardly any houses and nearly in the
> same primitive state as if it was left after the flood!![211]

In scenes reminiscent of *Dad's Army* some of the older guards
cannot keep up with the young detainees. To lessen their load it
becomes commonplace for the detainees to carry elderly guards'
guns as a favour and hand them back on their return to captivity.
This happens without the Commandant's knowledge until a shortage of personnel at the Camp brings all route marches to an end.

18.

'The birds are very plentiful around here and I often
deal out a supply of crumbs in the morning – they are
surprisingly tame too. Thrushes, goldfinches, sparrows
and various other sorts hop around within a few yards
of me and pick away undisturbed. One little sparrow
flew in the door today and immediately made for
the windows – unsuccessfully dashing itself against
the glass. I caught it easily and let it soar off again.
I never was much in favour of caging those cheery
little warblers – but now after having undergone
the experience myself I am totally opposed to it!'
– Frank Shouldice, Frongoch, 15 July 1916

If there is any nervousness in Ireland about the general atmosphere post-Rising, it is certainly not assuaged by Neville Chamberlain's county-by-county assessment. Reporting confidentially
to the Home Secretary on 'The State of Public Feeling in Ireland',
the RIC Inspector-General finds that outside of Ulster, 'the majority of County Inspectors report that the number of sympathisers
and Sinn Féiners is increasing and that it is only the continuance of
Martial Law that keeps the extremists quiet at present.'[212]

He reports Sinn Féin 'extending their influence' throughout
Connacht and 'large amounts are being subscribed' to the Irish
National Aid Association. Some counties merit particular mention
– like County Clare, where, 'if a German landing was effected the
majority of the people would join the rebels.' County Longford ('a
very sullen feeling throughout the county'), County Roscommon
('undercurrent of sympathy with the rebels'), County Galway ('the
people exhibit a sullen and unsatisfactory demeanour'), County
Dublin ('a general feeling of uncertainty – the lower class Nation-

164

alists are restless and sullen'), Tipperary North ('hurling matches were held by the GAA in spite of the County Inspector's warning to the leaders that his permission was necessary. The leaders refused to ask for this permission . . . prosecution has been recommended . . . this deliberate defiance of authority is significant').[213]

Chamberlain can see that the Rising has transformed attitudes. 'The people generally do not approve of the proposed Home Rule settlement,' he writes. 'Many nationalists now think that, but for the physical force party, Home Rule would have been allowed to die.'

Somewhat prophetically, he adds, 'The Nationalists in Belfast and throughout Ulster are . . . firmly convinced that the exclusion of the Six Counties is merely temporary, whilst the Unionists are equally convinced that it will be permanent.'

Though much of what it does is for appearance sake the Advisory Committee in London ploughs on through its heavy caseload. Even without the cooperation of appellants it is clear that hundreds of the men brought in – including Bertie Shouldice – are entirely unconnected with the insurrection. Under pressure to cut the numbers at Frongoch, the Home Office is highly sensitive about how this reduction is handled. On July 12 senior official Edward Troup writes to the Under Secretary at Dublin Castle.

> It is not proposed to hand the men individual notices stating that the orders of internment made against them have been revoked, because the matter is urgent and the preparation of the individual notices would take a considerable time. It is therefore recommended to ensure that they should not be re-arrested on their arrival in Ireland.[214]

In another letter addressed that same day to 'The Commandant, Prisoner of War Camp, Frongoch, nr. Bala, North Wales' the Secretary of State issues clear instructions to Heygate-Lambert regarding the release of 460 named prisoners.

> These releases must be carried out within a week from today, but the Military Authorities in Ireland are anxious that they should travel in as small parties as pos-

sible and that there should be as little opportunity as possible for any demonstration.[215]

The Home Office proposes clearing out the prisoners over six days, ferrying them to Greenore (for midlands and points north), Rosslare (for men from the southern counties) and for Dubliners the mail boat to Kingstown (Dun Laoghaire). 'The route to North Wall', it adds, 'should not be used.'

> It is especially important that no men should be released in a Sinn Féin uniform or wearing a Sinn Féin badge. If any man order (sic) for release has no other clothing you are requested to supply him with ordinary civilian clothing, and if you have any difficulty in obtaining it you are requested to report that fact at once by telegram.

From its first sitting on June 16, the Sankey Committee gets through 1,846 hearings before completing the last case on August 28. Many of the 'interviews' were met with silence yet the Committee recommends releasing 1,273 prisoners. However benevolent this might appear it raises fundamental legal questions regarding what grounds the men were apprehended in the first place. His job done, Justice Sankey goes on holidays to the Polurrion Hotel in Cornwall.

The Camp authorities are advised who they must let go. A list of prisoners' names is read aloud at assembly every other day. Those who are released are sent home at irregular and unsociable hours in order to prevent pro-Sinn Féin demonstrations at home. For those whose names are not called, omission is a daily disappointment.

Joe Lawless begins to feel it.

> As each group left the Camp to the cheers and farewells of those left behind, a certain discontent and unsettledness entered into the less fortunate. The Advisory Committee had apparently made its decision as to what was wheat and what was chaff . . . for a little while the thinning of the Camp population created a feeling of loneliness – friendly groups having been broken up and dormitories more than half emptied. But much the same thing had been happening in the North Camp and

as the number of prisoners remaining in both Camps could now be easily contained in either, those from the North Camp were moved down to join us in the South.

North Camp huts noticeably colder than South Camp
(Courtesy S4C Cymru)

As expected, Bertie Shouldice is one of the names called for release. He packs his bag and heads homewards for Ballaghaderreen, leaving Frank at North Camp. He writes to his brother upon reaching Dublin.

Dear Frank,

Arrived here safe and sound. Going to Ballagh to-night. All's well here . . Ena is in the pink. Also all in The Crescent. It seems Jim was held in Liverpool, can't say for what tho'. May be here in a few weeks tho', hope so. It's hard lines when a fellow coming on hols is prevented travelling. Well how are you since? Keep the heart up.[216]

The weeks afterwards leave Frank in thoughtful mood. It feels a long time since the heady days of open, deadly confrontation at Jameson's malthouse and Reilly's Fort. The open-ended nature of incarceration at Frongoch makes it feel like a sentence without end, a time of great uncertainty leavened by sport, study and some satisfaction that the Rising has made a genuine impact. And so begins a consideration of what lies ahead, whether it's a debate on the prospects of military re-engagement or at a broader level, what sort of independent Ireland these men envisage. It is from these discussions ideas emerge of economic independence. In more concrete terms it is the birthplace of the future New Ireland Assurance Company, a home-bred competitor in the insurance market. Five of the company's founders are ex-Frongoch internees.

Despite censorship and the prohibitive rules against camp visits, the men are quite aware that shots they fired in Easter Week continue to reverberate at home and abroad. Outside parts of Ulster, conscription to the British Army has tapered off. The political momentum is decisively with Sinn Féin and the Irish Parliamentary Party is fighting for its survival.

There is a dull reality to being held captive in damp and remote conditions yet camp life remains relatively stable. Under the surface however resistance is stiffening. With the inmate population whittled down to a more hardcore element, the implications of internment in North Wales takes on long-term significance.

World War One dominates the international agenda but local events in Frongoch are not so easily brushed away. Sensing a huge change in the collective mood at home the Irish Parliamentary Party tries to co-opt the Irish Volunteers into a reframed nationalist policy. In a parliamentary debate at the House of Commons on August 7, 1916 William Field, nationalist MP for Dublin, questions Samuel on how much longer Irish prisoners will be interned. The Home Secretary replies he is 'not in a position to say'.

The following day Alfie Byrne, MP for Dublin Harbour, establishes from Samuel that 579 Irish prisoners are currently interned in Britain. Byrne pushes the matter further, demanding to know how long detention without civil trial will last.

> *Samuel*: I have nothing to add to the reply which I gave yesterday to the Honourable Member for the St. Patrick's Division of Dublin.
>
> *Byrne*: Will the Right Honourable Gentleman state whether these men will ever have an opportunity of receiving what you boast of as British justice or will they ever get any justice?

With the Sankey releases completed Grandpa is one of a final count of 573 prisoners not going anywhere. W.E. Johnstone, Chief Commissioner of the DMP, wants to keep it that way. Dublin Castle categorises the prisoners into leaders, influencers and rank and file. Unaware of his specific role in North King Street Frank Shouldice, #192, falls into the latter ('C' category) as a 23-year-old clerk who 'was in Four Courts during the Rebellion and in general surrender.'

Johnstone writes to Under-Secretary Chalmers saying that even if the police had no records of those still interned it was better to keep them in Frongoch.

> I am also against any of these men being released because they would swell the ranks of the disaffected in the city to a dangerous extent although few of them are of the calibre necessary to make leaders.[217]

Feelings at the Camp are running high following Roger Casement's hanging at Pentonville Prison on August 3. Convicted of high treason, Casement becomes the fifteenth person to be executed for his role in the Rising. His lawyer, George Gavan Duffy, is ostracized by legal colleagues in England for taking the case and upon completion of the trial finds his name removed from the Ellis, Leathley, Willes & Gavan Duffy legal firm. Gavan Duffy's request to have Casement's body buried in consecrated ground is declined by Home Office insistence that he must be interred within prison walls.

Ten months later Jack Shouldice would spend his last night in captivity in an empty wing in Pentonville. He, Harry Boland and Gerald Doyle make their way to where Casement is buried and 'said a prayer for a brave rebel and a noble fellow countryman.'[218]

It is a benediction of some poignancy. Forty-eight years later, on the day of Jack's own funeral, Casement's body is finally brought home to Dublin, also to be interred at Glasnevin Cemetery. Meeting up with Eamonn Dore, Tom Sheerin, Frank Burke and feeling the sadness of the occasion, Grandpa notes a consolation in his 1965 diary, 'Everybody pleased with return of Casement remains for which we have been trying for nearly half century!!'

19.

*'Frongoch since then has been aptly termed the University
of the Irish Revolution, and so indeed it was'*
– Joseph Lawless, Irish Volunteer, Swords

Ena writes to say Jim is on his way from the United States aboard the liner *Finland.* The New York attorney plans to make his way home to Ballaghaderreen and then visit Jack and Frank in England. Arriving from New York he is completely unaware that the authorities, tipped off by close scrutiny of Ena's correspondence, are waiting at Liverpool and will not let him step ashore. Mindful of Irish-American sentiment complicating official U.S. support for the Allied war effort, Jim's sphere of influence in New York legal circles presents a cause for concern.

Ena keeps Frank updated, completing a circle of surveillance whereby MI5 can observe a target's reaction to their clandestine operations.

> Jim has arrived but they wanted to send him back. He was kept in L'pool from Sunday till last Thursday night . . . He got no explanation or apology for being kept. Anyway TG he's here. It will do M* good. He's looking splendid – fatter than when home last. And in his usual good form. He intends going to see Jack. Perhaps you'll be out before he goes back. He's sailing on the 2nd Sept.
>
> Bob didn't change – only he seemed a bit paler. Hop you don't get fat! Bob is to send you some eggs. Wish we could know definitely when you are coming out. [219]
>
> *Mother

Jim then writes directly to Frank when he finally lands in Dublin.

I was detained on board five days, then allowed to come in. Had a nice time on the steamer, apart from not being allowed to land. Had a few letters from M Merriman to Ena and to yourself which were sealed and they made some difficulty about bringing sealed letters into the country under the D of the R Act. They opened them and read them but of course there was nothing of a political nature in them.

I expect to be over to see you sometime in the week of Aug. 25th on my way back to N.Y. I also hope to see Jack.[220]

Jim Shouldice, District Attorney's Office of New York

After visiting the family in Ballaghaderreen Jim takes the ferry for England, heading south for Dartmoor. Despite having crossed the Atlantic he gets no concessions or extra time for his visit. Jack, Prisoner q101, writes about it in his statement to the Bureau of Military History.

I had a visit from a brother of mine home from NY on a holiday during that period. We could only converse through an iron grille with a space for a warder intervening between my compartment and my visitor's. A warder was present during our conversation which lasted probably about ten minutes. My brother told me afterwards he got a shock when he saw me with the prison haircut and the convict uniform. We could not say very much to each other as I was forbidden to discuss anything except purely family or personal affairs.

The warden's intrusiveness is not imaginary. Each prison warden is instructed to listen closely to Sinn Féin visits – according to a Home Office memo:

When the S.F. convicts were sent to Portland and Dmoor one of the instructions sent to the foremen was as follows: When the visit is paid it must be in a room with an officer present, so that he can hear the whole conversation. No conversation in Gaelic would be allowed.[221]

Following each visit notes are made about any remarks of interest and forwarded to the Governor. For instance, a June visit by Dubliner Mrs Pearse to two Irish prisoners in Dartmoor is meticulously noted by a warden named Stone. He hears that Mrs Pearse has been to a private dinner with Alice Ginnell, 'wife of Ireland's MP'. The other diners are identified along with respective remarks from the evening. All details were sent on by Dartmoor's Governor Reade to the Home Office 'in case they should be of use'.[222]

After Dartmoor, Jim takes the road north for Wales. As Frank tells his mother, the Frongoch visit, closely observed by a guard, is equally uncomfortable for both men.

> Well I had Jim around here last week and needless to say had a very unsatisfactory ½ hour's chat with him. Of course you know that a 'third party' had to be present – I don't know for what reason I'm sure!! He's looking much the same as usual and it's a pity his holiday was so short.[223]

After all the drama it's almost anti-climactic when Jim returns to America. It has been a difficult and troubling journey for him. Before he leaves Liverpool he sends a telegram to Jack and Frank; rather than send it to either prison he sends it home to Ballaghaderreen.

> To: Shouldice, Ballaghaderreen, Ireland
>
> Good-bye take care of yourself Jack and Frank fine Love, Jem.[224]

Ena writes to Frank.

> Jim is on his way to NY. He sailed on the Ordanna last Saturday, an English line. Hope he gets across safely...[225]

Telegram from Jim in Liverpool

A large section of her letter is blanked out by the censor. Hiding her disappointment she mentions that a prospective liaison with a certain Englishman has come to nothing.

> I mustn't get too hot or the censor will stop my letter
> – and I'd consider that hard luck anyway. But I hope
> he's a sport. If Englishmen would only put us on same
> footing with themselves as far as freedom and develop-
> ment for our country's good goes, we could call them
> neighbours. And talking of Saxons I never heard from
> my one-time friend in Essex since the rebellion!! And
> am not sorry I assure you. Am glad I never allowed <u>that</u>
> to happen. Though when I think of it I know there was
> never any danger.
>
> I suppose there'll be a little stew when Parliament re-
> opens. Ginnell will be back. Things are drifting. The
> great majority are crying for Redmond's exit. If he had
> any decency left he resign and not wait to be kicked
> out. However the people are alright.

Despite uncertainty about their fate the internees keep themselves occupied, taking classes in the Irish language, even macramé
lessons. A concert is held to commemorate the 108th anniversary
of Wolfe Tone. The prisoners somehow manage to print a circular,
'The Frongoch Favourite,' which serves as their own underground
newspaper. Though more like a college pamphlet it's a symbolic,
defiant gesture that they can do this under the noses of the camp

authorities. Volume One of a short-lived publication strikes its own rebellious note:

> Good morning! Hats off to the 'Frongoch Favourite' ...
> read by everybody in Frongoch, except the censor.[226]

It's a boost to morale and is not averse to sparking a bit of gossip about the place.

> Who is the lovelorn lad in Room 3 who talks in his
> sleep at 2 am every morning?

There is no sign of conditions easing at home. Ena sends Frank an update with characteristic vigour.

> Do you still get the newspapers! They are trying hard
> for Conscription here. So you may be better off than the
> fellows here (tho' I know you'd rather be with them). It
> will be the biggest mistake England ever made if they
> try that one!
>
> Arrests being made same as before Easter. A blind fid-
> dler 80 years of age was arrested in Galway under De-
> fence of Realm Act for playing Irish airs!! Poor Realm
> must be in a bad way!! (Get your blue pencil out Cen-
> sor!!) I'm sure you won't let that pass![227]

Frank gets another letter from an old girlfriend in Ballaghader-reen. From her new quarters in midtown New York Máire Merriman is feeling nostalgic. Moved on from Atlantic City she is intrepidly carving out a new life in the new world while he is fenced into the old, sitting in a wooden hut, cleaning mud off his boots.

> Well we are back in New York and somehow I don't
> like the change. I'm so lonely – did you ever feel like
> that in a great big city? When I settle down to work and
> get to know people and places I may feel better. Won't
> you be glad to get home dear – I hope you'll be there
> by the time you have this . . . I'd give the whole world
> just to see you Franky dear – sure there is nobody like
> you – you are so good and noble. I'd love to hug you. [228]

Another letter comes from an ex-girlfriend in Leicester named Sorcha.

> It is too bad to think you are not getting off for Xmas but cheer up better luck next time. I am beginning to think Frongoch air is not agreeing with you as you seem to have changed a lot of late. You will be 'past redeeming' by the time you awake in the old land if you do not keep your heart up.[229]

To keep himself occupied Frank signs up as Secretary of the Sports Tournament Committee chaired by Eamonn Morkan. On August 8 internees hold a sports day in which Michael Collins wins the 100 yard dash in a time of under 11 seconds. The famously competitive Corkman also takes the long jump and pips Grandpa by three inches in the running hop, step and jump. The Secretary of the Committee consoles himself by winning the 16lb shot and the long kick, thumping a placed football 184 feet, 7½ inches.

Indeed in some ways Frongoch was a strange place to intern Irish prisoners rebelling against English rule. Three decades earlier Thomas Davitt had visited nearby Blaenau Ffestinog to give a public address about agrarian developments with the Land League in Ireland. Welsh peasants and small farmers could identify closely with Irish grievances – in north Wales local landlords, including the Rhiwlas Estate owned and run by the Lloyd Price family, were very much in the ascendancy. 'I rejoice that there is now a kindlier feeling and a better understanding between the Irish and the Welsh than that which obtained in years gone by,' Davitt told the rally.

Among Davitt's audience that day was a 23-year-old by the name of David Lloyd George. Little did anybody know that by the end of 1916 Lloyd George would become Prime Minister of Britain. On his first day in office Lloyd George would order Irish prisoners to be released from Frongoch. He would also play a decisive role five years later negotiating the Treaty with the Irish delegation in London, reaching agreement with historic and tragically divisive consequences.

Frongoch lies in a strongly Welsh-speaking area near Bala. Local landlords and gentry were widely regarded as part of the British establishment whose privilege was rigorously upheld at the expense of the Welsh poor and landless. In normal times London might not presume absolute loyalty to the Crown in these independent-minded parts but of course these are not normal times.

Wales is gravely afflicted by losses through World War One. Upwards of 35,000 Welsh soldiers serving in the British Army will not come home – marginally more than the official Irish losses but proportionally far higher in a country of about 2.5 million. This dismal toll and the daily announcements of local casualties hardens sensibilities in the valleys.

Besides, the relationship between the Welsh and Irish settlers has a chequered history. Post-Famine Irish immigrants came to South Wales in droves, looking for jobs in mining, particularly in the coal industry. As Paul O'Leary points out in *Irish Migrants in Modern Wales*:

> The idea that the Irish were responsible for taking jobs that rightfully belonged to local people, and working for lower pay, thereby forcing down wage rates, was commonly expressed in the wake of anti-Irish rioting in Wales.[230]

They gained – both fairly and unfairly – a reputation for undercutting local labour rates, which led to widespread resentment and violent skirmishes but, as O'Leary suggests, there was a lot more to it.

> Anti-Irish protests showed no sign of abating in the second half of the 19th century. In 1853 there were attacks on Irish inhabitants in Ebbw Vale and Brynmawr, and the trend intensified in the 1860's as anti-Irish tensions grew in response to increase Fenian terrorist activity in Britain. Fears of Fenianism were widely disseminated by the press, causing anxiety among the public and increasing anti-Irish sentiment throughout South Wales.

Gradual integration over successive decades reduced those tensions, but the sudden replacement of German POWs by Irish nationalists in a North Wales internment camp reawakens any residual distrust. The point is not lost on a pithy dig in the *South Wales Weekly Post*.

> Some of the 'Sinn Féiners' should hear what their compatriots in Swansea think of them.[231]

The perception of Irish republican prisoners arriving into Frongoch is of a strange bunch of disloyal subjects guilty of stabbing Britain – including Wales – in the back. The local press, including the Welsh language newspaper *Y Seren*, are unsympathetic.

And so if the rebels tasted a hostile goodbye in Dublin they are hardly met with open arms in Wales. In his study *Frongoch Camp 1916 and the Birth of the IRA*, historian Lyn Ebenezer claims he cannot 'eradicate the blot from the Welsh collective conscience' the fact that the Welsh 'treated the Irish just as harshly as did the British in general. We now pride ourselves as being proud fellow-Celts. But some Welsh people were amongst the very worst of those that sought to keep Ireland unfree. Thankfully, there were other Welsh people, including many of the inhabitants of the Bala area, who treated the Irish internees and their ambitions with compassion and respect.'[232]

But the prisoners are not without support. As early as Easter Week itself the Irish National Relief Fund (INRF) is set up by Art Ó Briain in North Ealing, London.[233] It opens offices in Glasgow and Manchester and by June 8 Ó Briain reports that the Fund has amassed £150. Like the Gaelic League, whose offices in London are raided by police, Ó Briain discovers that the Home Office is far from enamoured with having a charity set up on its doorstep to support a seditious movement. The Home Office denies permission to allow a representative from the INRF to visit Frongoch in July.

Samuel and Asquith may wish to keep Irish prisoners out of sight in North Wales but the untidy knot is beginning to unravel, with each slip further loosened by increasingly vocal Irish parliamentarians, particularly Ginnell and Byrne.

The INRF maintains its campaign undeterred and Eva Gore-Booth, sister of Countess Markievicz (jailed in Aylesbury Prison), and Alice Ginnell, wife of the MP, are high profile participants on its Appeal Committee. When it winds up in 1918 it will have dispensed a total of £138,000 to prisoners, their dependants and whatever else they feel merits support.

Back home, the Irish National Aid Association combines with the Irish Volunteers Dependents' Fund set up by Tom Clarke's widow Kathleen. In a rare show of unity the two groups amalgamate into the Irish National Aid Association and Volunteers Dependents' Fund (INAAVDF) whose stated aim is:

> To make adequate provisions for the families and dependants of the men who were executed, of those who fell in action, and of those who were sentenced to penal-servitude in connection with the insurrection of Easter 1916 and in addition to provide for the necessities of those others who suffered by reason of participation or suspicion, in the insurrection.

The INAAVDF, in turn, links up with Ó Briain's UK operation. On release from Frongoch Michael Collins will take charge as National Secretary of the Fund in Dublin joined by Michael Staines as National Organiser. Like so many national institutions yet to form in Ireland – including Dáil Éireann – graduates from Frongoch's political university will be very well represented.

20.

*'Last night I dreamt you had come
home. I met you at the station'*
– Letter to Frank from Bertie Shouldice, 16 October 1916

Jim Shouldice is not the only American interest in the camp. The U.S. embassy in London receives a number of complaints on behalf of American citizens numbered among the internees. In correspondence with the Secretary of State in Washington, Ambassador Walter Hines Page simply conveys the official line given him by the British Foreign Office: 'There appears to be no foundation for the statement that the rooms are over-crowded,' says Page. The Foreign Office cites three separate reports to conclude sanitation was 'satisfactory' and 'the food was good and the prisoners told him that they were satisfied with it.'

All three inspections were commissioned by the British Government – two by the Home Office and one by the War Office. They are hardly independent but the Americans, still wavering about committing themselves to World War One, aren't really interested in 'certain American citizens . . . interned for complicity in the recent rebellion in Ireland.'

The British Foreign Office assures Ambassador Page that 'any complaints about the food receive prompt attention from the Commandant of the camp, who has made representations where necessary with a view to improving or changing some of the supplies.'

Equally well spun is the matter of prisoner treatment. 'Any definite complaint which Your Excellency may desire to transmit to this Department will be investigated. A number of prisoners had to be punished for refusing to perform a certain portion of their fatigue duties, but this punishment was remitted by the Secretary of State for the Home Department after it had lasted some little while. No complaint of rough treatment of the prisoners has reached the Home Office.'[234]

It is a peculiarity of Frongoch that the prisoners never attempt a mass break-out. From an inmate population peaking at almost 1,900 men there is only one recorded escape – and even that is described more as a lapse. Daniel Devitt literally walks out the front gate past the prison guards. He makes no attempt to hide from authorities and goes walkabout. He is recaptured soon afterwards.

Despite an ongoing war of attrition between prisoners and Camp authorities Frongoch is less a challenge by physical force than a drawn-out battle of wills. At one point violence is considered an option but the idea is soon dropped. Enniscorthy Volunteer Thomas Doyle tells of an IRB meeting called by Collins. As both an IRB man and Hut Leader #14, we might presume Frank to be present.

> It was discussed at that meeting that we should attack the guards the next morning when they would come into the Camp. He told all the leaders to take a vote on it in each hut. When they did, a good many of the prisoners, including myself, were against it. We were only going to give them the chance they were looking for, to shoot us down like dogs. [235]

The deteriorating quality of food becomes a focal point. Rations of frozen meat are deemed unfit for human consumption by the Camp doctor, as, on occasion, are potatoes and tinned milk. Many prisoners refuse to eat Friday's special, vinegar-salted herring. The issue is raised at Westminster by MP Lawrence Ginnell. The prisoners also maintain pressure on other Irish MPs, including O'Brien, T.M. Healy and Alfie Byrne to keep Frongoch on the agenda. On October 14 they write again to O'Brien to report the third occasion meat supplies have been condemned.

> This morning when the prisoners ration party attended the for the purpose of drawing the daily meat ration, the prisoners' Quarter Master complained to the Or-

derly Officer of the day that the meat, in his opinion, was unfit for human consumption, as the stench from it was very noticeable. The officer admitted that the stench was bad, but that 'if it was washed with vinegar and water the stench would disappear'. . .[236]

Substandard nutrition and poor ventilation at the old distillery are blamed for an outbreak of scurvy among prisoners as well as skin, dental and respiratory problems. While these complaints are somewhat exaggerated for impact – several prisoners, including Gerry Boland and Oscar Traynor, refuse to put their names to the complaint – the prisoners, untried and unconvicted, have legitimate grievances.

Several MPs are unmoved, including Conservative MP for Faversham Greville Wheler:

> They are receiving one and a half pounds of bread, half a pound of meat, and eight ounces-of vegetables and other component parts, making up a ration equal to anything that the German prisoners of war get . . . These men are not doing any work and yet they are fed quite as well as the ordinary infantry soldier who is in full training, with the exception of the small difference in the meat ration . . . in addition to that they get many parcels sent them by their friends, and their condition consequently is very satisfactory indeed.

The packages sent by relatives break any hold the camp has on prisoners. Frank's wish-list to his mother Christina is usually food-related. Sometimes it's a way to supplement camp fare but often it's a way of replacing what the camp kitchens dish out. Letters that follow are often used to confirm the delivery of food parcels.

> Your parcels have all arrived ok. I've just got the last one today – with the scones – and the chicken, as well as the other two previous ones landed safely – and were 'despatched' again, of course, with very little ceremony. The butter seems to have improved somewhat of late – tastes stronger and more like the 'rale' homemade sort.[237]

Christina and Lily are happy to raid the larder in St. John's Terrace and do so at regular intervals. Frank even takes to ordering fresh eggs – however not every conveyance is successful. Lily, 18, attaches a note to one fairly ambitious package.

> Well Frank I sent on a box of eggs the other day and also a parcel to-day of homemade bread, butter and sweets. I hope you will get them all safe + sound.[238]

Frank duly replies:

> My Dear Mama,
>
> I just got Lily's note and enclosure yest also the br. + cakes. The eggs arrived a day or two ago but there were about 5 or 6 mashed up with the sawdust! It's a pity – because they are so nice + fresh – and I suppose they are very scarce too.[239]

Next time round Lily is taking no chances.

> I am after sending you a parcel and the postmistress would not take because it was overweight, it was over 15 lbs. So sent it by railway. So you must look out for it. It was a large parcel, paper was dark and a tiny sort of rope around it. It contained a chicken, 2 homemade cakes, a sweet cake in paper, ½ doz of apples, a box of pineapple slices, bottle of Bovril, cigarettes, chocolate. Be sure you see that everything is in it and write immediately. As we forgot about your birthday present on the 23 Oct this parcel will do in its place.[240]

Given the shortages of wartime Britain it is surprising that quality food packages from Ireland usually, if not belatedly, make it past covetous hands to the mouths for whom it is intended. Even so, it angers the prisoners when incoming parcels are held up for days at the censor's office, particularly when perishable goods are rendered inedible by the time the men get them.

With prison numbers reduced by the big clear out, internees are shifted *en masse* to the old distillery in South Camp. POW status remains top of the political agenda. Through 'Head Camp

Leader' Michael Staines, the prisoners formulate a letter to Cork MP William O'Brien, comprehensively detailing their many complaints. In a theme too indelicate to raise publicly he writes,

> Owing to the pest of rats which infest the whole place it is impossible to keep private supplies of food in the rooms without it being damaged, partly or in whole by the rodents. And in one case a prisoner had his face bitten by one of the rats and was in for some days under medical attendance on that account.[241]

Though many internees make no mention of the plague, Prisoner #3030 Thomas Doyle from Enniscorthy is casually specific.

> The old brewery was full of rats. We could see them crossing over our beds at night.[242]

Another Wexford man, Comdt. Joseph McCarthy, describes a scenario not suitable for the squeamish:

> A number of dock workers from the Citizen Army, who had some skill in exterminating them, were put in charge. When we were locked in at night, the rats could be seen in uncountable numbers in the compound and on the roofs of the dining room and cookhouse. When the prisoners were sleeping in the dormitory at night I often woke up and saw hundreds of them running and playing along the floor and over the sleeping men. Frequently, men got up to frighten them away, but found it was impossible to do so. Donal Buckley was bitten under the eye one night by one and he got medical treatment . . . [243]

Due to continuous rain in October the camp leaders report a serious infestation at Dormitories 1, 2 and 3. MP for Cork North East, T.M. Healy returns to the issue at the House of Commons, describing Frongoch as 'the scene of desolation, of hunger, of hunger-strikes, of rats gnawing the unfortunate prisoners, and of terrible bitterness and ill-feeling.'[244]

His description is disputed by MP Wheler, who claims to have visited the camp.

> There may be a few rats running about, but then there are always rats in camps. The huts have been boarded down to the ground in order to stop draughts, and it is very difficult indeed to dislodge the rats which take refuge underneath. But every step is taken to get rid of them, and in many cases with very great success. These exaggerated statements, therefore, might very well be stopped in the interests of accuracy.

Even so, North Camp is reopened. Using what is nicknamed 'the Irish Republican post office service' Frongoch becomes national news in Ireland. Michael Collins smuggles a detailed report on conditions to the National Aid and Voluntary Dependents' Fund. Offering an eye opener to life within the Camp *Cork Free Press* publishes it on November 11. Edited by Frank Gallagher – subsequently editor of the *Irish Press* – Page One declaims: 'Tales of Horror From Frongoch' while a series of tabloid headlines blaze across Page Three:

> The Need for Amnesty
> Shocking Stories from Frongoch
> Wretched Conditions and Harsh Treatment

Lastly – and somewhat puzzlingly:

> Irish Girls Among English Prostitutes

Whatever about hyperbole the inference is clear – Frongoch is far from the model camp the Government says it is. Having smoothed away American enquiries about conditions the British Government takes exception to being openly contradicted. Mustering a response under highly restrictive Defence of the Realm Regulations (DRR), Baron Decies, Chief Press Censor for Ireland, suspends the *Cork Free Press*. The newspaper, owned by nationalist MP William O'Brien, will cease publication completely by the end of the year.

Meanwhile, for the rest of Frank's family at home, life goes on.

> In Ballagh things are as usual, in fact the same all over. Only any people ye know are always enquiring after you and Jack. Remember you are not forgotten.[245]

The thorny issue of conscription returns once again when prison guards come to North Camp looking for two brothers, Fintan and Michael Murphy. According to a statement issued on behalf of the prisoners:

A bearded Frank as sketched by P Ua Ceallaigh

> The military sergeant came into the prisoners' compound and explained that they were specially required as the wife of one of them had died. As neither man was married it at once became evident that another subterfuge was being attempted.[246]

The prisoners gear up for nonviolent confrontation, stating:

> It is stupid for the English authorities to think that men have not only just fought against them are likely to fight with them and it is the extreme of meanness and cowardice to try and force them to do so.[247]

A roll-call proves fruitless when the prisoners do not respond. One of the guards recognises Fintan Murphy and takes him away. A total of 201 unidentified men are disciplined. The search for Michael Murphy continues.

A second roll call is met with relative silence. In frustration, the guards deliberately apprehend the wrong man – Prisoner #716, 22-year-old Peter Barrett from Craughwell, County Galway – and send him to London for trial alongside Fintan Murphy. Gavan Duffy represents the hapless duo, explaining to the military tribunal that one of the accused is the wrong man. Barrett is hurriedly returned to Frongoch where behind the wire Michael Murphy remains unknown.

In a now familiar and consistently petty routine the Colonel withdraws all privileges from South Camp. Except this time all 201 prisoners go on hunger-strike. The 48-hour fast ends after the intervention of Fr Larry Stafford, a Dublin-born priest who irritates prisoners by appearing in British Army-issue khaki. The men are soon demanding the chaplain's resignation when those who come off the fast find their post withheld as punishment. Order is restored when deliveries resume but the trouble is only beginning.

Within four days Col. Heygate-Lambert demands to see all the Hut Leaders from the North Camp. Frank and the others are escorted to his office. The Hut Leaders are asked to identify the occupants of each hut. To a man, the Hut Leaders refuse.

In a clear escalation the Camp guard is bolstered by additional troops from the Cheshire Regiment in Wrexham. Accompanied by his staff the Camp Commandant visits North Camp to demand a roll-call from each hut. Some 342 prisoners out of a complement of 546 refuse to identify themselves and are expelled to the South Camp for lock-up at 6.15 p.m. with loss of all privileges

The men who answer the roll-call are left in North Camp with access to the kitchen and full privileges. They soon set up a 'very successful smuggling racket to their late comrades in the South Camp.'[248]

All 15 Hut Leaders are then court-martialled on charges of insubordination. The Camp Commandant says he holds them responsible for failing to enforce discipline among the prisoners. They are placed in cells under guard. In the upcoming trial Gavan Duffy, who has defended Casement and various Frongoch cases, will represent them.

Writing a letter (November 8) he does not sign, Camp Leader Michael Staines evades the Camp censor to keep Alfie Byrne MP informed of developments:

> This letter for many reasons is not been (sic) signed but
> if you compare it with the previous one you will have
> no doubt of its validity.[249]

Perhaps in a change of mind, the signature is replaced with a valedictory:

> On behalf of Irish prisoners who lost their identity.

Staines follows up with a letter to the Secretary of State, outlining the background to their courts-martial.

> The Commandant's only reply to this was to the effect
> that if he had to have in the camp nothing but dead
> bodies he would have discipline in it.[250]

In parliament, MP Alfie Byrne raises the matter with the Home Secretary.

> *Samuel*: I have received the letter to which the Honour-
> able Member refers. Fifteen Hut Leaders at Frongoch
> are awaiting trial by a Military Court for refusing to
> answer to their names when the roll was called. These
> men set the example of disobeying orders, the rest
> merely imitated them. Apart from this incident the
> camp is in good order.[251]

The 15 men are brought before a military court in North Camp by royal warrant for the 'Maintenance of Discipline Among Prisoners of War'. It is ironic – even strange – that the status accorded the accused is 'Prisoners of War', the denial of which is the root of tensions in Frongoch. Quizzed by John Dillon, the Home Secretary tries to clarify what legal forum the Hut Leaders now find themselves.

> *Samuel*: They are tried, not by a court-martial, but by a
> disciplinary military court, such as may be held under
> the Royal Warrant dealing with disciplinary matters
> in any internment camp . . . in pursuance of the pow-

ers conferred by the Defence of the Realm Regulations 14B. [252]

Laois MP Patrick Meehan then asks what everybody is trying to figure out.

> *Meehan*: What is the exact difference between a court-martial and this disciplinary military court?

> *Mr Speaker*: That question does not arise.

Prohibited from entering an internment camp, press reporters are not admitted to the trial. Staines smuggles another letter to MP Byrne.[253]

> Yesterday both English and Irish papers were prohibited from entering the South Camp. We don't, as yet, know the cause but suspect that you had made Question Time a lively period once more. We have a high appreciation of all the good work you have already done.

The prisoners also manage to publicise their situation in the now doomed *Cork Free Press*.

> While emphasising therefore, the truth of our previous statements on the subject of bad food, bad conditions and tyrannical management of the camp, it is well to make it plain that our present penal condition is due to our efforts to shield certain men among us from seizure by the British Authorities under the Military Service Act . . . the belief is also strongly held that these seizures are only the preliminary to conscription for Ireland itself, and assuredly if the Irish people do not face the situation now it will have to do so later in far graver circumstances. [254]

Gavan Duffy outwits the prosecution when the authorities try to hold the court-martial out of sight from the outside world. According to the *North Wales Chronicle*:

Mr Duffy drew attention to the position, and claimed that the court, to comply with the Royal Warrant, must sit in public. The Judge Advocate advised the press must be admitted. The President then sent a sergeant with a message to the Commandant, who replied that he had orders from the Home Office to admit no strangers to the camp. On this the court decided that the proceedings must be public, and they therefore removed their sitting to one of the camp offices outside the barbed wire and accessible from the main road. Here the reporters were admitted.[255]

Frank's case for Military Court is scheduled for November 25 at 10.00 a.m. The court-martial is overseen by Lieut.-General W. Pitcairn Campbell. Two officers from the camp testify against him, led by Adjutant Burns.

At Frongoch on the morning of November 7th 1916 the whole of the Hut Leaders were paraded at the Orderly Room and were personally ordered by the Commandant to inform the men in their respective huts that a roll call would be held in each hut commencing at 11.0 a.m. on the above date. The accused was present and the order was given to him in my hearing.

On calling the roll, as ordered by the Commandant, the accused to answer his name or number, he being present at the time.[256]

Proceedings are covered by the *Irish Independent* and *Manchester Guardian*, adding to what the authorities see as troublesome publicity about the Camp. The *Irish Independent* reports:

One of the accused put the whole case in a nutshell, said the Judge Advocate, when he said he did not answer the roll-call, as to do so would be to inform on a comrade.[257]

So that 'the Court may understand this better' Camp Leader Michael Staines makes the comparison of a German deserter held captive among English prisoners – would the Court disapprove if

189

the English soldiers refused to hand him up for compulsory service to the German Army? According to the article:

> Members of the Court, at the mention of the German analogy, smiled and remarked that they had not looked at the affair in that light before.

Ena follows the news at home.

> We were waiting to hear result of your trial but no news forthcoming. Hope everything has gone well. There was an a/c given in Independent Mon/Tue . . it spoke very highly of ye and Gavin Duffy praised ye all sorts for your conduct. We are hoping against hope that you will be home for Xmas. They're trying hard and if it fails perhaps you may get home on parole. Am going down on Xmas even. Have nearly a fortnight but I'm thinking it will be a dull holiday this time. However we will keep the best side out.[258]

In summary, Gavan Duffy tells the court:

> The roll-call in this case was part of the machinery for identifying certain unfortunate men whom it was proposed to thrust into the army and therefore to thrust into prison – that follows because these men had been interned as being connected with the Irish Rising. It does not matter how much you deplore it – they cannot be expected to take up arms for the Crown when they 'took up arms against it.'

> The accused were entitled to be treated as political prisoners, and, in any event, punishment would be utterly useless against men of honour acting solely from motives of principle and conscience.[259]

Afterwards, Frank writes to his mother in Ballaghaderreen.

> Well our little affair came off in very impressive style last Sat and Mon. I was up on Mon. I suppose you have seen the Ind reports so you know as much about the results as mise. One has been acquitted – Tannam . . .

we 14 are awaiting the final result which will be known in a few days probably.[260]

While the trial concludes at Frongoch, a wider discussion is aired at the House of Commons. MP for East Mayo John Dillon – whose Ballaghaderreen home is a stone's throw from Christina Shouldice at St John's Terrace – demands to know who is behind the courts-martial. Secretary of State for War Henry Forster denies he is but the exchanges become more heated when Dillon pushes further to know if the Military Service Act, passed in January 1916, is being used to coerce Irish internees to join the British Army. The Home Secretary intervenes.[261]

> *Samuel*: A number of the men at Frongoch refused to answer their names when the roll was called and otherwise combined to conceal the identity of certain persons who were charged with the evasion of military service, and consequently it was found necessary to take disciplinary measures.

> *Dillon*: May I ask the Right Honourable Gentleman whether it is not the fact that the Hut Commandants in the camp were informed by the Commandant that the roll call was for the purpose of identifying these men, and were they not thereby informed that they were acting as informers and assisting in getting their comrades arrested?

> *Samuel*: I believe that the Commandant did inform the men the reason before taking the roll call.

> *Dillon*: He must be very ignorant of Irishmen if he thought that they would give the information.

Over the next weeks Col. Heygate-Lambert's reputation is shredded by Irish parliamentarians. MP Byrne openly questions the Colonel's fitness for command, asking the Home Secretary:

> *Byrne*: . . . if he will now cause the Commandant at Frongoch to be mentally examined and report on his suitability to be in charge of 570 unarmed men?

Samuel: I have nothing to add to the answers I have given in this House on several occasions to the Honourable Member's questions on this matter.

Byrne: Will the Right Honourable Gentleman answer the last part of the question – whether the Commandant there is insane and will he have him examined? Has the Right Honourable Gentleman no answer to that? And are our countrymen always to be treated like slaves?[262]

Galway South MP William Duffy asks the Home Secretary does he realise that keeping Irish political prisoners there is a policy 'leading to unrest and exasperation and certain to keep open the sore created by the Easter Week.'[263] Public sentiment in much of Ireland has sided firmly with the prisoners. Dublin Corporation passes a resolution to send a three-man delegation to inspect the camp. The tiny village in North Wales is almost better known in southern Ireland than it is in South Wales.

Dogged by stalemate at the Battle of the Somme and facing insurrection within his own cabinet, Prime Minister Asquith resigns before the year is out, to be replaced by Secretary of State for War, David Lloyd George. Home Secretary Samuel resigns and in the new coalition the vacancy is filled by Conservative MP George Cave.

As war rumbles on in France it falls to Lloyd George to galvanise the troops. While cabinet focuses its attentions on trying to bring an unpopular war in Europe to a victorious conclusion, the business of Easter Week provide a growing distraction from the main business of the day. Tension continues to ratchet upwards with British policy in Ireland facing increasingly vociferous criticism.

Cave's appointment as Home Secretary offers no let-up in the criticism of Col. Heygate-Lambert, most particularly by Alfie Byrne, MP for Dublin Harbour, who asks:

Byrne: . . . if any new conditions have been agreed on as regards the treatment of the Irish prisoners of war; if they have been now eight months imprisoned; whether he proposes to release them at an early date; and, if so, when?

Cave: I am not in a position to add anything to the answers given by my predecessor and by the Chief Secretary for Ireland on this subject.

Byrne: Having regard to the fact that the blundering and stupidity of his predecessor in the past have been the means of the Right Honourable Gentleman occupying his present position, will he not say whether the blundering and stupidity will now cease?

The embattled Home Secretary is rescued by James Lowther, Speaker of the House.

Mr Speaker: I should like to see that question on the Paper.[264]

The trial of the Hut Leaders reaches its verdict mid-December. Grandpa is found guilty and sentenced to 28 days hard labour. The same sentence is passed on 11 other hut leaders. Two more – Richard Mulcahy and Tom Sinnott – get 38 days and William Tannam is acquitted on grounds of mistaken identity.

Following his profound disappointment over the Casement trial, Gavan Duffy is pleased with the verdict at Frongoch. He declares:

This is a very signal victory (for in all the circumstances the sentences are very light) over the high-handed methods of the Commandant but the question (sic) arise as to the whole body of men who were transferred and punished to the South Camp for committing the same offence as the Hut Leaders. These men are still in punishment in the South Camp unless the Commandant has chosen to release them now that the Hut Leaders have been dealt with . . . and it is most important that you would take steps to see that the Irish press voices loudly the demand for no further punishment against these 300 men.[265]

Having been detained for the duration of the trial Grandpa serves six more days in a punishment cell before rejoining the other men. The episode is recounted in a song called 'The Frongoch Roll Call' which begins:

> Fifteen forgetful rebels filed into the Frongoch 'clink'
> Shouting out the battle-cry of Freedom,
> In a state of blank abstraction – of their names they couldn't think
> So they shouted out the battle-cry of Freedom.

With prisoners suspicious of all approaches by Camp personnel, they refuse to identify themselves even when sick. A local doctor, Dr. David Peters – and his nephew, Dr Robert J. Roberts – visits the camp daily. Poor ventilation in South Camp leads to an overload of respiratory cases – three men die from pulmonary illnesses shortly after release. Under strict orders from the Commandant the doctors cannot treat prisoners who don't give their names. Dr Peters is well-regarded by prisoners and he is clearly frustrated at being unable to perform his duties. The men hold the Commandant responsible for the neglect of patients but all are shocked when Dr Peters' body is found in the River Tryweren.

The *Liverpool Daily Post* reports 'Frongoch Camp: Doctor Bothered to Death'[266] citing Cave's explanation that 'he had not been in robust health lately and was much worried by annoying and untruthful statements made by Irish prisoners at the camp.' Local newspaper *Yr Adsain* publishes that prior to his 'tragic death' the Bala doctor was 'worried by conduct of Irish Rebels'.

> He had left his house the previous morning, saying he was going to the Frongoch Camp, and nothing more was seen of him till the following morning when a search party in charge of Supt. Morgan found the body in the river. On his person was found his written resignation as camp medical officer. He was 50 years of age.[267]

At the inquest in Bala his widow testifies:

... when her husband let the house at 9.30 a.m. the previous day for the camp he was not in his usual health,
having had a very restless night. He had been worried
lately on account of the conduct of the Irish prisoners
at the camp ... Dr. Robert J. Roberts, Corwen, who had
been working with Dr Peters at Frongoch Camps since
July last, said there had been a good deal of trouble
lately with the prisoners and that had caused Dr Peters
to worry a great deal. His health was affected and in his
opinion, he might have fallen by accident into the river.
The jury returned a verdict of Suicide 'while temporarily insane.'

The Colonel calls an assembly of prisoners and berates them
for driving the doctor to suicide. The prisoners are riled by the accusation. In his memoir *With the Irish in Frongoch*, W.J. Brennan-
Whitmore recalls:

The prisoners broke out in a storm of protest. They
charged the colonel with being the cause of his death,
in that he would not allow the deceased to perform his
professional functions unless he consented to become
a political instrument of torture.[268]

The Colonel and the coroner lay blame at the feet of the prisoners and that line is maintained by Home Secretary Cave who
says the doctor's 'mind appears to have been unhinged by the false
charges made against him and his staff.'[269] Dublin MP Byrne says
the prisoners utterly reject this and demand an enquiry.

Word about resistance at Frongoch spreads wherever Irish
prisoners are held. Referring to his time in Portland Prison on the
south coast, Gerald Doyle tells the Bureau of Military History of:

... an awakening of ideas on how to combat the jail
system and start a movement for the status of political prisoners ... Larry Ginnell had raised questions
in the British House of Commons about the prisoners
in Frongoch Camp and, with these tit-bits beginning
to come through, we also found that there was a new
spirit amongst the prisoners in Portland.[270]

News gets around in dribs and drabs, even to a place like Dartmoor where all communication is forbidden. The prisoners somehow get wind of what is happening but are often too hungry or too cold to be interested in what's going on outside. Jack remembers eating dandelion leaves to fill his stomach at Dartmoor. Unlike Frongoch, the Irishmen there serving long terms of penal servitude and are thus treated as convicts. They are not allowed receive food packages – for some, the sudden deprivation of cigarettes is punishment enough.

Late autumn and early winter bring another abiding memory for Dartmoor inmates of mist and fog coming off the moor to the point that 'the prison walls literally ran with moisture'. De Valera and two other Irish prisoners are transferred to Maidstone for disciplinary reasons. Jack moves from an end cell to the one vacated by de Valera, where it is marginally warmer.

In December the authorities decide to gather all Irish convicts into one place. Lewes Prison becomes home to 123 men, Jack among them, transferred from the harsh regime of Dartmoor to a more relaxed one in Sussex. When he writes to his mother from there he has some inkling mid-December that releases at Frongoch are imminent.

> It is quite probable you will have Fk home for Christmas. I sincerely hope so at any rate though he seems to be in splendid form, from what I hear from yourself and Ena.[271]

> Frank 'the boyo' seems to be thriving on the life and enjoying himself as if he were on holiday. I would give a good deal to be able to have a lash at a football occasionally here or a game of handball, but never mind. There is a good time coming D.V. [272]

Putting his best foot forward, Jack looks to make his new 'little house quite cheerful and homelike'.

> I wd like to have one of Frank's letters (and photos) if available, giving some account of his life since we part-

ed. However I suppose I shall have to be content until
we meet again, which may not be so long.

Christmas is drawing near and the waiting game goes on at
Lewes, Aylesbury and Frongoch – and everyplace else Irish prisoners are helf. Frank writes home.

> My Dear Mama,
>
> Well how are ye all faring; I suppose ye are expecting
> news – like myself – every day and I'm afraid I can't
> give anything fresh yet! . . . well Mama I didn't expect
> to be here so long, that decision is taking some time to
> arrive at – perhaps we may not be sent off at all now!
> At any rate as Jim says 'I should worry!' Am feeling fine
> mesel' and hope Lily, B. and yourself are ditto.[273]

At year's end incoming Prime Minister Lloyd George begins
his address to the House of Commons. From the weighty burdens
of World War One Lloyd George switches track to a predicament
closer to hand.

> I wish it had been possible for me to have said some-
> thing today about Ireland. I had hoped to be able to
> do so but the circumstances to which I have already
> referred have made it impossible for me to devote my
> time and attention to the problems which have arisen
> in that country . . . All I should like to say is this: I wish
> it were possible to remove the misunderstanding be-
> tween Britain and Ireland which has for centuries been
> such a source of misery to the one and of embarrass-
> ment and weakness to the other . . .
>
> I have always thought and said that the real solution of
> the Irish problem is largely one of a better atmosphere.
> I am speaking not merely for myself, but for my col-
> leagues when I say that we shall strive to produce that
> better feeling.[274]

To which Michael Flavin, MP for Kerry North interjects, 'Let
out the prisoners!'

The Home Office is not particularly concerned how Irish prisoners spend Christmas but MP Byrne presses the Secretary of State.

> *Byrne*: . . . whether he is aware that the Irish National Aid Association are anxious to supply a Christmas dinner to the Irish prisoners of war at Frongoch Camp if they are not released before that time?

> *Cave*: Yes, sir. I have given permission to this Association to send into Frongoch camp a consignment of Christmas fare. The men who are still in the South Camp will be allowed to share in it.

The Home Office duly telegrams the National Aid Association in Dublin to confirm 'Dinner and parcels will be allowed north and south camps.' Naturally, the prisoners and their families take this to mean that there will be no general release before Christmas. Whether it is merely indecision or a deliberate ploy, the late announcement has relatives in Ireland scrambling around to get parcels and letters across to Frongoch in time.

Following Lloyd George's first address as Prime Minister, John Redmond makes an impassioned plea to him and Henry Duke.

> *Redmond*: You are holding in English prisons – it is an extraordinary thing to think of – between 500 and 600 untried prisoners . . . you may say they are dangerous men and you do not want to let them loose because they have extreme opinions. Surely that is going back to the old evil English rule in Ireland. These men are dangerous so long as they are where they are. They cease to be dangerous – they become far less dangerous – the moment they are released, and if the Right Honourable Gentleman wants to create a better atmosphere in Ireland and a better feeling, let him instantly release these men. Let him do it tomorrow. Let him do it as a Christmas gift to the Irish people . . .[275]

The next day, five days before Christmas, John Dillon makes another heartfelt, if long-winded, appeal to let the Frongoch internees go home.

> *Dillon*: What better action could have been taken to improve the atmosphere than to announce to the Irish people that all these prisoners at Frongoch and the gaols in England would be released by Christmas?

In a lengthy, even windier reply, Chief Secretary Duke dismisses any comparison between the internees and 'the men who are fighting with such brilliant valour with the Irish Division at the Front.'

> *Duke*: There is no need to stir up feeling in this country about a matter of this kind. What is the true position in regard to the men who remain interned in Frongoch, and why it is that grave deliberations have necessarily marked the conduct of those who had to answer the question, 'Has the time come when these men can be released?'

The Chief Secretary points out that of some 3,000 originally arrested after the Rising, the number detained has been whittled down to 562 'who were held by the Advisory Committee to be involved in actions of treason.' Duke maintains that for 'the peace of Ireland' he must stick by the rulings of the Committee.

Yet in an unforeseen U-turn the following evening, December 22, he suddenly announces that the Frongoch internees will be released. Helena Molony and Winifred Carney who, unlike prisoner Countess Markievicz, are categorised as internees at Aylesbury, will also be released. No reason is given for the government's change of heart. In an effort to reduce the possibility of violence in Dublin Under-Secretary Chalmers telegrams Chief Secretary Duke with preparations for their arrival.

> Unless you otherwise direct I shall tell police that the existing prohibition of all demonstrations of welcome on homecoming of interned prisoners must not be

enforced on occasion of this wholesale release. As a measure of conciliation but that such demonstrations should be allowed as long as they are not a menace to public order or an occasion for seditious language and merely watched and reported on. Inspector General agrees. Glad if HO will give date and time of earliest discharges.[276]

The men gather in the camp mess hall and are told they are on their way home. Suspecting another trick they ask how they are supposed to sign out. A solution is found that the prisoners can leave without being identified individually. In wintry conditions they gather their meagre possessions and file out through a blizzard to await the train from Frongoch. Some of the men sign each other's autograph books as they leave the camp, aware that this is a journey not without significance. Transportation is two hours late. Saturated, they board the train and are held up again at Holyhead before they finally board the night mailboat.

Grandpa is coming home. The boat is packed with Irish people making it back for Christmas. Also aboard the boat that night is Helena Molony, Winifred Carney and Seamus Ua Caomhanaigh, who had four brothers active in the Rising. Ua Caomhanaigh originally worked as a telegram boy at the GPO but when he refused to join the British Army at the age of 16 he was dismissed. On Easter Monday Seamus and his brother Micheál went back to the GPO to report for duty under Padraig Pearse.

Cheered by the festive mood the boat is full of song before leaving port. Homebound passengers discover that they have been joined by the Irish prisoners just released from Frongoch. Ua Caomhanaigh recalls the scene for the Bureau of Military History.

> We bore a very disreputable appearance at that time. Our clothes were in tatters and, with standing so long in the snow and sleet we looked even worse than usual. We were not long on board when a man came up to me and asked would I like a cup of tea . . . then a lady gave me an enormous hunk of Christmas cake. Another gave me a large piece of cheese. I drank the tea, and with the cheese in one hand and the cake in the other

I would take an alternative bite out of each and by the time I had got it all down I was feeling fine.[277]

But the crossing gets very rough. Storms and high seas toss the mail boat in its swell. The singing subsides and nearly all the passengers are seasick. The boat, with its lights switched off to reduce the risk of submarine attack, zig-zags the channel at full speed, Grandpa among its now distressed human cargo struggling for balance and respite in the turbulent murky waters, until finally, in the early hours of a new day they catch a first view in the distance, the embrace of Dublin Bay.

Grandpa, former sniper and now released prisoner, steps gingerly ashore.

21.

'You take it when we were deported I don't recollect
a cheer of a smiling face at all. We were spat at and
jeered. But it was different when we came back.'
– Irish Volunteer, Sean Nunan[278]

Getting home, Grandpa and other released prisoners can see that attitudes have really changed. To their general astonishment the returning Volunteers are welcomed back, the vitriol of their send-off replaced by sympathetic, enthusiastic approval. Their emotional homecoming is reported by the *Irish Independent*.

> Numbers of relatives and friends kept an all-night vigil at the North Wall to welcome back the released men. The spectacle of the anxious groups of people in the early morning, with wind and rain following frost, was strikingly pathetic. They stood outside the gates of the L & N.W. Railway, greeting their friends as they passed through the portals. It was a touching scene, having in it nothing of the effusively demonstrous – just a quiet family meeting in every instance.[279]

Previous distinctions between Irish Volunteer, Irish Citizen Army and Cumann na mBan are redrawn in broader strokes and Sinn Féin is on the march.

> A big body of the prisoners left from the Great Southern Station at the North Wall for Cork and Limerick and about 40 from the West marched to Fleming's Hotel, Gardiner Place, where they breakfasted. A number of members of the National Aid Association met the boat on its arrival and gave instructions to those who were in need of funds to call at the offices in Exchequer Street during the afternoon. Here there was a busy

scene throughout the afternoon. Among those who called to welcome the men back was Mr L. Ginnell, M.P. . . all the prisoners looked in robust health. Many of them wore beards.[280]

Finding his feet after a difficult crossing Frank discovers that the Volunteers Dependents' Fund[281] has set aside £10 14s 4d to provide cooked breakfasts and connecting taxis for westbound and southbound returnees. Great Western Railway ticket No. 209, courtesy of the UK Home Office, will take him 'one-way' from Frongoch to Ballaghaderreen with 'break of journey not allowed.' His mother and Ena send a telegram to the Bolands in giddy anticipation lest he make an unscheduled pit stop in Fairview.

> Greetings. A thousand welcomes. If coming by 8.50 to-night could get car Kilfree love Mother Ena[282]

He catches the night mail train for the West and steps off at Kilfree sub-station, six miles outside Ballaghaderreen. Family friend – and future brother-in-law – Joe O'Kelly picks him up with a hearty welcome. Frank is back home after nine very eventful months but as his foot hits the platform Joe O'Kelly is not the only one watching.

In fact from the minute the mailboat landed in Dun Laoghaire he is on Dublin Castle's radar. He is unaware that reports and information about him will originate and pass between MI5, Special Branch's 'G' Division, Dublin Metropolitan Police, Royal Irish Constabulary, British Military Forces in Ireland,

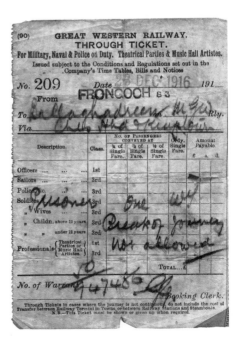

Frank's train ticket from Frongoch to Ballaghaderreen – one-way

the Lord Lieutenant and Chief-Secretary's office. His file, 78S / 75590, at Dublin Castle will be heavily thumbed over the coming years.

Frank might think his release from internment in North Wales will be his last encounter with the British authorities. In many ways it is only the beginning. He will spend almost half of the next four years locked up.

That train journey home marks the beginning of a handwritten police file entitled 'History of Frank Shouldice', which keeps a confidential record of his movements in and out of Ballaghaderreen, up and down to Dublin. Ruled into three columns it leaves room for the date (punctuated like a psalm) and the name of the officer recording the information. The central event is given most space – where he goes, who he meets, what time he gets home. File 78S / 75590 is stored by Special Branch 'G' Division at Dublin Castle and will leave the country, along with hundreds of thousands of secret and confidential official documents when the British administration prepares for evacuation from Ireland.

I re-read his 'history', distracted momentarily by the black comedy of its title. The file is part of a larger surveillance folio on the Shouldice Family currently stored at the vast British National Archives in Kew, London. Discovering that a secret file about

Handwritten police file on Frank Shouldice 1916-17
(Courtesy British National Archives, Kew)

Grandpa should even exist jolts the attention. There's an immediate sense of state power tightening, the focus of its attention this returning 24-year-old and his family in Ballaghaderreen.

Whatever about Frank getting home from Frongoch in time for Christmas there is no prospect of his brother being released. On the back of courts-martial Jack and his 122 fellow prisoners ring out the New Year behind bars.

The Home Office has moved them all to Lewes Prison near Brighton and Countess Markievicz remains in Aylesbury. The Governors at Dartmoor, Wakefield, Portland and Maidstone are told that the men 'will be given special privileges'[283] at Lewes. Previously, they were all assigned jobs like making coal sacks, mail bags, horse halters, bookbinding and helping out in hospital; now, the 'Irish Rebel Convicts' will be accommodated in a special part of the prison, allowed free association, civilian clothes, monthly letters and visits – all subject to good behaviour. In effect, the prisoners are promised Prisoner of War status in everything but name.

In return, should a prisoner a break the rules he 'will be immediately transferred to the ordinary conditions of detention in an ordinary prison.' This proposition faces its first test when the prisoners are transported to Lewes. They are requested to promise in writing that they will not try to escape. Somewhat affronted, the men refuse any such guarantee and, as Jack tells the Bureau, they are soon reminded who is in charge.

> When we were removed from Dartmoor we were chained together in batches of six by means of a steel chain through handcuffs.[284]

Bound together like slaves for a 12-hour rail journey conjures its own sullen picture. Typically however, on a bitterly cold winter's day, their camaraderie is irrepressible and makes a mockery of the situation.

> That journey was very enjoyable. We sang rebel songs on the way and even danced. When changing from the Dartmoor railway line to the main line we had a delay – it may have been Plymouth station. On the platform

our squad who were chained together consisted of Bob Brennan, Harry Boland, Dick King, Con Donovan and another whom I cannot recollect. Bob asked Dick, another Wexford man, to give an exhibition of Irish dancing, Bob lilting in great style. We held up the chain and King, who was a Leinster champion dancer, gave us a selection of jigs and hornpipes which delighted us and even the English travellers and railway officials who were on the platform and they warmly applauded the performance. When we arrived at Lewes Station, all in great form, we were transferred to prison vans but before entering the vans we insisted on singing 'The Soldier's Song' . . .

Reunited with de Valera and other familiar faces, the Irish contingent at Lewes numbers about 130. Although conditions are appreciably better than Dartmoor they remain prisoners, not Prisoners-of-War. On Day Two in his new surroundings Jack writes to his mother. There is no mention of handcuffs or chains.

My Dear Mother,

Well we have got the first steps towards emancipation. We were changed here yesterday from Dartmoor and needless to say, the change is all for the better. Extra food but no variation. Allowed to write once a month and I understand – but not definitely – that we will be allowed a letter in lieu of a visit once a month, which means a letter once a fortnight . . . in fact only for the change I would not be able to write you until the New Year. Now I may be able to have a reply from you by Christmas.[285]

Provided with warmer comforts and better food there is a sense of give-and-take about the new regime. According to the rules at Lewes, 'Money, Books, Postage Stamps, Tobacco, Clothes etc should not be sent to Prisoners, for their use in prison, as nothing is allowed to be received at the Prison for that purpose.'[286]

Jack's comrades welcome the improvement but have no intention of being absorbed into the British penal system as criminals when they regard themselves as Irish political prisoners. They are heartened at hearing their cause ventilated at the House of Commons. Like he and other Irish MPs did for prisoners at Frongoch, Dublin MP Alfie Byrne requests special yuletide arrangements from Home Secretary George Cave.

> *Cave*: The dietary of convict prisons is regulated by statutory rule and depends on the nature of the industrial employment. Special facilities at Christmas cannot be allowed, but prison diet on Christmas Day includes beef and plum pudding.
>
> *Byrne*: Does not the Right Honourable Gentleman think that the time has come for the release of all prisoners?[287]

A familiar complaint over delays in the post – as well as frequent incidence of letters not reaching their destination – soon leaves prisoners wondering how good Lewes' privileges really are. Writing to his mother months later, Jack says he is waiting for a reply from Jim in New York but has heard nothing back.

> It is annoying and ridiculous to be holding up letters like this. The two letters per month we are entitled to are certainly not turning out very satisfactory for us so far. It means writing two letters at least before receiving a reply to the first.[288]

22.

'Such is the terrorism of Ireland, and it does not augur
well for a peaceful settlement of that distressful country'
– M.L. Waller, Home Office, June 1917

Frank lives it up when he gets back. Held captive for eight months it's time to let loose. There are plenty around town who want to hear about life in Frongoch and get a first-hand account of the Easter Rising. Those who know him better will resist asking.

Impervious to the covert fuss around him, he writes to Harry Boland at Lewes.

> It felt a bit awkward at first not having to get up at 6 a.m., and being compelled to wear a collar and appear a bit civilised, but after a week or so I succeeded in suffering on in bed till 11 or 12 (and more'n that sometimes) and am now more or less civilised again.[289]

Up at the RIC barracks Constable Kenny gets the surveillance ball rolling with an entry two days late. He's not exactly making history but he is the one writing it:

> 25:12:16 Frank Shouldice arrived at Ballaghaderreen from prison 25 December 1916 and was met at Kilfree Railway Station by Joseph Kelly (now in custody for attempted murder of two Constables).[290]

A more detailed report is filed separately, correcting the arrival date (December 23), identifying who met him, where Frank is living ('with his mother and brother and sister who reside here') and noting that although he used to be in the Land Commission 'he has presently no occupation.' It also adds that since getting home at Christmas 'he has been drinking a good deal and keeping company with the Sinn Féiners especially P.J. Ryan.'

Furthermore, unconfirmed – and inaccurate – references to Frank's grandfather being a German national are now stated as fact.

> He is a son of the late ex-sergeant Shouldice of the RIC whose father was a German in the employment of the King Harman family at Rockingham Boyle.[291]

The transition from prison life to Christmas holidays in Ballaghaderreen is sudden and surreal. Confinement and shortage is suddenly replaced by drinking, eating, dancing. His miniature 1917 diary remains blank for January before he makes the first entry of the year.

> Saturday, February 3. Dance (all night).

Yet amid these festive celebrations Frank will feel a pang of regret, even guilt, for leaving his older brother behind. The spectre of five years' penal servitude hangs over the family like a shroud – if the Lewes sentence runs to full term Jack will be 39 by the time he is released.

It would be natural for Jack to feel envious of Frank's newly bestowed freedom but he writes from Lewes with genuine warmth, a magnanimous nod between two brothers aware of what sacrifice means. They know what each other has gone through. If Jack is feeling low at Christmas he doesn't let it show. In microscopic handwriting he sub-divides a letter to Christina with a page for Frank, Jack tests the censor – and his mother – with coded references and an in-joke for his brother.

> Well Prionsias a mhic,
>
> So you are back on the land again after your 6 weeks diversion in Dublin. The 'natives' up there must have made a fuss of you to keep you 5 weeks longer than intended. I expect through it was something akin to a 'shy but willin' attitude on your part. Of course I can 'guess' too as you say what an interesting time you probably had. Miss Blawklee and her friend are warm customers

I know and generally welcome their friends with open arms.[292]

By way of encouragement, there are clear signs that whatever sent the brothers out on Easter Monday has set in train a slow transformation of Ireland's relationship with Britain. General John Maxwell, the man who oversaw the executions, signed Jack's court-martial and ordered Frank's deportation, is gone but not forgotten. From a position of almost absolute power in Ireland his appointment is unceremoniously terminated by his superiors. He is re-called to Britain to steer the calmer waters of Northern Command.

Had Maxwell ever come across a copy of the equally ill-fated *Cork Free Press* his ears would sting with rebuke. Declaring 'the Military Dictatorship of Ireland thus rendered vacant' it announces:

> For all Irishmen the hour has come or is coming for weeping and gnashing of teeth, false or otherwise. The nation is to suffer a great grief. Sir John Maxwell is going to leave us.[293]

Such derision may be the sting of a dying bee – the newspaper's tangle with the British censor proves terminal over its unsparing coverage of Frongoch – but if *Cork Free Press* is going out, it goes out with a bang. Lighting an unsympathetic pyre for Maxwell, it throws a few sparks in the direction of censor Baron Decies as well.

> There will be no 'keening' in Ireland over the departure of General Sir John Maxwell. There is only one thing to report about it – it comes six months too late. After the very first execution General Maxwell should have been removed from office . . . General Maxwell being very stupid lost his head when he was made powerful and it was he more than any other person who gave the Dublin Rising the worldwide importance it has since assumed, to the dire detriment of the objects which England says are here for this war. At first the Easter Week revolt was merely the courageous protest of a brave knot of men against a shockingly corrupt parliamentarianism. In its first days it inspired a little admiration perhaps but there was no general approval or sympathy in Ire-

Secret DMP/RIC surveillance report (Courtesy NLI Archives)

land. Then the wise Coalition Government sent General Maxwell to quell the rebellion and in two weeks it leapt from unimportance to the greatest tragedy and the greatest protest in Irish history.

It was the Prime Minister who had spent the last five years speaking platitudes about the right of the Irish Nation to freedom and who Mr Redmond spent the same five years lauding as an ideal statesman, who bears the greatest share of the guilt in General Maxwell's regime. One word from Mr Asquith and not an execution would have taken place. But Mr Asquith also know the right way to solve the strange situation that arose after the rising, like all other Englishmen when faced with problems they do not understand, he remembered only that the British Empire was the strongest in the world, and thought a display of its strength in Ireland was the very thing to frighten that wild race into new centuries of submission. England through all her connexion with Ireland made exactly the same mistake and always with the same result.

Even with Maxwell out of the picture, the imposition of martial law and unrestricted application of Defence of the Realm Regulations (DRR) underscores a day-to-day reality that the administration in Ireland now functions as a police state, dependent on surveillance and control as a means of maintaining some semblance of order.

DRR provide the police with an ever-expanding set of powers. County Wicklow provides a typical example when a concert held in Baltinglass town hall on December 27 raises funds for the local Workman's Club. A festive crowd of almost 500 people enjoy the evening but a police informer reports that 14-year-old Joseph O'Neill gets onstage at the concert to sing 'Easter Week.' The song begins, 'Who fears to speak of Easter Week?' Otherwise, according to the informer, the evening 'passed off quietly.'[294]

A couple of days later a detective inspector named Egan approaches Edward O'Neill, the boy's father. O'Neill, a painter, fearfully assures Detective Egan 'that his boy will not sing the song in future and that he would not allow him to associate with anything or person of a disloyal or seditious nature.'

Such a minor infringement hardly seems worth investigation yet the file passes to a senior officer for consideration. 'I think this should be sufficient for the present, concludes Egan's superior. 'If there is any repetition of conduct the boy can be summoned.'

Eight months since The Rising there is a sense of anticipation that something is about to give. Patriotic songs may be temporarily subdued but it is a harbinger of change that political loyalties are shifting decisively away from the Irish Parliamentary Party (IPP). Even in Ballaghaderreen, John Dillon's home town, the old certainties are no more. Esteemed both locally and at Westminster, Dillon will be Redmond's successor as party leader; at the end of 1916 he has no inkling that his political career will be over in 23 months.

Events have prompted deep introspection in the most unlikely quarters. Easter Week inflicted the heaviest military losses on British army regiments from Nottingham and Stafford. The impact of such a broadside is reflected in a remarkably candid contribution by Nottingham South MP Col. Henry Cavendish-Bentinck to a debate on the Military Service Bill when he strongly opposes introducing conscription to Ireland.

> There is no reason why, because we are fighting the greatest tyranny the world has ever known, that we should become tyrannical and domineering ourselves . . . we have great Allies in this War, but I am not sure that

the greatest allies of all are not our ideals, our ideals of liberty and of freedom. It is those ideals which have sustained this country in two years of unexampled trial, and it is the belief that we are honest in those ideals that has brought our fellow countrymen rolling up from every part of the Empire. It is because we unfortunately do not believe those ideals apply to Ireland that the Irish people are now turning their backs upon us. To do the English people justice, I believe they fully realise the necessity for the application of our ideals to Ireland.[295]

He is followed swiftly by Arthur Lynch, MP for West Clare. Australian-born, Lynch was himself tried for treason and sentenced to the hangman's rope for siding with the Boers against British forces. His sentence was commuted and he later got a pardon, after which he volunteered for the British Army. Lynch calls for a general amnesty of all Irish prisoners still held in British jails. It is past 11.00 p.m. when he closes the Commons session with a lacerating attack on British administration and an emotive defence of the Irish desire for independence.

> With respect to the Chief Secretary (Duke) I will say this; that whereas in private life I admire him as an admirable and courteous gentleman, yet as the Chief Secretary I abhor him, because I abhor the office which he represents, and which in itself is the very seal placed on the subjection of Irishmen. I abhor in that respect the Lord Lieutenant also, and I hope that in any bold scheme both will be swept away. Remember that you cannot coerce Irishmen; you cannot drive Irishmen. You may grind them down under your heel, and they will still fight. Even if you kill them outright, their very ghosts will come back to haunt you. I hope that Irishmen will never lose that spirit.

Comparing Belgian resistance to Germany with Irish resistance to Britain he asks why one people's desire for freedom should outweigh another's.

If your own country – I pray that the omen shall never be realised – were to be subjected to the heel of a conqueror, what Englishman would you respect – the man who made obeisance to the new Government, who learned to speak German and cry 'Hoch' to the Kaiser, or the man who through every misery and disgrace still kept his soul pure in its ideals, burning strong with the aspiration to the liberty of his country? Do you think Irishmen are inferior to that? No! Irishmen have many faults, but I believe there are no people in the world in whom the ideal is found burning more brightly than in the breasts, not only of the educated and cultured Irishmen, but of those in the very lowest ranks, not of humanity, but of the ordinary work-a-day world of profit. Many a time I have stood before an ignorant Irish peasant and have respected him – I was going to say as a king, but no! – higher than I place any king – simply for that bright and burning spark which he exhibited, and in the readiness with which he would defend it with his life . . .

It's a heartfelt speech to disinterested listeners. But whatever Lynch's talk of dreams and glory the reality is suspicion and scrutiny. Constable O'Toole tells the DMP on January 11 that Frank Shouldice has boarded the 3.50 p.m. train for Dublin.

He is here since 25th ult. Having come here on his discharge from Internment. He is well known to D.M.P and I sent following cipher wire to DMP Dublin 4¼ pm 'Frank Shouldice by three fifty pm train to Dublin'

Further information is furnished by the Roscommon RIC two days later.

Three members of the Shouldice family were arrested in connection with the rebellion. One of the three is presently undergoing penal servitude. The other two, Frank & Bertie, were recently released from internment.

By the first week of February Special Branch detectives don't know where their target is. No sighting locally in Ballaghaderreen or in Boyle either. 'His whereabouts is not known presently,' confirms Constable O'Toole. 'Enquiries are being made.'

Had they looked harder they might have found him up the road. Although unemployed, Frank is helping set up Sinn Féin clubs throughout the wider locality.

The party gears up for a critical by-election in North Roscommon. On February 5, Count Plunkett, deported father of the executed Joseph Plunkett, emerges victorious, comfortably defeating IPP candidate Thomas Devine. Politically seismic – and extremely alarming to Redmond, Dillon and Lloyd George – it's a massive advance for the party, the first time a Republican candidate will win an MP's seat and then give two fingers to Westminster.

On February 11 RIC Roscommon notify the DMP that Frank has again left for Dublin. The job of watching him is passed like the baton in a relay. A secret report filed by the Superintendent at DMP's 'G' Division indicates Frank stayed with the Bolands at 15 Marino Crescent from January 11-22. 'Since that time, Shouldice has not been seen or traced in the city, and he may have returned to Ballaghaderreen.'

For a couple of weeks they again lose track of him. Constable McMahon of Roscommon Special Branch in Boyle reports to Dublin Castle on February 12:

> I beg to report that I have made very discreet & careful
> inquiry re the above named and I can find no trace of
> him in or around this locality at present nor neither did
> he visit this place during the election.

Dublin Castle is told 'no trace of the suspect has been found' and this remains the case until February 26. The RIC confirm his arrival back in Ballaghaderreen on the 10.00 p.m. train from Dublin in the company of Patrick Towey, a local man returning home for his mother's funeral. 'Shouldice,' it says, 'has remained indoors all day . . . and his movements here will be kept under observation.'

Special Branch in Roscommon is keen to maintain this level of surveillance. The office communicates with Dublin Castle on March 1, 1917.

Please have discreet supervision kept over Shouldice and if possible notify police (by wire) of whatever place he visits. What evidence is available in this case? Please submit it.

While MI5's all-consuming interest in Frank and Jack is hardly a surprise, the entire Shouldice household sets the nosehairs of police and military intelligence twitching. In fact anybody who comes into contact with the family becomes 'a person of interest'. For the watching eyes of Dublin Castle's Special Branch – either through 'G' Division detectives, the DMP or RIC or their local informers, all comings and goings, every football match and every social event is treated with circumspection. Repeated file observations of the mundane bears an uncanny resemblance to regimes yet to emerge behind the yet unformed Iron Curtain. Under Defence of the Realm Regulations it seems that any patriotic remark pricks a listening ear, every utterance dutifully scribbled into a notebook and stored away for future use.

Frank receives a letter from Jack in Lewes.

> You seem to be having the time of your life down there 'doing the country,' visiting old friends, going to dances, 'fitballin', farming and generally making your presence 'felt' . . . I'm afraid I will have forgotten the 'light fantastic' by the time I will have my next' swing.[296]

It is not without irony when detectives in Dublin Castle note Frank and Jack's father Henry was an RIC sergeant. Frequent reference is made to the 'fact' that Henry Shouldice was son of a German national who worked for the Rockingham Estate in Boyle, County Roscommon. In a time of international war with Kaiser Wilhelm II, the provenance of German ancestry, albeit long-departed, and two rebel grandsons proves irresistible to investigative minds at 'G' Division, highlighting the connection as a dot-joining aid to anybody who might not see the all too obvious.

The ever-expanding 'History of Frank Shouldice' sees him accompany Joe O'Kelly on March 3rd to Frenchpark at 11.00 a.m. and return at 7.00 p.m. Eight days later he goes to a GAA tournament in Ballaghaderreen which raises money for National Aid Funds, a support agency for Volunteers and their families. '£5 gate money realised,' the police note. He attends a similar GAA tournament the following week.

Strengthening his connection with the GAA – and getting in a game of handball when he can – he is elected Vice-President of the Mayo County Board. The authorities suspect – with some justification – that he uses this role as cover to get around the county on Sinn Féin business. However police intelligence stretches into flattery when the RIC files say:

> Last year the GAA club here was affiliated with County Roscommon, Shouldice has got it transferred to Mayo.

Perhaps the RIC just want this to be true. The county border was redrawn in 1898 to bring Ballaghaderreen into County Roscommon but the town's GAA club stayed with County Mayo. The club did transfer to Roscommon for one year only in 1905 only to return to the Mayo fold the following season. Frank was 12 at the time.

He is monitored meeting with President of the Mayo GAA County Board, Padraig McManus, in Swinford on April 10. He returns home the next day.

> April 13 Attended a dance in Swinford accompanied by Joseph Kelly and his brother Bertie Shouldice.

> April 27: Was met by patrol 1:20 a.m. in Ballaghaderreen accompanied by Joseph Kelly (now in custody). Suspected of erecting Republican flags.

Three days later O'Kelly is no longer in custody. Five RIC officers (Kenny, Scully, McCarthy, Hegarty and O'Toole) add individual notes to Grandpa's file.

> April 30: Met at 11½ p.m. in company with Joseph Kelly and he was seen going home at 1½ a.m. following morning.

Following Sinn Féin's shock win in North Roscommon the next big political showdown is South Longford's by-election on May 9. In a radically innovative move, Sinn Féin nominates Joe McGuinness, a fellow-inmate of Jack's at Lewes. McGuinness is a reluctant candidate but agrees to go forward. Eamon de Valera is unconvinced about the strategy as is George Gavan Duffy. British Intelligence notes that Michael Collins is actively involved behind the scenes.

The strategy is hugely successful, a 'put him in to get him out' electoral formula reprised successfully in July when de Valera is nominated for the East Clare vacancy. W.T. Cosgrave repeats the trick a month later in Kilkenny City.

In the manner of history repeating itself, the political establishment would be just as stunned in 1981 when IRA Volunteer Bobby Sands takes Fermanagh South Tyrone as an 'Anti H-Block/ Armagh Political Prisoner' candidate. Less than a month later at Long Kesh Bobby Sands MP is dead aged 27, succumbing to 66 days without food. Sands' victory at the ballot, some 64 years after Joe McGuinness set the template, triggers the passage of the Representation of the People Act (1981). Its purpose? To prevent long-term prisoners being nominated as candidates in British elections.

Frank is seen travelling by car with the O'Kellys and Sinn Féin supporter John Anderson on May 6. They leave Ballaghaderreen at noon and are headed towards Longford. They do not return home until midnight. Furthermore:

> The motor carried 3 Sinn Féin flags and all the occupants wore Sinn Féin colours.

Additional reports (May 8) from Ballaghaderreen state that:

> . . . since 24th April last Sinn Féiners have been active here in spreading disaffection. Since that date 11 Republican Flags have been taken down here and two Consts were shot on 7th inst. at 3½ a.m. by Joseph Kelly, a released Sinn Féiner . . .

Constable Sheridan, one of the policemen 'wounded,' makes a statement on the shooting. He stretches his testimony to incorporate Frank Shouldice into the account and place him close to the scene even if he wasn't there.

I saw other Sinn Féiners besides Kelly who fired on us about the street. John Cooney and John Anderson of Flannery's staff, also Frank Shouldice. I saw John Cooney and John Anderson parading up and down about 2 ½ am and up to the time of arrest. I asked them under the Defence of the Realm Act what they were doing out and Anderson said they were in Longford and Cooney said they had a perfect right to be out. Frank Shouldice was with Kelly up to 3a.m. and went home then.

Grandpa's peripatetic diary offers a different explanation.

6.5.17 – In Longford with Kellys. Grand drive to B'mahon. Great enthusiasm for McGuinness. Back about 12. Joe K. got into shooting biz after I left him. Beer!

The shooting incident gives the authorities a first opportunity to make a move on their main target in Ballaghaderreen. Then senior officers begin to grumble in a policeman-like way about a lack of evidence.

According to RIC Roscommon's secret file:

May 9: Left for Longford 12¾ p.m. Not yet returned.

Grandpa's diary account says:

9.5.17 – Down to Longford. McC, all the boys, Frong-och everywhere. Joe taken to Dublin from Castlerea. Great excitement. Tight contest.

Opposed by the Catholic Church and local business, Joe McGuinness pulls off a sensational victory, edging out Patrick McKenna by just 37 votes. Barring a Houdini-like turnaround Dillon and the ailing Redmond fear the writing on the wall – at the 1918 general election the Irish Parliamentary Party will shrink from 80 seats to six. And while Frank and Ena toast the historic occasion in South Longford, Jack, who describes the McGuinness win as 'the biggest thrill of our prison existence,' joins in the celebrations at Lewes.

There was nearly a riot in the Prison when we got the news – discipline broke and we cheered Joe in the Prison Hall and put him up on a table to make a speech. Joe obliged and the Prison rang to the cheers of 130 Irish convicts.[297]

Dublin Castle is informed that Frank Shouldice returns to Ballaghaderreen at 2.21 p.m. on May 11. A couple of days later Frank gets a handwritten letter from Joe O'Kelly at Arbour Hill Prison:

> You must have got a great surprise when you heard I was taken away and especially on such a charge. I had a visit from Ena on Wednesday eve, the poor girl was frightened out of her wits. [298]

Shouldice has nothing to do with the shooting incident but RIC Detective John Kearney at regional headquarters in Boyle sees things otherwise. He wants to make an arrest using Defence of the Realm Regulations as he feels it 'quite useless to have these men dealt with by a Court of Summary Jurisdiction.' Detective Kearney advocates 'a swift, strong hand.' His report, a confidential handwritten document, incorporates a number of inaccuracies which assist him in arriving at a strong personal conclusion.

> 12:5:17 <u>Frank Shouldice who is the Sinn Féin leader now in Ballaghaderreen</u> was employed as a Civil Service clerk in the Irish Land Commission Office Dublin prior to the rebellion. I believe he held the rank of Lieutenant in the Irish Volunteers and surrendered during Easter Week at the Four Courts. He was interned at Frongoch till 23/12/16. His brother John was Captain in the Irish Volunteers during Easter Week in Dublin . . . Frank is living with his mother in Ballaghaderreen. He is unemployed. He was recently elected V.P. of the County Mayo G.A.A. Board. He has been suspected with the Kellys and others of hoisting republican (Sinn Féin) flags around Ballaghaderreen. He was <u>in the company of Joseph Kelly a short time before Kelly fired at and</u> <u>wounded two police at 3.30 a.m. on 7th inst.</u> I sug-

gest that this man be removed from Ballaghaderreen. His presence has an evil effect.

However Special Branch 'G' Division first wants some explanation from RIC Roscommon and wants actual evidence of sedition.

13:5:17 For what purpose its it believed that these suspects were out at this our on 7th inst? Had F. Shouldice been in Longford?

Previous file re Shouldice attached.

Joe O'Kelly is detained in military custody in Arbour Hill charged with the attempted murder of two RIC policemen. He faces trial in July but in a secret memo marked 'Conduct of Sinn Féin suspects at Ballaghaderreen' it is clear who Special Branch is after. With emphasis, they note regretfully,

A great deal depends on the trial of Joseph Kelly and his comrades now in military custody charged with shooting two Constables at Ballaghaderreen – as to whether Sinn Féin actively will continue there. <u>Undoubtedly Frank Shouldice is the moving spirit</u> but there is very little evidence to connect him with the shooting of the police.

On May 19, Special Branch in Dublin receives a confidential update from Roscommon on 'Frank Shouldice released Sinn Féiner of Ballaghaderreen.' Of wider concern to authorities is the clear momentum behind the republican movement as a new political

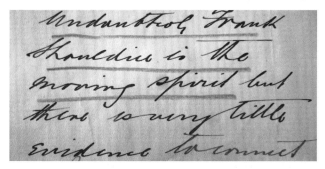

For Special Branch, 'Undoubtedly Frank Shouldice is the moving spirit ...'

force. Sensing a clear shift in public support Sinn Féin plans to confront John Dillon on his own patch in East Mayo at the next general election.

In handwritten notes the police report underlines:

> Shouldice is possessed of much ability and works secretly and discreetly in furthering the Sinn Féin movement. He has been practically living with the Kelly family since he came here from prison and they have been specially active since April. All the Republican flags taken down here were made in Kellys.
>
> May 20: Shouldice is now practically in command of the G.A.A. in County Mayo – a maritime county; and, can use that organisation to further the Sinn Féin object. He has made frequent visits to various places with Joseph Kelly, now in custody.

This update is passed to Major Price, Director of British Military Intelligence in Ireland. In response, further information is sought 'regarding this man, F. Shouldice,' pending which, Price 'does not intend to make any order as regards Shouldice at present' because according to police files:

> There does not appear to be sufficient evidence as yet for action under DRR 14 & 14B.*
>
> *Defence of the Realm Regulations Section 14 and 14B

Over the next weeks in good weather Frank clears the O'Kelly bog in Edmundstown. He cycles frequently to Swinford and sets up Sinn Féin clubs around the county. In between it all he plays senior club football for Ballaghaderreen and is selected to play for Mayo county team. Two years after winning the Croke Cup he's leaving his Dublin crest behind.

The RIC in Roscommon watches closely, noting on May 25:

> Shouldice's movements and associates should be very discreetly watched and reported on when anything suspicious is noted.

23.

'What a reception!'
– Jack Shouldice on arrival back in Dublin, 17 June 1917

Much to Jack's relief, he is given a gardening job at Lewes, enabling him to pass a lot of time outdoors. It's also a lot easier on his eyes than spending hours in poor light at a sewing machine. He writes to Christina.

> The work I am at in the garden is light for some time as it has been cutting grass with a lawn-mowing machine just in front of the prison where I can see plenty of traffic – mostly motor – and people passing on the road to Brighton and into Lewes. It is a pleasant change from inside, as there are plenty of trees and some nice flower beds about, and the entrance looks more like a large country house of the castle type than the outside of a jail.[299]

On the face of it Jack, Harry, Dev and others sentenced to penal servitude would seem a more straightforward matter than the blurred legal definition of internees. Immediately after the Rising, military courts ordered executions as well as passing 72 custodial sentences. Seeking to extricate the military from the equation however, Home Forces HQ then asks 'whether the Secretary of State Home Office will be good enough to agree to take over all such male civilians, sentenced in Ireland by Field General Court Martial to penal servitude.'[300]

The Home Office complies with the request – with one exception.

> ... with reference to the female convicts and the Countess Markievity (sic) in particular, that the latter is the only case and that in view of the wishes of the Secretary of State, Home Office, arrangements are being made for her accommodation in prison in Ireland.[301]

So although sentenced by court-martial, most of these 'political convicts' are now serving time in civilian prisons. This handover from military to civil authorities sidesteps the key issue of status. On June 5 the Prison Commission returns to the Secretary of State about 'the Sinn Féin rebels' to clarify 'whether their offence constitutes a felony or misdemeanour'. The Government in Ireland advises that 'all persons who were originally sentenced to death or to p.s. come within the category of "felons".'[302]

The Home Office fudges the issue of Prisoner of War status for the next five years and, inevitably, the bitter melodrama played out in Frongoch is set to run again and again. Emboldened by resistance shown by the internees Irish prisoners will not accept to being categorised as convicts. In short, they want to be treated as Prisoners-of-War. When they start agitating towards this goal it throws the Prison Commission and Home Office into a legal abyss. Correspondence between relevant officials reveals widespread uncertainty about how to proceed; more specifically, how to define these prisoners. The Prison Commission proposes irritably to the Home Office that the military takes over Lewes Prison so that its 123 Irish inmates can be managed by the authority that convicted them in the first place.

> These men should not be dealt with in Convict Prisons, but removed to the care of the Military Authority by whose Tribunals they were sentenced . . . There is at present no Convict Prison for Military Offenders, and I am not aware of any legal difficulty in the way of surrendering Lewes Prison to the War Office for this purpose. It would then be open to the Military Authorities to provide for their treatment as they may deem wise and suitable, and it would relieve the Directors (at Lewes) and their officers from the grave difficulty in which they are placed in trying to maintain convict discipline under circumstances which render it easy for those under their charge to defy their authority. [303]

Just as in Frongoch, the situation at Lewes creates serious tension between the military, the Home Office and the Prison Commission which operates the jails housing the Irish prisoners. In one of the early challenges on status, de Valera and Robert Brennan demand study facilities at Dartmoor. At the time the Home Office advised the Prison Commission:

> . . . if these men are to remain in convict prison they must be treated according to ordinary rules . . (it appears) that there is no intention of treating them as prisoners of war.[304]

A minuted note from the Prison Commission remarks:

> Dealt with. Brennan refused. De Valera informed that he is not yet eligible for the privilege for which he asks.[305]

Eleven months later the political wind has changed. De Valera writes to the Governor of Lewes on behalf of the Irish prisoners, stating there will be a withdrawal of labour until Prisoner of War status is granted.

> Sir,
>
> The Irish people demand that we be made prisoners of war.
>
> Until the government declares our status as such we refuse to do any services except those related directly for ourselves e.g. cooking, laundry etc[306]

With no progress made on status the prisoners adopt more militant tactics, announcing that they will smash their cell windows unless the situation improves immediately. De Valera is, once again, the conduit with a handwritten warning to the Governor.

> Sir, I wish to inform you that if on tomorrow evening we are still confined in this manner we shall be compelled to take steps of our own to secure a proper supply of fresh air.[307]

It is only the start of their campaign.

On the basis of intercepted mail and police reports from Bal-laghaderreen, it is quite inevitable that Ena Shouldice – whose republican sympathies burn as brightly as any of her brothers – is deemed to have gone too far. Unaware of machinations behind the scenes she is suddenly told by the GPO that she is being trans-ferred to Sligo. Considering the number of agencies weighing in to prise her out of the job, it's just as well she has no idea what forces are behind it.

For the time being her work continues at Amiens Street. She divides her hours between telegraphic ennui and fending off many suitors, including a Superintendent named Doyle who proposes marriage to her on a regular basis. A stronger candidate and fer-vent admirer is Harry Boland, a good friend of the family and pres-ently a prison mate of Jack's in Lewes. As Jack tells her, Harry is no model prisoner.

> Harry is in the clink as usual, tell them at home (they probably know by now) that they may not hear from him for a month or so as he has 'lost some marks' ow-ing to breaches of the regulations! You can assure them he is in his usual good 'fighting form,' fit and well.[308]

Ena knows about postal censorship but is unaware that vari-ous letters she sends Jim in New York are intercepted. Several are never delivered. Her brother hopes to make another visit home soon – although he senses a change in attitude towards him at work since his difficulties in Liverpool. It is unclear whether the Attorney-General's office in New York has been approached by MI5.

> (Jim) thinks he's not in such favour in his office since he returned. Funny isn't it. But I told him not to worry only push ahead with the right crowd – where he ought to make some good friends.[309]

Jim, a busy man, telegrams Ena on April 8, 1917.

> Everything as usual will keep you informed.

Even an attorney could have little idea of the flap created in the intelligence community by such a cryptic message. With a red flag raised by the censor Cable 0627 is intercepted by the War Office in Liverpool who refer it to MI5.[310]

Suspicious text in message to Ireland.

It is sent to Major Price's intelligence unit at Parkgate HQ and prompts a flurry of 'Secret' correspondence to and from 'G' Division, Special Branch. Marked 'Very Secret and Immediate,' Irish Command HQ advises:[311]

> Attached copy of telegram is sent for VERY DISCREET inquiries as to its meaning and as to the sender or addressee.
>
> If the sender is perfectly loyal and the telegram is believed genuine and harmless, please wire to this Office as follows: – 'Message No. 0627 correct'.

The response from Dublin Castle[312] is quick. Evidently, Message No. 0627 is not 'correct'.

> I beg to report that there is hardly any doubt as to the sender of this telegram being James B. Shouldice, an American Attorney of New York . . .

Suspicious text in message to Ireland.

Forwarded to	Copies sent to	Action taken at Cable Office	Action taken at War Office	Initials and Date
			I. O. I. C.	
			For enquiry please.	
		HELD.	*J.J.*	**9.4.17.**
			M. I. 5 - O.	
			10 · 4 · 17	

W343—6385 120,000 1/17 HWV(P1131) G16,593
313 6385 110,900 2/17

'Suspicious text to Ireland'

227

This man, who is an American citizen (Serial No. 5564) arrived here on 4/8/16, left for Ballaghaderreen on 12/8/16, returned 15/8/16, left again 22/8/16, returned 25/8/16, and finally left for Chester 28/8/16.

His Identity Book, No. 24158, issued by Store Street Police Station at 5/8/16 has been surrendered as per file – 11535/16. The family are natives of Kingsland, County Roscommon and <u>two</u> of them were connected with the Sinn Féin Rebellion.

At this stage the political and military authorities feel they have seen enough.

The family history points to disloyalty, and I am reliably informed the (sic) Miss Christina Shouldice is a Sinn Féin Sympathiser. The meaning of the telegram of course cannot be ascertained, and I doubt if an interview would be of any use.

Handwritten into the typed report from Dublin Castle is a police inspector's note:

The employment of this lady (C. Shouldice) in the GPO is a matter for regret, but there is not at present any <u>further</u> evidence against her available.

While the House of Commons continues to shuffle through 'Disturbances in Ireland' those rumblings inch a lot closer to home. The violent outbreak at Lewes threatened by de Valera has materialised. According to a visiting Home Office official:[313]

It is quite a new experience in prison life to have howling going on, punctuated by crashing of bed boards against the doors, and window smashing. When they commenced on the gas box glass there was a tremendous hullabaloo with cheers etc . . .

In response, the Home Office splits the Irish prisoners into smaller groups and redistributes them once again. Their transfer is observed by Inspector Winn of the Prison Commission.

Of course the shouting and singing could be heard beyond the prison walls; as most of the shouting is in Gaelic, it sounds like howling.[314]

A 'Private' report to the Home Office by the Prison commission says that prison chaplain Fr O'Loughlin personally feels the men have crossed a line by staging a revolt after attending Sunday Mass which renders the men 'completely out of hand as far as he is concerned'.

> He thinks that if this is stated in the House, and thus made known in Ireland, there would be no sympathy felt for them. He says that no real Irish Catholics would have ever contemplated such a proceeding, but Valera (a half-breed) he considers capable of any enormity, and he thinks when once proposed by him, the others had not the strength of character to refuse to carry out his suggestion.

> Colonel Winn telephones this morning that he had been informed by Dr Cook, the Medical Officer, that many of the men stated that they were sick of it, but would have to go on with it because otherwise after discharge their lives would not be worth living – that they were all members of a Secret Society.[315]

With the Irish prisoners moved out of Lewes, Governor R.A. Marriott reports a restoration of calm. He does his rounds of the cells vacated.

> I found that P. McMahon had chalked in large letters on the floor:
>
> DIRECTORS
> DAMN THE RULES
> WE DEFY THEM.

The venom of the message surprises Marriott.

> This prisoner is a miller by profession, in a very good social position, and has been quite well-behaved hitherto.[316]

When Ena gets wind of the rioting she worries about Jack. She hears tell that he is getting thinner and his eyesight has deteriorated. The family is spared knowing Jack finds himself back in chains for transferral to Maidstone in Kent along with Harry Boland, Tom Ashe, Tom Hunter and Eamon de Valera, regarded as the ringleader. Other prisoners are spread between Portland and Parkhurst but the protests will continue. Jack tells the Bureau of Military History:

> It was arranged that wherever we were sent we should carry on with non-cooperation of the prison regulations, that was – to refuse to work, talk whenever we could, or shout or sing in our cells and demand political prisoner's treatment from the prison authorities.

Boland physically resists the wardens and in a remarkable episode detailed by David Fitzpatrick[317] seizes his chance to drop a hurried note on the street. Unseen by the guards he casts it to the mercy of the wind with the entreaty: 'Friend – Send on this note to Mrs Boland, 15 Marino Crescent, Clontarf, Dublin, Ireland and earn the prayers of her son who asks this favour of you.'

A young girl finds the letter and brings it home. Incredibly, her parent performs the kindness by posting it on with an anonymous note that 'as I, too, have two sons doing their bit, it is with pleasure I forward it to you as the writer wishes.'

Kathleen Boland receives the note, scribbled on toilet paper, which reveals the scale of violent protest at Lewes unknown to the outside world. The men are determined to maintain this resistance until they are treated as Prisoners of War. As a mother she is alarmed by the dim finality of his closing lines:

> Good-bye, give my love to dear sister, brothers, and aunt. Pray for the good soul who directs this to you. You won't hear from me again till my time comes. Your loving son, Harry.

Kathleen Boland brings the letter to the Irish National Aid Association and Volunteers Dependents' Fund to see what can be done. With this new information Michael Collins and Michael Staines, both Frongoch graduates, expose the vagaries of life behind prison walls and ramp up the campaign to get the men released. On hearing of events at Lewes a banned public meeting at Beresford Place in Dublin erupts into violence which claims the life of DMP Inspector John Mills.

Ena is infuriated by the revelations from Lewes. Writing to New York on June 9 she refers to Jim's queries about her previous letter being censored. If she is aware of it, she blithely disregards the rule that the outspoken word will invite further scrutiny.

> It must have referred to the government as interpreted to Irishmen in this country. But we won't be muzzled always and anyway I think you know <u>how</u> to read the newspapers from these parts . . .

The censor duly extracts meaning, underlining passages for emphasis:

> Am sorry to say I haven't good news of Jack. At least they are all in the same boat. There has been trouble. The men have been refused their rights. Result was they were taken away in batches of about twenty to unknown destinations a few days ago but <u>if you realised ever there the inhumanity of the Huns you would come in your thousands and murder them</u>. It's brutal and shocking and <u>we're going round with black hearts</u>, I can tell you.

The censor takes umbrage, commenting:[318]

> In spite of her anti-English sentiments and rebel connexion, writer is still employed in the Telegraph Dept, GPO Dublin, she is being transferred to Sligo for three months from the middle of July.

Irish Military Command at Parkgate picks up the case with another 'Secret' communiqué sent by Lieut-General Mahon, Commanding-in-Chief Forces in Ireland, to Under-Secretary William Byrne.

Evidently this woman – CHRISTINA or ('ENA') SHOULDICE is a most unsuitable person to be in Government employment, and especially in such an important post as telegraphist at the Post Office at Amiens Street, through which most telegrams go between Ireland and England. The reference to the Huns is evidently to the English or to loyal Irishmen.[319]

Two days later Under-Secretary Byrne orders:

Communicate extract from letter confidentially to Sec. GPO

This is done from Dublin Castle on June 26:

I am directed by the Lord Lieutenant . . . to forward to you, for your confidential information, the accompanying extract from a letter from her to J.B. Shouldice . . . It is understood that Miss Shouldice . . . is about to be transferred to Sligo for three months about the middle of July . . .[320]

The GPO Secretary acknowledges the letter two days later and advises the Lord Lieutenant that the matter 'shall receive attention.'

Following the Lewes 'mutiny' Jack is placed in solitary confinement at HMP Maidstone and, like others, put on bread and water. Each time the prisoners are brought before the Governor they repeat their demand for Prisoner of War status. In a game of cat-and-mouse privileges are restored, then withdrawn but the men hold out. Alone in his cell Jack's ears perk up when he hears 'Harry's well-known voice from his cell rendering "Twenty Men from Dublin Town" . . .'

In just over a week the Irish prisoners at Maidstone are assembled.

The Governor, referring to the gracious action of the government, made a little speech and said that they now hoped that on our return to Ireland we would be good boys and cease our extreme methods of political agitation. His little speech was received in silence.[321]

A pardon signed by Chief Secretary Cave 'graciously pleased to extend our grace and mercy unto the said prisoners and to pardon and remit unto them the remainder of their said sentences.' As part of a general amnesty Jack and Harry, along with de Valera and 20 others at Maidstone, are transferred one last time for an overnight stay at Pentonville where Jack pays his respects at Casement's grave.

Making a point of buying Irish goods when possible, the London branch of INAAVDF spends £114 and three shillings to procure 14 pairs of boots, 17 suits of Irish cloth and overcoats, hats and Irish caps, underwear, ties and collars for the returning prisoners. One of the men requires dental care.[322]

The men are not measured so the clothes don't really fit and they're a motley looking crew when deposited at Euston Station 'like schoolboys going home on holidays.' On arrival home Michael Collins and Dick Mulcahy will ask Jack to assist Frank organising the East Mayo Brigade of the Irish Volunteers. He will immediately start working on Sinn Féin campaigns in East Clare and East Mayo, putting huge effort into the election of Harry Boland in South Roscommon as well as less fruitful outings in East Tyrone, South Armagh and Antrim. That's all in the days ahead; first, it's time to enjoy the journey.

Harry (1) and Jack (2) return to Dublin with other prisoners,
17 June 1917 (Courtesy Irish Independent)

At Euston Station the ex-prisoners are each handed five shillings and a packet of ten cigarettes. After such a long break from nicotine Jack feels almost sick by the time they reach Crewe. They board the boat at Holyhead and set their course, homeward bound. It's an auspicious moment.

Frank makes room in his miniature diary.

> 18.6.17 – Convicts released today after breaking up Lewes Gaol!! Terrible scenes of excitement when they landed in Dublin! Vols took possession of streets and flags floated over GPO for a week!

For two days solid Frank works the bog. And then, Saturday, June 23, it's time to hit town and roll out the green carpet for Jack.

> 23.6.17 – Down to Boyle with McK + Bob to meet the rebels. A very wet evg. Big night in BD afterwards.

Countess Markievicz joins the homecoming at Westland Row
(Courtesy RTÉ Stills Library)

24.

'The Shouldice family is most disloyal, one was convicted
and sent to penal servitude and another was interned in
connection with the rebellion. Their father was a member
of the R.I.C. whose father was a German employed
by the King Harmon family at Rockingham, Boyle'
– Under-Secretary William Byrne,
Dublin Castle, 25 June 1917

Unaware that she is at the centre of a military intelligence pick-
le, Ena writes to Jim from Ballaghaderreen on July 10. She
makes no reference to working in Sligo – just as her transfer was
announced without any explanation it is abruptly cancelled.

> My dear Jim,
>
> A thousand apologies for not writing sooner.

She does not know this letter will never be delivered. The British censor seizes it and examines it forensically, extracting anything of interest. The censor could put the letter back into the
postal system for delivery onwards and nobody would be any the
wiser. In this case, however, MI5 opts to retain the original letter,
diverting it instead to the Shouldice folio kept at Dublin Castle.

With palpable enthusiasm Ena relates public reaction to the
prisoners' homecoming. Jack's return has brought 14 months of
anguish to a temporary close.

> I wouldn't have time or vocabulary to describe the lat-
> ter. It was immense. Nothing like it seen in Dublin be-
> fore. I'll tell you all about it sometime. When the con-
> vict train got in to Westland Row everyone lost their
> heads. We were carried off our feet. I expected to see
> old Jack with drawn face sunken eyes etc but he actu-

ally looked as if he were returning from a picnic. Brown + plump. He and a few more looked miraculously well but the majority were haggard and ill.

I nearly forgot to mention the reception he got here. It was splendid for B. Better than John D. MP in his heyday! Local band procession torchlight + tar barrels, illuminations, speeches etc!

The next parts of Ena's letter catch the censor's attention.

J. doesn't like all the fuss he gets but he has to stick it for propaganda work. He's in the pink and so are all of us T.G. Jack has proceeded to Ennis County Clare for de Valera's election – another convict! He is expected to be returned. If so it will be the third!

Jack is home just three weeks and for the most part he and Harry B. have been holding meetings and forming Sinn Féin clubs all over the district! You wouldn't believe J. could stand up and make a speech. Well I've heard him and it wasn't bad . . .

The envelope also contains a one-page note from their mother, Christina. If the censor is unsure about this family's disposition, any uncertainty will soon be dispelled. Christina has no enthusiasm for Jim joining the U.S. Army – or any army that might support the Allies. Curiously, though, she leaves the incriminating word blank, as though omission might earn a benediction from the censor.

You never think of joining the Army especially the –––.

The letter is held by MI5. It is likely that for some time all correspondence to and from the Shouldice family home in Ballaghaderreen has been intercepted. However the sentiments expressed in this letter do confirm many suspicions for those who have been watching Ena for the past 15 months.

Notified of updates on 'Christina (or Ena) Shouldice, Telegraphist' Major Price at Irish Military Command, Parkgate, demands

to know from Under-Secretary Byrne 'are any steps being taken as regards the above named Post Office
employee as a consequence of the
GOC in C's letter No. G/2064/1 of
23/6/17.'[323]

The Under-Secretary duly follows
up with the Secretary of the GPO 'to
inquire if any action has been taken.'
Furthermore:

> I am directed by the Lord Lieu-
> tenant to forward to you the
> accompanying further extract
> from a letter written by Miss
> Ena or Christina Shouldice . .
> . and I am to ask that you will
> be so good as to say whether
> any action has been taken as
> regards Miss Shouldice. [324]

Ena's letter to Jim,
confiscated by MI5

The GPO Secretary formally acknowledges the enquiry and
gives the Under-Secretary another *pro forma* response that the
matter 'shall receive attention.' On July 26 the GPO clarifies its
position in a way neither Dublin Castle nor Parkgate anticipate.
Marked 'Secret and Confidential' the GPO holds that 'No action,
it should be stated, has yet been taken as regards Miss Shouldice.'

The GPO's reluctance to remove Ena irritates Price who demands the Under-Secretary exert further pressure. On August 2,
a letter marked 'Confidential' from the Secretary of the GPO prof-
fers a courteous but robust defence of their telegraphist.

> Sir,
>
> With reference to your letter of the 25th ultimo, No.
> 15223/S, relative to Miss C. Shouldice, Sorting Clerk
> and Telegraphist, Dublin, I am further directed to state,
> for the information of the Lord Lieutenant, that Miss
> Shouldice performs her duties in a satisfactory manner,

and that she has not come under notice in connection with any irregularity in her work which would indicate that she is disloyal. It is considered that no action can at the moment be taken by the Post Office other than to maintain a careful watch for any overt act of disloyalty on her part.[325]

The authorities beg to differ. Reaction from the Chief Secretary's office comes in red ink across the bottom of the page:

Her letters prove clearly that she is disloyal and therefore untrustworthy.

While this discussion goes back-and-forth, Ena, unaware that her thoughts are pored over by British Military Intelligence, puts pen to paper once more. She has no idea Jim never received her previous correspondence. Considering the vagaries of wartime, particularly the hazards of transatlantic shipping, perhaps people simply don't presume that letters posted to America will reach their destination

From her flat in Clontarf, Dublin on August 3, 1917 Ena begins a far more personal letter, unburdening herself in what are almost the notes of a reverie. She will never imagine this letter is also withheld and Jim will never know how she entrusted him with personal confidences. For whatever reason MI5 decides against releasing the letter onwards to New York so it instead joins Dublin Castle's growing folio on the Shouldice family. For months – even years – afterwards Ena might wonder why Jim never referred to it or even acknowledged her trust in him. Perhaps she mistakenly takes his silence for reticence or even embarrassment, small tragic splinters of collateral damage when state powers get to play with the lives of ordinary citizens.

To my astonishment I discover several of Ena's original letters on file at Kew Military Archives. On a glorious day in April 2015 I find myself sitting in the library upstairs opening personal letters she wrote 98 years ago. It feels wrong to have to request access from a British library to see a letter sent by my grand-aunt to my grand-uncle, correspondence that was improperly confiscated by MI5. I have to resist the temptation to steal her words back.

There is something profoundly sad about the August 3 letter. It feels like a violation, the brute realisation that Ena's most intimate thoughts ended up on a desk at the Directorate of Special Intelligence.

I never met Ena – she died in 1965, two years after I was born – but there is a restlessness in her words, like somebody charged for a life that does not come her way. Reading such a deeply personal letter is a strange and affecting experience.[326]

> My dear Jim,
>
> . . . you probably have got my letter since written from home few weeks after he (Jack) got out. Has he written you at all? Wouldn't be surprised if he didn't. His hands are more than full with propaganda work + now he's got the Leinster Secyship of GAA which means £120 a year. Nothing much in itself + wouldn't keep him here so he's staying on at home + will travel to Dn when necessary. It would be alright with his other job – but so far no sign of that. However things are moving – rapidly – I don't know how you are there – no news coming. There's a great rally + all the boys are happy. Heard Tay Pay* got a bad reception. The Irish Party down + out at last! Rumour has it that the war will be over very soon. Well D.V. it will + then the whitewashing all round to cover up the mess will be in full swing.
>
> The much talked of Convention is already making its promoters tired. The 'Play' deceives nobody. It's neither representative or sympathetic. <u>We</u> have nothing to do with it. The Peace Conference will be tried no matter <u>what</u> comes from the foxy saxon.
>
> *T.P. O'Connor, Nationalist Party MP

She asks Jim about the glamour of New York. It reads like an introspective pause. Clearly, on this occasion, she wants to talk to someone.

You see some life anyway. It's the one thing here always
– I get badly bored at times. One doesn't feel getting
old + there's not much fun only worry to be had mostly
always. Of course it's fine since Jack came home – but
I rarely see him or Frank . . . those fellows always have
a crowd with them – at least while he was up here he
didn't get a moment . . .

As regards the Supt. I mentioned he is too old – I don't
care much for him at all. He's kept at it so long (four
years!) + a few times last summer I felt desperately
lonely + miserable. I was inclined to favour the idea but
when I was myself I absolutely couldn't bear to think
of it. I'm weary refusing + snubbing him but he's like
India rubber – rises again every time just as tho' nothing happened!!

The censor notes her disparaging comments about the Lloyd
George-engineered Peace Convention but poring through the
next section of her long letter, the censor finds a nugget about a
'released Rebel' who MI5 know is bound for America on a Sinn
Féin fundraising mission. The censor's notes are forwarded to Major Hall and Major Price, director of British Military Intelligence.

You may probably hear of my engagement soon to
Harry Boland. One of the Bolands at the Crescent. You
didn't see him as he was in (prison) with Jack. I rather
liked him before the Rebellion – used to go to dances
etc with Jack and crowd. He has nothing at present –
but will get back his job in Todd's as a cutter soon. He
doesn't want to go back however. Wants something
better . . . if it comes off you will meet him. He's a bluff
hearty fellow – has a bad temper tho'!! and isn't quite as
refined as I would like. He's a wee bit rough.

Pity how I can't get what I really want – it's not in my
sphere here – and people have told me I'm too hard
pleased – and I better not go on refusing each one.
There were a few others – I don't know whether I told
you – none of them were much to look at or even had
anything! If I was once settled perhaps I should be con-

tent. I'm really afraid to go on with it fearing H. would not understand me – or be kind enough always. He rushed me into promising him and now I feel nervous. I wish I could see light somewhere and also that I could be cured of our sensitiveness. If it weren't for the latter I'd be saved many an ache and pain but can't help it.

Boland's active service with the IRB and Irish Volunteers, his spirited resistance at Dartmoor and Lewes and, more particularly, his close connection with Collins, makes him a significant target for British intelligence services. A GAA-related trip to London first brought him into contact with Collins. From that encounter, Boland was instrumental in getting Collins into the IRB. The two men became close friends and political allies but will ultimately part ways over the Treaty and find themselves on opposite sides in the Civil War.

Harry and Ena

Ena, bolstered by the privacy of her silent audience, speaks more candidly than usual. She continues here, lovelorn, forlorn. A previous romantic encounter with a man from Essex has not faded from her memory. Heightened by solitude, a pen in her hand, she confesses to how mixed up she feels.

It's queer – but that blessed Englishman whose face you didn't like – always has come back on three or four occasions when I had such an offer and I thought I was happy. I was quite happy for first week or two after H. + I fixed it up + now I find this Englishman disturbing my peace once more and imagine no one understands me like him. He was altogether more refined than anyone I've known and maybe that's the reason I can't forget him. Of course I'd never marry an Englishman – but there are plenty of Irishmen I wouldn't marry either.

Anyhow if it all goes well and I'm fairly happy – it may come off this time next year.

But this is not how things will work out. In the public imagination at least, Harry's romantic adventures usually relate to his tug-of-love with Michael Collins for the attentions of Kitty Kiernan. However long before his competitive joust for Kitty he will propose to Ena and she will accept. The proposal will wilt on the vine and the engagement will not crystallise even if their friendship outlasts any liaison. They drift apart for a spell but largely thanks to Harry, unemployed Ena will get full-time work at Sinn Féin headquarters in Harcourt Street where the pair of them, once betrothed, then disengaged, get on very well.

The bond between the Shouldice and Boland families survives without undue fuss. Jack and Harry will later clash over a GAA ban on civil servants under oath to the Crown but their close collaboration on the campaign trail in 1918 is key to Harry taking South Roscommon with 72 per cent of the ballot. Just two weeks after Frank breaks out of Usk Jail in Wales, Boland and Collins will spring de Valera from Lincoln Jail. Harry's combustible star, at once both endearing and abrasive, will burn brightly until the Civil War when Irish Free State Army troops gun him down at the Grand Hotel, Skerries. At the age of 35 he dies from his wounds at St. Vincent's Hospital, refusing to identify the men who shot him. Twenty days later Michael Collins will die in an ambush at Béal na Bláth and his remains brought to the same hospital.

Even in a time of violent killings Harry's premature death in July 1922 comes as a deep shock to Jack, Frank and Ena. If Ena's intercepted letter to Jim reveals the truest beat of her heart it would be misleading to overplay the prospects of their doomed romance. But it would be equally unfair to underplay how dear a friend Harry became to her and to the Shouldice brothers.

As for Ena's romantic horizons, numerous other suitors will present themselves to her. Supt. Doyle asks her again ('The thought of marrying him nearly paralysed me,' she shudders). Yet thoughts of 'the Englishman' will not leave her, the unknown chance of a kindred Anglo soul to whom she could not allow herself acquiesce.

She may rue a missed opportunity or just accept the personal sacrifice of principle. Or in her late years she might question what actually guided such a pivotal decision in her life.

Ena

> You mustn't mind my talking like this to you but I have to let it out to somebody. I wouldn't <u>talk</u> to you thusly if you were here. You'd make too much fun of me . . . I think I'm turning into a sour old thing. Say something nice in your next letter and forgive your silly but affectionate sister.

Ena will never marry. Perhaps she was not made for such a conventional arrangement but the abiding impression is of someone for whom life did not work out. And on a rare occasion that she summoned the courage to confide in someone by letter, her raw confession found only an audience of pencil-wielding strangers.

She signs off, as though fast losing her nerve to send it.

> And please burn this at once. I'm not <u>really</u> as blue as it looks. It's only in spasms. Best love from yr affectionate Ena.

25.

'And we bore him through the lone narrow passage
And up the stone stair where he oft tread'
– 'The Funeral of Dick Coleman in
Usk Gaol' by Tadhg Barry

Boyle RIC Constable John Kearney's burning desire to curb the 'evil effect' of Ballaghaderreen's chief suspect is thwarted when prosecutors cannot connect Shouldice to the shooting incident that left two policemen injured. Joe O'Kelly claims he was defending himself at the time but, found guilty, he is sentenced to jail for two years.

What adds to Kearney's disappointment is he knows 'G' men don't really need evidence. Under DORA they can arrest whoever they like, and, in the volatile political climate of 1917, that's what they do. Suspicion is sufficient as grounds for arrest and when they open File 78S / 75590 they are already way more than suspicious.

In a passage almost suggestive of Flann O'Brien, John P. McPhillips, a member of the Volunteers' Ballaghaderreen brigade, recalls their training regimen watched from afar by bemused RIC constables.

> Intensive training was the order of the day when Frank Shouldice was given command. He used to take us across bogs and swampy fields so as to leave our pursuers stranded with their bicycles on the roadside. I think that the police in those days were delighted to sit by their bicycles along the roadside while we were going through field manoeuvres.[327]

Food shortages prompt Sinn Féin to discourage local growers from exporting goods that are needed at home. Frank and Jack are both committed to breaking economic ties with Britain by disrupting in the sale of foodstuffs – butter, potatoes, vegetables – to English agents. Frank is quizzed about what is described as a 'third period' during his application for a Military Service Pension (MSP) in 1937.

> Q: Your activities were chiefly organising, drilling. Taking census of crops, enforcing the letting of land at a fixed price, commandeering of foodstuffs at markets and retailing locally to prevent export. That was in anticipation of conscription?
>
> FS: Yes. It was at the time.
>
> Q: You were full-time on this job?
>
> FS: Yes. I was (at) that time.[328]

Jack elaborates further at his MSP interview.

> JS: About that time there was great activity as regards the export of food and there was a general whip-up by the British Government to try and get as much food as possible and our people got active to try and keep the food at home. In connection with that I was sent down to the country. There were several markets around Ballaghaderreen for the sale of butter and potatoes for export to England. My brother, Frank, was more or less in charge there at the time. In the case of butter, that was sold locally to the people and whatever they got for it was paid to the farmers it was sold at a fair price.
>
> Q: You were sent from HQs to originate this campaign?
>
> JS: To give a hand. It was there at the time. There was a kind of framework of an organisation built up there.
>
> Q: Was it fairly successful?
>
> JS: It was as regards that area.[329]

Frank takes up working a parcel of land outside the town but when he's not farming his twin commitments with Sinn Féin and the GAA keep him continually on the road, whether around County Mayo or back and forth to Dublin. His diary entries are sporadic and vague, although the possibility of arrest is good reason for leaving large gaps day-to-day, month-to-month. He is, as those pursuing him might conclude, not one for the limelight.

> 26.6.17 – Sinn Féin club started at Rooskey. Maiden speech. Don't like spouting. Harry a topper tho! Met Alec in C + Hegarty's of Tubber. Great night. Home at 5.30 a.m!

In fact it's largely thanks to the diligence of police and military surveillance that we have any idea of Grandpa's frenetic schedule through 1917-18. Military Service Pension records confirm he is organiser in East Mayo for the IRB and named as company captain of the Irish Volunteers.

He is called upon to organize a service to honour Bill Partridge, a leading trade unionist and Irish Citizen Army officer as well as former inmate with Jack at Dartmoor and Lewes. Facing a 12-year sentence Partridge was released prior to the general amnesty because of ill-health. He passes away in July and his funeral is one of the biggest Ballaghaderreen has ever witnessed. John P. McPhillips is called to guard duty lining the road from the cathedral all the way out to Kilcolman Cemetery.

> A contingent of the Citizen army under the command of Countess Markievicz arrived by train from Dublin, a company of Volunteers under the command of Mick Brennan arrived from West Clare, all in uniform. Our local company was under the command of Frank Shouldice. A guard of honour was formed . . .[330]

If Special Branch in Roscommon regard the Irish Volunteers as a purely local operation Partridge's funeral shows the town's brigade is clearly plugged into the national grid. Markievicz leads a graveside salute, firing her pistol into the air and extolling Partridge as 'the purest-souled and noblest patriot Ireland ever had.'

Over the next months Frank's travels around the county sees Sinn Féin 'clubs' established in Brosna, Edmondstown, Carracastle and beyond. If this work is building the party at local level, the broader picture is already in view. Jack travels with Harry to campaign for de Valera in East Clare. Shortly afterwards Jack gets a remunerated position as Secretary of the Leinster GAA Council, based in Dublin.

Frank's solid friendship with Joe O'Kelly leads to spending much time over in the O'Kelly house off the market square. Put it down to fellow-feeling for Joe's hardline republicanism but their ongoing collaboration coincides with the development of another initiative, Joe's sister Cissie (née Winifred). Romance begins to blossom although there is so much happening it's too early for anything to really settle.

Cissie O'Kelly

The O'Kellys are also more than passing interest to the R.I.C. – Joe is now behind bars in Mountjoy and Cissie is very active in Cumann na mBan. Brief hints of optimism speckle Grandpa's 1917 diary.

> July 10 – Polling in Clare. Great hopes!
>
> July 11 – Up De Valera!! In by nearly 3000! Big night after circus procession and fires etc. A glorious win!

Countess Markievicz returns to Ballaghaderreen with de Valera to review Sinn Féin clubs across The West. Frank travels along with them, met by Joe McGuinness and Harry Boland at a town hall meeting in Ballymote, then Keash. They stay on Sunday night for the dance in Keash where Cissie joins them.

He is on the road constantly, all around Mayo and Roscommon. When he comes up to Dublin he stays with the Bolands at The Crescent. Frank, Cissie and Harry visit Joe in Mountjoy but the steady expansion of the Irish Volunteers-cum-Sinn Féin is attracting a lot of attention.

> 15.8.17 – Tons of arrests for drilling, wearing uniform
> etc. Sentences from 3 mos to 2 years!!

A serious knee injury – picked up playing hurling – confines him to bed for a week. Decommissioned amid so much activity he's an impatient patient.

> 16.8.17 – Getting tired of this bed tack! 4ᵗʰ day today.
> J. & Harry home – his ankle like a football. Hurt it on
> Vinegar Hill with Des and the Enniscorthy lads. More
> misfortune! Harry got a wasp sting in the palate. Nearly
> did for him.

W.T. Cosgrave follows up with another by-election win for Sinn Féin, this time in Kilkenny City. Yet for all this excitement, the sombre and tragic is never far away. Late in September Joe O'Kelly joins about 40 republican prisoners, including Fionnán Lynch and Austin Stack, on hunger-strike demanding political status. The protest is led by Tom Ashe, a former prison-mate of Jack's at Lewes and ex-President of the IRB Supreme Council. In a dreadful and convulsive episode Ashe loses his life when force-fed by the prison authorities.

> 25.9.17 – Tom Ashe died in Mater as a result of hunger
> strike after forcible feeding – 5 hrs after being admitted
> from Mountjoy. Terrible excitement over the country.

> 1.10.17 – Ashe's funeral yest was the biggest ever and
> no excursions up!! Vols in uniform and <u>firing party</u>
> turned out!!!!

Things are stepping up in other ways. Frank's work on the bog has prompted him to consider setting up a farm. He calls to the local Hibernian Bank to ask about a loan and to see what is on offer around Ballaghaderreen but nothing is within his price range.

As ex-prisoners, Frank and Jack apply for assistance from the INAAVDF to compensate for loss of income and loss of employment. The Fund works like a sort of insurance policy. Awards are made to individual Volunteers or their families, depending on rank and circumstance. Settlements are also reached for families of the executed men although different values – contentious but unpublicised – are placed on each Volunteer.

Prior to the tragedy at Mountjoy, £500 was set aside for Thomas Ashe upon his anticipated release from prison; in other 'Life Cases' a sum of £500 is allocated to Countess Markievicz; Eoin MacNeill (eight children) is due £1,000 on release. Down the line Payment #1855 provides £100 for Dick Coleman; Tom Cotter (#1922), a co-worker of Frank's at the Land Commission, receives a contribution of £25. The Fund considers the Shouldice brothers' application, noting that their mother received stipends including a payment of £4 in August, 1916 while Jack got a clothing allowance at Lewes.

Reviewing Jack's application, internal Fund records note,

> Recommend £250 to close 23/10/19 which includes 4 weeks grant in advance and brother's case to be considered later. Department of Agriculture, not reinstated. Is now Secretary of the Leinster Council GAA, worth from £80- £100 in pre-war days. Was thinking with his brother Frank of buying a farm which would cost est £1,200 to £1,500. How far could the Executive assist them for this?[331]

In October Payments #1763 and #1764 furnish Jack and Frank with £250 and £200 respectively.[332] It's a huge boost, which merits an enthusiastic line in Grandpa's diary.

> 13.10.17 – Heard from Jack that N.A. have recommended me for £200 and J for £250!!

Jack shares the good news in a letter to Jim, which is immediately intercepted by the British censor.

No. USA 22865/ 10.1.18

Writer says: –

INAAVDF payments to Frank (£200) and Jack (£250) (Courtesy NLI Archive)

Frank is still at home and I understand he is keeping a look-out for a suitable farm. He appears to like the farming idea best of all. I got 250£ and Frank 200£ from the National Aid, so we did not fare badly after all considering that 'Rise' that got us the 'push' . . . do you know they have made me President of the E. Mayo Sinn Féin Club . . . Enclosed a Sinn Féin Christmas card.

References are made to 14 other intercepted transatlantic letters to and from Jim. The information is passed confidentially to Irish Army Command at Parkgate HQ[333] regarding 'Grants given by National Aid Fund to Sinn Féin released prisoners John & Frank Shouldice.' Major Price suggests forwarding this to Dublin Castle.

Possibly the Under-Secretary wd like to see this. These men are brothers of Miss Ena Shouldice, post office telegraphist who is said to be engaged to Harry Boland, released convict. See USA letter of 8/8/17 no. 18352 attached.

RIC Special Branch in Roscommon adds further details:

Previous papers are attached. John Shouldice is now at home at Ballaghaderreen. He attended meetings at Gurteen, Co Sligo 31/12/17 and Bunamadden Co Sligo on 6/1/17 (L Ginnell MP and others). With his brother Frank he drilled men near Boyle on 13th inst.

It is then forwarded to the Under-Secretary.

See attached extract which goes to prove that the funds of the National Aid Association are being used in a way that does not comply with its constitution viz relief of <u>dependents</u> of rebellion sufferers.

October's Convention at the Mansion House effectively merges Sinn Féin with the Irish Volunteers. Eamon de Valera, who was largely ineffectual through Easter Week but did show leadership mettle in prison, is elected President of Sinn Féin and Executive President of the Volunteers. Grandpa notes:

25.10.17 – Sinn Féin Conv in Mansion Ho. About 1700 delegates rep over 1000 clubs. Great day. Sitting up to 11pm.

26.10.17 – Conv. on today also till 5pm. Dev elected President. Griffith and Plunkett withdrawn. Dev made a glorious presidential add.

27.10.17 – I.V. Conv today. Met tremendous lot of Frongoch and Lewes soreheads.

Frank and Cissie O'Kelly are now seeing each other regularly, both in Dublin and in Ballaghaderreen. Marking his 25th birthday he makes a decision that she is the one for him. 'Practically 'squared it up," he tells his diary. It has to be something big to get three exclamation marks. 'Plain talking!!!'

He visits her brother Joe several times at Mountjoy. After Ashe's traumatic death, the prisoners' dispute has been resolved and the hunger-strike ended.

29.9.17 – He's in great form. All political prisoners now!

Frank's payment comes through for £200 and Jack's £250 is imminent. 'Won't suffice for our farm scheme tho', he feels. Joe is transferred to Dundalk Prison where the promises made in Mountjoy are quickly broken. Incensed, Joe and others resume their fast.

Dear Frank,

Just a few lines to let you know we landed here at 7 yesterday morning and are now in a 'state of hunger strike' with John Bull, for not fulfilling the concessions regards treatment, food, etc which he made to us while at Mountjoy.[334]

The dispute is eventually resolved and Joe released from prison. His republican beliefs do not waver but lasting damage inflicted by hunger-striking means Joe O'Kelly will suffer from stomach complaints for the rest of his life.

Frank gave up idea of farming full-time

Widespread tensions have yet to flame but the return of republican prisoners from England has certainly galvanised the movement. Despite an impressive rally by the Irish Parliamentary Party – winning three by-elections on the trot – the IPP faces well-organized opposition from a political and militarized movement. Sinn Féin is on its way to becoming the dominant political force in Ireland and the authorities are straining to hold back the tide. Frank returns to Ballaghaderreen and finds the pressure and strain has taken its toll at St. John's Terrace.

> 5.11.17 – Ena's been down for a few weeks – nervous breakdown.

The demand for change is irresistible but personal lives are routinely sacrificed amid the turmoil.

26

*'They may not be the individuals, but they may be
equally dangerous to the State. The position is this:
The one thing Germany wants is trouble in Ireland'*
– Edward Shortt, Chief Secretary of Ireland, 5 August 1918

Constable Kearney's ambitions in Boyle may have been frustrated but help is at hand. Using martial law conditions, plans are afoot between Irish Command – as the Competent Military Authority (CMA) in Ireland – and Special Branch in Dublin Castle to draw up a fresh list of deportees. Except this time the suspects are going to neither prison nor internment camp; they are being deported to selected towns in Gloucestershire, Worcestershire and Herefordshire.

The Under-Secretary is notified when 11 English towns are selected to accommodate a total of 150 Irish deportees. A secret document from Irish Command HQ to Dublin Castle names Wooton-under-Edge, Morten in the Marsh, Newent, Cranham (near Stroud), Malvern, Pershore, Upton-on-Severn, Leominster, Bromyard, Ledbury and Ross.[335]

A month later Home Forces HQ in London reduces the list of locations to two – one in Southern Command (Cranham, Gloucestershire) and one in Western Command (Ross, Herefordshire).[336] A shortlist of 25 suspects is drawn up by Irish Command and Special Branch and sent to Chief Secretary Henry Duke. Jack Shouldice is Number 22 on the list; Frank is Number 23. After some consideration 19 individuals, including the two brothers, are finalised as cases to 'intern or deport.'[337]

They should be told they must leave Ireland 'forthwith' and will be taken to Arbour Hill prior to a sailing to Holyhead. Arresting officers are provided with guidelines in the event they are asked any questions:

> If the persons arrested ask for the reason for their arrest, they should be informed that they have been arrested under D.R.R. 55 because their behaviour is of such a nature as to give reasonable grounds for suspecting that they have been acting and were about to act in a manner prejudicial to the public safety or the Defence of the Realm.[338]

A deportation order is drawn up for Frank under the DRR by Lieut-General Bryan Mahon, General Officer Commander-in-Chief Forces in Ireland. The order states:

> DO HEREBY ORDER that FRANK SHOULDICE of Ballaghaderreen, County Roscommon, shall not reside in or enter IRELAND and I FURTHER ORDER the said FRANK SHOULDICE to leave IRELAND within 48 hours of service of this Order upon him.[339]

Grandpa is to be sent to a town called Ross. He will report every day to local police station and cannot stray more than two miles in any direction. No mention is made where he is supposed to stay or how he is to support himself. Or how his family in Ballaghaderreen will manage without him. A similar expulsion order is drawn up for Jack.

But the orders for suspects #22 and #23 are never issued. In months to come Lloyd George's government will devise an alternative means to lock up the entire Sinn Féin leadership rather than deploy such a bizarre and contentious deportation strategy. And so Grandpa never discovers the quiet enchantments of Herefordshire.

Others, however, including Terence MacSwiney, Sean T. O'Kelly, Tomás MacCurtain, Darrell Figgis, J.J. O'Reilly and Eamon Waldron of the Gaelic League bear the brunt of this brutal and largely unpublicised policy – Irish Command confirms to the Assistant Under-Secretary and Attorney-General 'the removal from Ireland of 28 suspects in February.'[340]

Mícheál Ó Droighnáin from Furbo, County Galway recalls being put on a train by RIC officers at four in the morning. After a boat to Holyhead and another rail trip he and Padraic Ó Maille end up in a town near Hereford.

> When we arrived in Kington it was near midnight and the sergeant of police didn't know what to do with us and he seemed embarrassed when he told us he would have to send us to the workhouse.[341]

Ó Droighnáin and Ó Maille, both native Irish speakers, objected strongly and were housed at the Cambrian Hotel at their own expense – at a rate of 50 shillings per week. Under DORA the press are banned from reporting these deportations but their severity is repeatedly highlighted in parliament by John Dillon, Arthur Lynch and Lawrence Ginnell. Henry Duke is challenged to explain the legal grounds for deportation without charge or any prospect of trial. The Chief Secretary falls back on the DRR mantra by way of justification.

> *Duke*: Twenty-eight persons have been arrested under Regulation 55 of the Defence of the Realm Regulations, which empowers the police to arrest any person who is reasonably suspected of having acted or being about to act in a manner prejudicial to the public safety or the Defence of the Realm. It is not proposed to try these men, the Competent Military Authority having decided to issue orders under Regulation 14 of the Defence of the Realm Regulations prohibiting them from residing in Ireland, which has been done.[342]

Dillon points out that many of the deportees were released from jail before Christmas only to be re-arrested six weeks later and then deported:

> . . . without any charge being made against them and to the declaration of the Government that it is not their intention to put them on trial . . . I ask this question, why were these men arrested?

Lynch: What are these mysterious crimes?

Duke: Honourable Members have no responsibility in this respect. The responsibility of the Executive in Ireland is to see that if there are real grave grounds for anticipating sinister action on the part of individuals it shall be prevented in the humanest way possible.

Flavin: Will the Right Honourable Gentleman say what these cases were? We who have been living in Ireland do not know anything about them.

One of Ó Droighnáin's travelling companions – an IRB member named Seamus O'Doherty – takes his case directly to the man who issued the order. Using two pages of a school copybook he writes from his enforced exile in Leominster to take issue with Lieut-General Mahon. Justifiably out-of-sorts, O'Doherty struggles to contain his anger in contesting the legality, if not the fairness, of his extradition:

> Dear Sir,
>
> I have been taken out of Ireland by the military authority there, and I presume you are not unacquainted with the order under which I have been so deported . . . I am now living in the village of Leominster, a village in Herefordshire, by direction of the chief of police for that county.
>
> As no provision has been made for my sustenance here, and as I have been advised by the people around here that it would be useless my looking for work, and as I also have my wife and children in my home in Ireland depending on me to provide them with food and clothing and a house to live in, I demand that the ordinary human rights not denied to the Belgians, the Rumanians or even the Serbians who have come under German rule, be accorded to me.
>
> You sir, have not tried, condemned or even charged me with any offence against your country, yet you drag me from my home and my family and send me under

armed military escort out of my country and throw me amongst a hostile people and when I enquire what provision, if any, has been made for me, I am told I may go to the workhouse!

You talk of your love for freedom and your fight for small nationalities and have blinded and persuaded thousands of young Irishmen of our generation, to leave their bones whitening on the shores of Gallipoli or their bodies rotting in the fields of France or Flanders – and for what? For freedom? For Ireland? Yes! Freedom for the English Government in Ireland to do as she pleases with the few Irishmen who remain!

Were you other than a British soldier I should appeal to your sense of Justice and humanity, but not being such, I make a public demand, for I am sending this letter to the press, that the few rights remaining to me as an Irishman be restored to me, that I be taken back to my own country and allowed resume my ordinary occupation which you deny me here, so as to provide food and clothing and a home for my wife and little children.

Yours truly,

J. O'Doherty[343]

The Chief Secretary resists all calls to have the 28 men repatriated but under persistent questioning at the House of Commons a concession is made May 3 to provide maintenance to the deportees at a rate of at least £1 per week.

In a strange twist, Lieut-General Mahon, a Galway-born militarist, will be appointed by W.T. Cosgrave to Seanad Éireann after independence in 1922. His appointment would hardly have been welcomed by O'Doherty, who, like other deportees, was not allowed return home until June.

* * *

The clamour for enrolling Irishmen into Britain's war effort gains impetus following a major German offensive in March, 1918. Pro-

John Dillon addresses an anti-conscription rally in his home town, Ballaghaderreen, 1918. Fighting for his political survival it was the first and only time he shared a platform with Eamon de Valera, leader of fast-emerging Sinn Féin. (Courtesy Underwood & Underwood/Corbis)

vision is made to extend the Military Service Act to Ireland. The British Army urgently needs manpower and a virtual collapse in voluntary enlistment, even before the Rising, signposts southern Ireland as a largely untapped source. Public speculation galvanizes the anti-conscription movement as Sinn Féin's ace card for mobilizing mass support. Frank is involved in organizing a monster rally in Ballaghaderreen in April 1918. The Irish Parliamentary Party is fighting for its survival and Dillon shares the platform with de Valera for the rally which draws an estimated 20,000-strong crowd. The carve-up of the town into rival IPP and Sinn Féin factions tragically claims the life of Thomas Doherty, a Dillonite supporter from Kilmovee. With the town crowded by supporters from both factions Doherty sustains a head injury after being tripped in the street by Thomas Maguire. A post-mortem reveals the injury was complicated by the onset of pneumonia and pleurisy. Maguire is remanded with Bertie Shouldice over the fatal incident but Bertie is soon acquitted without charge.

When the Military Services Act is passed at Westminster even the hitherto compliant Irish Parliamentary Party walks out in protest. Four days later nationalist parties reach consensus with the Anti-Conscription pledge, drafted by de Valera:

> Denying the right of the British Government to enforce compulsorily service in this Country we pledge ourselves to one another to resist conscription by the most effective means at our disposal.

The stance is supported by the Catholic bishops and more mass rallies are planned around the country. The trade unions call a highly effective one-day general strike. Seeing first-hand how united the opposition is in Ireland, Chief Secretary Duke is known to be averse to introducing conscription. Lloyd George and his Dublin Castle administration are unnerved by Sinn Féin's run of stunning successes at the polls. With a general election looming later in the year his coalition government has much to worry about if de Valera maintains course. The immediate remedy is simple – Duke is replaced by Edward Shortt on May 1.

Lloyd George and his new Chief Secretary forge ahead, clearing out potential objectors like Lieut-General Mahon (replaced by Lieut-General Shaw) and Viceroy Lord Wimborne (replaced by Field Marshall French). It was French, former Commander-in-Chief Home Forces, who previously despatched General Maxwell to put down The Rising. Now, two years later, French is entrusted to crush the mass movement Maxwell's clampdown has spawned.

The Military Service Act makes conscription legally – though not practically – enforceable in Ireland. It hasn't yet happened because of mass opposition and because Irish Volunteers – now Sinn Féin and soon to be the Irish Republican Army – keep fighting the wrong fight. Backed by Edward Carson, Prime Minister Lloyd George declares clear links between wartime Germany and Sinn Féin. His new Chief Secretary in Ireland can't produce anything conclusive but proof does not appear necessary. According to perceived wisdom, the rebels plan a Rising (Mark II) by getting more German guns to arm de Valera's reported reserve of half a million soldiers, stretching British forces across Ireland while Sinn Féin's

German allies continue a large-scale offensive in Europe. In wartime it sounds far-fetched enough to be plausible. The so-called 'German Plot' is born.

For Grandpa, it begins with a pre-dawn raid on St. John's Terrace. As before, he keeps a log of events.

> Arrested in bed at 3.45 a.m. at Ballaghaderreen, Sat. 18 May. Conveyed by military wagon (5 police and driver) to Boyle and left in cell until morning train to Dublin. Given 3 blankets and had to sleep on floor. Good breakfast – handcuffed then and brought to station in military wagon (about 9.30 a.m.). Escort of 1 officer, 1 police and 6 soldiers (armed). Handcuffs removed after train starting and officer civil.
>
> Met J. Clancy and JJ O'Connell at Mullingar (came on same train). Also George Geraghty and Sean Hurley and the Cavan election contingent; J O'Mahony, Des Fitzgerald, Dick Davis, Jn Dolan, J. Loughran. Went right through Dublin to Ktown where we heard Dev, Griffith etc were already waiting for deportation. Get served with deportation notice under DORA on man o' war which booked us to Frongoch as aliens. Arrived in Holyhead at about 10 p.m. Saturday – were expecting a bust-up on the way. Tadhg Barry, Pierce Ryan, F. Drohan, Brennan-Whitmore and several others were on boat. 46 in all including the Countess. Our party were shoved down in the 'hold' and locked in. Kept in military camp at Holyhead that night and until morning.[344]

Frank has been at liberty for 18 months but re-arrest shows him reverting instantly to the same cheery defiance as before. Even if it's partly bravado it appears as though detention, far from arriving like a bolt from the blue, was almost expected. He manages to get a message home.

> Dear Mama,
>
> Well I arrived this far safe + sound and am meeting a lot of old pals! Jack & Harry should be arriving soon! I stayed in Boyle on Fri night and was brought to Dn_

next day and shipped across. We are booked for Frong-och again and only put up here on the way – I understand. Don't know exactly when we'll get there but we are alright here, same huts etc as in Frongoch . . .

Meantime you can get the following things ready – night shirts, tooth brush + monkey brand (my brush is the one with the curved back) – one of those £1 notes in my pocket book – safety razor + brush – B. will find it in cig box on wash table – a few handkerchiefs, some sponges and tobacco (Gallagher Army & Navy cut plug) . . .

I suppose the folk around got a big surprise on Sat. morning to find me flown. Possibly you may have some of those 'mollies' in sympathetic mood now – but I'd give 'em a cool reception . . .

Well beannacht leat – now dear Mama I didn't think I'd be so far away this weekend.

As ever, your fond son, Frank

P.S. just told <u>now</u> we're not bound for Frongoch – nothing definite yet. Will write. F.

For the next weeks Christina has no idea where her son is taken and can get no information from the authorities. Sounding more like Ena in full flow she takes it upon herself to write to prison governors wherever she thinks he may be held.

To the Governor, Gloucester Prison.

Sir,

I demand immediate information as to whether my son F. Shouldice is among the Irish prisoners in your charge. It is now nearly three weeks since he was taken and imprisoned without trial and no tidings of him have been yet received. Also it has been stated by one of your MPs that the prisoners are entitled to communicate with their friends and receive parcels. This is another British lie – the plain fact being that we are not even aware of their whereabouts. This I take it is another sample of your tender humanity. In common justice be good enough to supply the necessary information to (Mrs) C. Shouldice.[345]

The Governor replies:

Madam,

Mr. F. Shouldice is not here – nor do I know anything of his whereabouts. You are in error re: communication to friends – the Under Sec. of State's reply in the House of Commons being in accordance with facts. Probably before this you have received a p.c. giving you information of your son's location and giving particulars as to how you should address a letter to him.

The Governor at Reading also replies.

Madam,

I have to acknowledge the receipt of your letter of the 4th instant and to inform you in reply that there is no person here in my charge named F. Shouldice.

Frank's arrest is part of a sweep of leading republicans – including four MPs (de Valera, Plunkett, Cosgrave and McGuinness) – on the grounds of alleged conspiracy between Sinn Féin and Germany. The immediate intention is to neutralize Sinn Féin but the legitimacy of the action is seriously undermined by Shortt's May 20 letter to Lloyd George.

We cannot and do not pretend that we can prove that each individual taken has been in active personal communication with German agents, but we know that someone has, and each of the interned persons has said or done something which gives ground that he or she is in it.[346]

As political repression goes it's a crude instrument. Evidence of Irish republicans being in league with Germany is flimsy, if there is any evidence at all, and by the end of the year John Dillon is openly accusing the British Government of 'pure invention.'[347] The charge is not refuted.

Arrested and interned as part of the so-called 'German Plot' 73 men – Jack Shouldice, Harry Boland and Michael Collins, among others, evade capture – are rounded up across Ireland on unspecified charges of assisting Germany in its war effort against Britain. No concrete evidence is produced of Irish-German collaboration and arrests are made under ever-pliable Defence of the Realm Regulations of 'persons suspected of acting, having acted, and being about to act in a manner prejudicial to the public safety and the defence of the Realm . . . and should remain interned until further orders.'

Credibility of a 'German Plot' is further shaken a fortnight later by former Viceroy Wimborne at the House of Lords. Pointing to a complete overhaul of the Irish executive prior to these mass arrests, he queries the Prime Minister's motivation for changes that 'had the effect of removing from the Irish Government all, or nearly all, of those of professed sympathy with the case of Irish nationality.'

> It is true that in partial explanation, at any rate, the Government have alleged the existence of a German plot in Ireland. One would like to know a little more about it. It is somewhat strange, in view of the highly specialised means of obtaining information which have recently existed in Ireland, that neither I, nor, as far as I am aware, any other member of the late Irish Executive, was aware of the existence of this plot until it was discovered by the British Government . . . perhaps it is better to regard the German Plot, and what has happened in connection with it, as evincing more the zeal of the new broom than as revealing any fundamental change in the internal situation of Ireland itself.[348]

27.

'The "darkest hour is that before the dawn"
and indeed we have had a lot of dark hours'
– Kathleen Boland, 17 June 1918[349]

The Home Office chooses to designate Frongoch for Irish internees once again and sends a batch of DORA orders to the
Chief Secretary. The order served to Grandpa aboard the British
Navy gunboat is signed by Edward Shortt. But it's an inauspicious
start – or a comical illustration of the 'German Plot' – because
Frongoch is already full to capacity with German POWs. Having
lain idle for a spell in 1917 the camp was reopened to accommodate more POWs captured in Europe.

Frongoch is ruled out as an option. New internment orders are
hastily forwarded to Shortt for a fresh signature. Meanwhile the
Irish detainees are kept in Holyhead for two nights until the Home
Secretary notifies the Under-Secretary by letter,

> As you are aware it has been decided that these prison-
> ers shall not remain at Frongoch but that they will be
> divided into small groups and will be interned in differ-
> ent prisons.[350]

The detainees are nominated for jails in Reading, Lincoln,
Durham, Birmingham, Gloucester, and Brixton. Grandpa joins 19
comrades to be taken by train to Usk, 12 miles east of Cardiff, 10
miles north of Newport. It will be his second and last incarceration
in Wales.

After being held in Holyhead he makes a note of his travels.

> Started at 7 a.m. per train after going through half Eng-
> land & Wales on a broiling day – go to Usk! At 7 p.m.
> (escort decent – Lieut. Close). Shoved into gaol there

264

(women's portion). It's in Monmouth on border of England and Wales, beautiful country all around. Grand
bank holiday (Whit) trip for us. Saw some sights on the
way. Saw Jack's warrant on the vessel but he nor Harry
and several others have been landed so far!! [351]

Mr and Mrs Thomas of Pontypool may have had an idiosyn-
cratic sense of humour when they christened their son Thomas. At
the age of 69 he was arrested for stealing a lamb belonging to Row-
land Bevan and is sentenced to three months hard labour. Thomas
Thomas has just completed his sentence at Usk Prison when 20
Irish prisoners in civilian clothes troop into town.

The town is used to exotic visitors. Newport, once a thriving
maritime base, was known for its ribald excesses portside. Stranded sailors with no permits to stay in Britain were frequently sent
to Usk to serve custodial sentences. Unusually, the prison is set in
the centre of town, situated between the colonial-style courthouse
and the local cricket ground. The front entrance is a squat design,
two main support columns with turrets astride a now disued central archway. The prison wings behind the wall extrude above the
parapet but most of the cell windows face inwards so visual contact between the inmates and the good people of Usk is kept to a
minimum.

Hired hand Henry Pierrepoint carried out three of the prison's
seven executions here between 1905 and 1910. Known for an assiduous manner in the strange precision of his craft the family
name is no stranger to Irish prisoners – his brother Thomas will
carry out 24 hangings in Mountjoy when appointed as official state
executioner for the Irish Republic after independence.

The Irish prisoners are led from the train station – long since
abandoned – along the River Usk, over the stone bridge and down
past the shopfronts and doorways of Maryport Street. The town
is in deep discussion how to honour local men sacrificed on the
fields of France and Belgium. Without question, in these parts the
preferred type of Irish hero at this time is the likes of Major Marshall of the Irish Guards, who, according to the *Llanelly Star*, 'has
been wounded a tenth time and is progressing favourably.'[352]

As far as anyone who reads newspapers is concerned, this bedraggled line of unshaven fugitives are German collaborators. Lloyd George has declared it so. Two years previously Irish rebels stabbed Britain in the back when Welsh soldiers were fighting Germans and dying in Europe for the rights of small nations. German guns were involved back then too except they sank to the bottom of the sea.

Two years later and Welsh soldiers are still fighting Germans and dying in Europe for the rights of small nations. Pontypool Urban District Council is soon to hold a Town Hall meeting to discuss where to plant a memorial to honour its glorious dead. And here are the Irish rebels again, ready to stab their Celtic neighbours in the back with the help, again, of a resurgent Kaiser.

The national press across Britain is happy to vouch for this Sinn Féin/German collaboration although the *Cambria Daily Leader* rushes to the defence of the beleaguered Irish community in Swansea.

> The revelations as to the Sinn Féin plottings today are distressing – but let us be fair and discerning. The Prime Minister said yesterday that the Nationalist leaders had nothing to do with it. We are very sure that not a spark of sympathy existed for it in Swansea, where nearly every Irishman of military age had joined up long before Conscription came in.[353]

Maligned in advance as criminally seditious the men walk under the prison arch to begin an indeterminate sentence on unsubstantiated charges. They are met by Governor William Young, already apprehensive about having enough staff to deal with potentially difficult and violent prisoners. Although Usk authorities have been photographing new arrivals since 1876 they do not photograph the Irish detainees. The admittance book is filled in. Frank is listed as Number 36 – George Geraghty from Roscommon is Number 37 – with committal dated as Ireland on May 17, the day before he was pulled out of bed.

Under the 'Sentence' category all the so-called 'German-plot' prisoners are listed as 'Interned'. The record shows Grandpa is

25 years, 5 foot 10 ½ inches with dark brown hair. His 'Trade or Occupation' is listed as 'Nil' – perhaps the first stirrings of non-cooperation have begun.

The men are segregated in a wing formerly used as the women's prison. They go to their cells, wondering what is in store for them and how long they will be here. On June 3, the Chief Secretary's Office at Dublin Castle finally informs Christina Shouldice where her son is detained.[354] Frustrated by delays with regular post Christina overlooks the extra expense of sending a telegram to Usk and even pre-pays for a response.

> 6.6.18 – Dear Frank only now learned your whereabouts wire immediately condition requirements cheer up love Mother.[355]

The drama back home seems to invigorate Ena. Opting against a return to Dublin she takes up secretarial classes in Galway and spends more time at home with her mother and Lily. Her full-time position at the GPO has finally come to an end but her spirits, after a difficult year, are lifting. As ever, she is the first correspondent to her jailed brother. Her letter, sent to Frongoch, is re-routed to Usk.

> We're feeling somewhat recovered from the shock. Hope you're in good form after all the knocking round that you got . . . the 'blues' stopped for two hours after you left and searched the house, but bless your heart they had their trouble all for nothing. We were all awake till about five or six a.m. I never <u>looked</u> as lively in my life. . .
>
> No word from Jack yet. If you don't meet him there soon we can only guess he's 'missing'. Somehow I think you'll be better off there in the heel of the 'hunt'. The boys at home will have a lively time. So far you're safe anyhow and that's consoling.[356]

Many at Usk with Frank are ex-Frongoch prisoners. Experience has hardened them. They feel they have been detained on fabricated charges and are in no mood to buckle. A standoff with Governor Young begins immediately over uniforms. He wants them to wear prison issue. They refuse. The prisoners have been through this rigmarole before and they insist they are Prisoners-of-War. As such they demand the status that distinguishes them from criminals. Flustered, the Governor contacts the Home Office and at its behest duly relents on rules about clothing.

For Governor Young – and for prison authorities throughout the U.K. – official policy on the Irish internees remains a muddle. Regarded as political prisoners without Prisoner of War status, the Prison Commission seeks clearer direction from the Home Office.

The tone of exchanges is set when the Commission asks what they are supposed to do 'in accordance with the arrangement made by the Secretary of State (for) the Sinn Féin prisoners brought to this country for internment.' Having witnessed the revolt at Lewes the Prison Commission fears trouble and wants back-up from the army.

> As these cases are for internment and consequently will be associated with possible risks of combination (many of them were concerned in the Lewes mutiny), a staff of more than average strength would be necessary, but owing to depletion of staff through the release of officers for military service, the prisons are being managed by a staff below even normal strength. It will be necessary therefore at all times when these men are out of their cells to have an adequate guard present and to provide it, it is urgently required that the War Office should be asked to instruct the military authorities in the districts named to supply such guard as the Governors may think necessary to supplement their staff..[357]

The War Office turns down the request. It can provide escorts to civilian authorities when internees are being moved. Otherwise, however:

> The Army Council much regret that they are unable to comply with the request that a military guard should be provided at the prisons wherein Sinn Féin prisoners are being interned.[358]

Minuted records from the Home Office suggest prison governors are expected to handle any crisis locally.

> I have told the Prison Commrs that any Gov who doubts the adequacy of his staff should apply to the G.O.C. of his district for a military guard without waiting to hear of the Army Council having actually instructions for guards to be furnished.[359]

Caught between the Prison Commission, the War Office and the Home Office, the governors at various prisons feel the blow back. A freeze on visits and post catches the Usk prisoners by surprise. They have been arrested, deported and interned on what they feel are trumped-up charges. The additional penalty of isolating them from the outside world is deeply resented. Governor Young writes to the Home Office:

> There are undoubted signs and hints that the men's patience will not hold out much longer in this matter and it is right that I make you aware of this [360]

He adds that the prisoners each carry a copy of their internment order with them, and regarding POW status, are adamant that 'it is laid down that they "shall be subject to all the rules and conditions applicable to persons interned in Frongoch Camp."' With little option to do otherwise, the prison regime at Usk is relaxed. Aside from not having to wear prison issue, the men are allowed free association and postal restrictions are lifted. It's a victory of sorts.

About 30 miles away Irish prisoners almost make up the full complement at Gloucester Jail. They have their 'Joe McGuinness moment' when Arthur Griffith, Sinn Féin founder, becomes MP for East Cavan in a June by-election. It's a critical win as the Irish Parliamentary Party was on a run of victories in South Armagh, Waterford City and East Tyrone. Lloyd George's move towards conscription has not helped the IPP's cause.

Cissie captures the mood in a letter to Usk.

Well Frank this is a queer world – one day trouble and the next day joy, but I must say yesterday evening was a happy one for me and a glorious day for Ireland; just fancy that victory in Cavan, a majority of 1,214* wasn't it marvellous? And all the opposition we had.[361]

*the majority was 1,204

Showing a flourish with the pen, East Cavan's new MP opines from his prison cell:

This being a cathedral city, an air of Established piety exudes from the officials who, on the whole, are quiet civil sort of men who open our cell doors at 6 and see us back to them at 8pm. [362]

One of the earliest letters Grandpa receives at Usk is from his old pal, Tom McKenna, who sends him 'American stuff' (chewing gum) in the post. It's as though everybody steps back into the rhythm and roles established during Frank's spells at Stafford and Frongoch.

. . . glad to learn that you accepted your enforced holiday philosophically. The weather was just becoming 'summery' when you were 'pinched' and just now it's far too nice to make gaol a suitable holiday resort.[363]

Once again, he cheerfully offers to search town in pursuit of unpredictable requests. 'Well Frank old man, here we are again,' he writes. 'Am sending at long last the macramé thread.'[364]

In Frank's absence neighbours at home help Christina cut the turf. Having just discovered her brother is not actually in Frongoch, Ena sends a registered letter to Usk.

Your very welcome and anxiously awaited letter arrived only this Fri morn. We had despaired of hearing from you – so I wired yesterday morning to you c/o Governor. As it was yesterday we heard for the first time we heard where you were! So you can imagine what sort of a three weeks we put in. we were thinking all sorts of things, that you would be starved and ill etc. however your letter was a great relief and it sounds brisk enough. But you haven't said how you were – and if food was sufficient etc etc

You will be glad to hear we had the turf all cut in a day about a week after you were taken – by 30 men . . . Fr Gildea was out working all day too! [365]

Frank writes to the *Roscommon Herald* in gratitude to neighbours, taking the opportunity to spur on the Sinn Féin clubs he set up the previous year.[366]

> . . . thanking most sincerely my numerous friends in Ballaghaderreen and the surrounding districts for their generous action in saving and carting home a supply of turf for me. They will understand that I am unable at the present time to thank them individually but nevertheless it is non the less sincere . . . the obstinate fact remains that we are prisoners and such kindly acts as those banish all doubts that we are forgotten in the old country . . . the few westerns who are here look forward with pleasure to receiving the Rosc. Herald and are proud to see from the reports of the various clubs that The West's Awake!

Satisfied that most key Sinn Féin leaders have been apprehended the authorities go to extreme lengths to penetrate the organisation by monitoring who contacts the internees and what's being said. A special censorship unit is set up at the Directorate of Military Intelligence to compile fortnightly reports on mail to and from 'German Plot' prisoners. Between July 14, 1918 and up to their general release on March 15, 1919 the unit examines 25,000 letters, 745 telegrams and 1,585 newspapers. Its findings are circulated to the Chief Secretary, MI5, Home Office and the Prison Commission.

Some 393 letters are referred to MI5, MI9 or other agencies for investigation and 484 letters are retained. The censors offer an overview of the dominant themes during each period, noting in November,

The news of the signing of the Armistice was the occasion for outbursts of sarcasm and open hostility in letters both to and from Ireland. [367]

For such a labour-intensive, time-consuming exercise however the Directorate concludes its work somewhat discouraged, particularly when material previously unseen appears in newspapers written by prisoners.

> From a censorship point of view the results have been practically valueless, owing to the fact that the internees in all the prisons devised means at one time or another to evade censorship, either by entrusting letters to prisoners released on parole, or by some method unknown to us.

This level of observation may not yield intelligence hoped for but the team of censors inevitably gets to know the humours and preoccupations of particular correspondents. [368] They evaluate each internee in every prison, citing particular extracts or declaring 'Nothing of interest' on each report. One censor at the unit takes issue with Tadhg Barry's December correspondence, picking for example a letter which begins:

> I hope in God I may never spend Xmas out of Cork again.

The censor is unmoved, commenting:

> Letters in his usual style of self-pity and grumbling, chiefly on the subject of his continued detention in Prison.

Barney Mellowes figures in the censors' notes, although it is the ire of his wife which attracts most attention:

> *Mrs Mellowes*: I hope when we have our own Republic you will demand damages for wrongful imprisonment – the demanded sum should be a good round one; not that even that would compensate the wives – moth-

ers – relatives for their time of enforced anxiety and desolate homes robbed with less compunction than a common robber would a hen roost.[369]

Grandpa's letters are discussed extensively in the Directorate's first report.[370]

> FRANK SHOULDICE: Was evidently a leader in Sinn Féin circles in Ballaghaderreen and is kept in touch with their doings by his brother Bertie Shouldice and other friends. Secondary meaning is frequently employed in his correspondence – 'concerts', 'teams', 'theatricals', being terms used to refer to Sinn Féin meetings and Conventions.

Profile notes are drawn up on the people he writes to, or those who write to him. Cissie, his sweetheart, is described as:

> An active worker in Sinn Féin interests in Ballaghaderreen, and professes the greatest patriotism and interest in the coming election. Letters are frequently suggestive of secondary meaning. 'Music', being used to cover political information.

As for Ena, having been let go by the Post Office, the former telegraphist no longer excites apoplexy at Dublin Castle. However when she starts work at Sinn Féin headquarters in Dublin the address of her workplace is immediately noted by censors.

> Employed at 6 Harcourt Street; gives personal news of friends there. Her letters frequently suggest secondary meaning, and are undesirable in tone.

And Frank's brother, Bertie.

> Letters are ambiguously worded and frequently contain allusions to matters not intelligible to third parties.

Bertie, who knows all about censorship from his stay at Frongoch, doesn't seem bothered who reads what he writes.

12.6 – Is there any word of a trial yet or has this fiasco of a plot all dwindled away, when proof cannot be brought to bear on it. Anyhow, rest assured the whole world knows a plot is ridiculous.[371]

14.7 – What on earth are ye being detained so long for and without even a trial, strange times we are living in. . . . Things here as usual. Am sick answering enquiries re you.[372]

Tom McKenna is simply dismissed.

Correspondence conveys unimportant political information and expresses great optimism and confidence in the result of the coming electioneering campaign.

Others, like Jennie O'Connell who writes to Frank c/o 'H.M. Hotel,' or Sheila O'Regan, make a joke of the surveillance.

My dear Frank,

It seems like old times to be writing to you again. I suppose I really should feel honoured to be in a position to correspond with one of his Majesty's most esteemed guests . . . I'm a great hand at the farming business now and I'll give my services <u>voluntarily</u> to the breaking up and tilling of your 'plot'! I don't think I'll say more for I might be violating some clause of the DORA regulations for which of course I have the keenest regard.[373]

However the satirical gem he receives from Alfie O'Kelly – brother of Cissie and Joe – would have censors scratching their heads. It is, unfortunately, the only letter he receives from Alfie.

Well Frank it looked so mean that you never came to say good bye to us before you left, and to say that you have been receiving communications from Herr von Kuhlmann or some other Herr or Von that I know nothing about, making tools of you for their own ends and now you are in a nice fix which I don't suppose they will try to get you out of, it simply makes me ashamed to say I am an Irish man atall.

274

> Well Frank if you could only see the position you and
> your fellow men have got Ireland into you would feel
> very much ashamed. First you have stirred the <u>quiet</u>,
> <u>fairdealing</u>, <u>honest</u>-<u>governing</u> mind of <u>Sir</u> <u>John</u> <u>French</u>,
> you have led him to proclaim ¾ of the Irish Nation,
> even led him to use violence in the governing of our
> country made half of what ye call the Sinn Féiners turn
> loyalists and even blackened the name of Ireland all
> over the world for the sake of a little <u>German</u> Gold.[374]

Frank settles into a routine at Usk although the delays on post
clearly rankle with everybody. In a letter home to Christina, he
says wryly:

> Your last lr written on 9th inst arrived here on 23rd. I
> don't know whether it went around by San Francisco or
> Hong Kong but it managed to get here all the same.[375]

After his experience with Jim at Frongoch he discourages any
plans for a visit.

> Just after hearing that visits are to be allowed every 3
> mos – if that's any news to you. I know of old the value
> of such a ½ hour's confab under the circs – so I'd advise
> anyone thinking of the trip to give it up! [376]

Fiancé-less back home, Cissie finds the house very quiet. She
is in regular contact with the Shouldice family in town but she and
Frank have yet to announce their engagement. The sudden disap-
pearance of her beau contributes to tense, empty days.

> I spent my day over in Usk Prison today but alas only
> in my thoughts … on the old road when I thought of
> you dearest. How often you cycled out there and how
> anxiously I looked forward to the weekend together.
> Oh when will that time come again I wonder. <u>Will</u> my
> patience hold out atall and how I long sometimes to
> see you.[377]

These are tough, lonesome times and the strain of separation
and general anxiety is patently obvious.

Having no consolation to find for anything but to write to you I'm sending you these few lines, just to let you know it has been a fortnight now since I had a letter from you. Needless to say I have been worrying for the past while and perhaps no necessity for it. Is anything the matter?[378]

She confesses to sometimes being 'in the dumps' and is glad to seek spiritual help – or pure diversion – by travelling to Lough Derg with Ena for a pilgrimage or getting her palm read by a gypsy in Frenchpark. At times Cissie ('my thoughts day and night over in Usk prison') appears very conscious that her letters will be read by a third party.

When the letters are censored it's hard to know what to write not indeed that the censor has seen enough of mine I'm sure when they are long like this he doesn't go through half of them.[379]

She takes succour from pleasant memories and holds dearly and in detail one particular afternoon at the Botanical Gardens in Dublin. Since then, much of their time 'together' has been time apart. The very act of writing offers its own catharsis and Frank's indefinite absence often prompts heartfelt emotions, censor or no censor.

My heart is aching for you more and more every day. When atall shall I see you out or have the pleasure of a good decent póg . . . strange to say I never loved you as I do now and it may be my imagination but certainly I would give my life were it needed to see you again and be in your arms once more.[380]

In response, Frank sends her a postcard with a picture of Usk Prison on the front and an arrow pointing to the Irish wing. He writes, somewhat mischievously:

This is the outside view of our present 'abode' and which is not altogether as forbidding a place as it may look!!

Postcard from HMP Usk with arrow pointed to Irish prisoners' wing

November's report from the Directorate of Military Intelligence makes fresh observations of Usk's post bag.

> Frequent reference is made in this correspondence to Shouldice's brother – alternately called 'Jack' and 'Larry' – who appears to travel about Ireland as a Speaker or Director of Elections.

Jack, described by the Intelligence unit as 'a Sinn Féin agent', is still very much at large. He spends much of the time with Harry Boland, fugitives on the run from DORA's internment order. Somehow he maintains his position as Secretary of the Leinster GAA Board and also acts a liaison between the Irish Volunteers Dublin Brigade and the INAAVDF. And, somewhere during all this, he finds time to begin a romantic liaison with Liz Merriman of Ballaghaderreen.

The censors' single out a remark made by youngest sister Lily.

> Jack come (sic) round sometimes, he is avoiding them yet.

Harry's mother Kathleen writes to Frank to say that Gerald Boland has just been sentenced by court-martial to six months for drilling and training Volunteers. In a reference to Jack's work with Harry she adds:

J & H are on holidays <u>surely</u> through rather early in the season God bless them. It's a dreadful thing to see their comfortable beds every night empty and wondering where they are but God will watch for them and all your dear comrades in English prisons.[381]

The world Frank now knows divides into those who are incarcerated and those who are not. Ena attends her evening classes in bookkeeping and shorthand. Typical of the time her news is a mix of good and bad.

Nothing very startling to relate since the E. Cavan knockout . . . Jack is knocking round and doing his work as usual. It's marvellous. H is in good form too I believe. Gerald is doing time in B'fast. They're getting treated badly there. Always did. Dundalk follows on hunger strike for Ashe terms.[382]

The indeterminate length of the men's stay in prison at Usk weighs heavily on them in the same way it did at Frongoch. Conditions are generally acceptable but there's a general torpor about their situation. Con O'Donovan, Jack's former cell mate on death row in Kilmainham, writes from Usk to ex-Frongoch stalwart Henry Dixon.

Paudeen O'Keeffe, B. Mellowes, F. Shouldice and myself . . . we are all more or less disappointed to find how difficult it is to lay ourselves out decently and stick to any course of study here. I think it must be that there are just too few and too many of us (if you allow the bull) confined in a limited space and that we are so continually knocking up against the same walls + doors + gates + persons without the least bit of change. Then again, we have nothing to do and all day to do it. [383]

For Frank, the arrival of a new kitten at the jail and a job in the kitchen make life a little easier. Christina and Lily keep the parcels coming too.

> Ye needn't bother much with bread – just an odd time
> – but butter of course is welcome and an odd tin of
> cocoa and bottle of 'Irel' coffee. I generally have some
> cocoa at night and a spot of coffee after dinner. So you
> can see we are looking after ourselves very well. [384]

To relieve the boredom the prisoners improvise a handball alley inside the compound. They clear an area leading to the high perimeter wall and get permission to remove a metal obstruction that impedes play. Governor Young takes to watching what is to him an unfamiliar and most unusual game. O'Donovan sees the impromptu alley as a great release for pent-up comrades.

> All here are in usual health and spirits making the best
> of things as we find them but incidentally doing a good
> deal of grumbling. Of course it is only natural to expect
> that owing to atmospheric disturbances, heatwaves
> and the like, there should be occasional fits of depression from which the sufferer speedily recovers on playing a game of handball. [385]

Happily, Ena seems to have regained her spirits. After the GPO debacle and the tangled affairs of her heart she's ready to return to Dublin, to take up a full-time position at Sinn Féin headquarters.

> My dear Frank,
>
> A thousand apologies for delay in answering your letter
> but I was waiting for news and then I came up to Dn last
> Wednesday. They wanted an extra clerk in Harcourt St
> and so here I am. Harry and Paddy pushed me into it
> although I am not prepared. Have to get shorthand up,
> but meantime I expect they can make use of me as they
> appear to be very busy.[386]

Frank might well feel that his own life has stalled behind prison walls while everything outside is moving on. He gets a telegram from his brother Jack and Liz Merriman – 'married this morning in Lisacul very sorry you are not present'. Typical of the anomalies of the day, Jack's brother-in-law Johnny Merriman fought in World

War One with the Connaught Rangers. He will later join the Free State Army only to lose part of his leg in a republican ambush during the Civil War.

Lisacul's family nuptials gives everybody pause for thought, including Ena.

> Nothing doing for myself. Seem to be out of the running. Well I have myself to blame I suppose.[387]

World War One is about to end. At savage cost to both sides, the Allies have finally overcome the Axis Powers. Cissie writes on November 11, Armistice Day. 'They cannot keep you much longer with the war being over,' she muses rhetorically. War is indeed over but news of peace breaking out in Europe hardly preoccupies those behind bars in South Wales. They see no change in Usk or anywhere else Irish prisoners are held. Typically, the end of war produces a potentially explosive situation in Dublin when a large, vociferous crowd – including 'G' men and military personnel – converge on Sinn Féin's HQ in Harcourt Street. Windows are broken and damage done to the premises before Jack and other activists arrive, fully armed, to defend it. Only then the mob withdraws.

But as the season heads into winter there is a new threat. 'We are having exciting times here,' writes Tom McKenna a little too jauntily. 'With an epidemic of what is called 'influenza.'[388] Ena is less flippant and with good reason – the Spanish flu' will claim an estimated 23,000 lives in Ireland and ten times as many in Britain.

> I see the plague is raging in England and South Wales particularly so hope ye are all safe. There are an awful lot dying here from it . . . it is a terrible business. Some families in Clontarf have lost father, mother and two or three sons. Others a father and three sons. So you can imagine it's pretty serious.[389]

At the prisoners' request families in Ireland are notified once weekly by the prison that there are no health issues. Through November and mid-December blue notes arrive in Ballaghaderreen, reassuring Christina of her son's welfare. Con O'Donovan is not so lucky and is taken to hospital in serious condition. Another prisoner, J.K. O'Reilly, keeps Henry Dixon up to date.

> Poor Con has had a very bad time of it. First a severe attack of the modern influenza followed by pleurisy, which is holding him in hospital still. He is out of danger now, thank God, but up to a few days ago we were anxious for him. Whitmore also was very close to the beyond.[390]

Christina expresses her concern directly to Governor Young who considerately replies to inform her that 'your son . . is still in good health.'[391] O'Donovan and Whitmore both recover. The same cannot be said for Dick Coleman, a 28-year-old Volunteer who fought alongside the Lawless family at the GPO.

The former Captain of the Irish Volunteers' Swords branch endured imprisonment with Jack at Lewes and hunger-strike with Tom Ashe at Mountjoy. He was transferred with Joe O'Kelly to Dundalk Prison and following release was again re-arrested as part of the 'German Plot' and despatched to Usk.

It is inevitable that the flu epidemic rampant in the hard winter of 1918 should find a way through damp prison walls. Cold conditions and poor quality food test the prisoners' immunity. Coleman's physical state is already weakened by previous hunger-strikes. On December 1 he is diagnosed with pneumonia and removed to hospital. He dies eight days later.

News of Coleman's death reawakens Christina's fears and with the mood dark and angry at HMP Usk Frank sends a telegram to reassure her. She does not receive the telegram for five days so he takes it up directly with the Home Secretary, letting off steam with a proverbially 'strongly-worded letter'.

> It is bad enough to be kept convicted for 7 mos. here on an invention of Mr Shortt's fertile imagination but this interference with and holding up of our correspondence – which has gone on all the time – is nothing short of scandalous.[392]

Thirty-three days later he receives an official reply to the effect that the wire was despatched in the normal fashion. In the meantime it is difficult to imagine what impact Coleman's death has within the walls at Usk. Grandpa, George Geraghty, Peter Hughes and Tadhg Barry act as pallbearers for a sombre funeral service commemorated by Barry's poem 'The Funeral of Dick Coleman in Usk Gaol'. The poem begins:

> We were four and we moved together
> Our gaolers near to keep watch and ward
> And like our hearts was the wild wet weather
> As we slowly moved across the prison yard.

Frank Lawless accompanies the body home to Dublin and Coleman lies at St. Andrew's in Westland Row where thousands of mourners pay their respects. However ingloriously horrific his death, it confers the status of martyr and renews public interest in the deportees' cause. In a show of defiance towards watching police he is given a military send-off in Glasnevin. At the graveside a prohibited firing party sends three volleys into the skies. When Lawless returns to Usk he writes to Henry Dixon.[393]

> The journey over with poor Dick's remains was sad enough. I feel lonely for him here since I came back. We were together, both in Dartmoor and here also we occupied adjoining cells. Well, the one thing is he has not died in vain.

December's general election signals the big-time arrival of Sinn Féin and a crushing end for the Irish Parliamentary Party (IPP). Sinn Féin takes a remarkable 73 seats from 105 constituencies; the IPP loses 61 seats but the focal point of the contest is de Valera usurping Dillon in his home constituency of East Mayo. Jack campaigns with de Valera and Ena also gets involved on the election trail. When Frank mentions it in a letter to Cissie the censors at Usk are quick to mark it for attention.

> I see where Ena made her appearance with Jack in Charlestown. Some girl! Well I hope she was successful in getting a lot of X's for our own Eamonn.[394]

De Valera gets more than enough X's, thrashing Dillon by 8,975 votes to 4,514, effectively ending Dillon's political career. Considering the strenuous – and unsuccessful – official attempts made to get Ena sacked from the Post Office, detectives and officials at Dublin Castle must find it galling to see her so openly involved with Sinn Féin electioneering.

Close scrutiny is paid when a letter arrives at Usk from Jack himself. Surprisingly he uses his own name although the contents are as oblique as you'd expect from someone on the run.

> Have done a little sprinting myself the past three weeks with Henry (sic) Boland and elsewhere. The latter is sure to be accommodated. I am more or less C.B. here as the air does not agree with my health here.[395]

Usk Prison is plagued with sickness and their comrade's death has tested the men's resolve. George Geraghty, 40, is paroled to visit his fatally ill sister – another Spanish 'flu victim. By the time he gets home she is already buried. He meets briefly with Jack and Ena in Dublin but when he returns to Usk the censors note a discernible change in Geraghty's mild manner.

> Is usually extremely guarded in his correspondence, but openly expressed his hostility in a letter to N Mc-Court, Roscommon

> Extract: –

> I was arrested without having time to bid my poor sister goodbye, and I never saw her again alive or dead. This only increases my long cherished up hate for those who are responsible for my arrest.[396]

The so-called 'Great War' is over six weeks and the so-called 'German plotters' are still in jail. Demanding change, the Irish electorate still await the results of a plebiscite that is going to produce a landslide. All these things whirl around Cissie's mind on Christmas night. She sits at her kitchen table in Barrack Street and writes Frank a 14-page letter.

> I am starting you a letter tonight quite lonely but very, very happy . . . you will soon be out again and perhaps in a little while it may be the will of the great God to unite us before we expect . . . [397]

Frank writes his last letter to his mother from Usk on January 13. Naturally, he gives no hint of what is to come.

> All our patients are recovering nicely now including O'Donovan & Whitmore – who have been a long time on the sick list now. I'm still keeping A1 and glad to hear ye are all the same . . . As to our release, well 'Blessed are they that expecteth little, for they will not be disappointed! That's the safest maxim under the circs!![398]

With a blue pencil poised might the censor raise an eyebrow? It couldn't possibly be a coded reference to an escape – or could it?

28.

*'In view of the outrage inflicted by the English military
Government on numbers of our fellow countrymen
by detaining them in English prisons without charge
or trial and on those others whom they continue to
degrade for purely political activities, the Executive
Committee of Sinn Féin order that hunting be stopped
throughout the country pending their release'*
– Nottingham Evening Herald, 25 January 1919

Public uproar over Dick Coleman has put extra pressure on the authorities to prevent any further deaths. With six other prisoners already diagnosed with 'flu, Governor Young is ordered to move all the Irish prisoners to Gloucester Prison. It's not that Gloucester is immune but it's not as damp as Usk and the Home Office needs to take – or be seen to take – preventative action.

But the Governor's office isn't the only place where plans are afoot. From the moment they were marched into Usk Frank and others have been thinking of a mass breakout. Coleman's death spurs them on but the idea is heavily compromised when the prison population is decimated by illness. Prospective escapee numbers are trimmed to four, two of which – Barney Mellowes, 28, and prison spokesman Joe McGrath, 28 – are physically weaker than usual.

For weeks they use ingenuity and cunning to overcome a series of disastrous setbacks. They cut an original key to open cell doors by sending coded messages through classifieds ads in the *Irish Independent*, fashion a replica key from diagrams and construct a rope ladder from kitchen towels and kindling wood. A grappling hook is made from the piping they cleared for their improvised handball court. When the transfer to Gloucester is announced all

285

four know the escape has to happen quickly or it will not happen at all.

The plan is put into effect on Tuesday, January 21, the day before the prisoners are to be shipped out. Partly due to staff shortages, regulations are relaxed that evening. Prisoners can move freely within the wing with cell doors left open all night. The customary 8.00 pm roll-call is suspended and there will be no check on numbers until breakfast. The duplicate key the escapees have spent innumerable hours preparing is no longer required.

Making their way to the yard by removing a window, they unfurl the rope ladder they had concealed in the cells. Geraghty uses his experience as a stonemason to assess the height and width of the outer wall. He climbs quickly, followed less assuredly by Mellowes and McGrath. Shouldice is the last man out.

Grandpa and George Geraghty co-wrote a personal account of the Usk jailbreak, published by Anvil Books[399] in 1971. It was unusual for Grandpa to speak publicly about those times but it did provide them with a chance to set the record straight. He keeps his own copy of the book at home, its yellowed title page self-inscribed:

> F. Shouldice 25/x/71. Late 1st Batt., F. Co., Nth King St. 1916.

In the chapter about Usk several passages are underlined in biro, as though Grandpa is delighted by such an audacious getaway and must remind himself that one of the four intrepid adventurers is in fact himself.

Once over the wall they ditch the ladder in the cabbage patch and walk towards Pontypool junction, spotting two newly arrived warders from Gloucester coming the opposite direction. They pass, unobserved. The escapees are hoping to catch the Fishguard express but find the local train station closed. They walk seven miles to Pontypool and, feigning American accents, catch a taxi to Newport to book train tickets for Liverpool via Shrewsbury. Incredibly, they bump into a familiar face on the platform, Tom O'Loughlin, a Volunteer from Dublin, who is doing some ground work for an imminent high-profile jailbreak.

Incredulous at meeting the four fugitives O'Loughlin is concerned that their escape from Usk will jeopardise plans being progressed by Collins and Boland to spring de Valera from Lincoln Prison. The four escapees assure him it won't and, splitting into pairs, make their way onwards.

Reaching Liverpool's Lime Street station they disembark and make their way through the early morning crowd. There is a disturbance on the platform behind them when suddenly a policeman races through and grabs Frank by the arm. His comrades are left with a split second to react. The wrong move will blow their cover and the whole escape will be exposed, even before the alarm has been raised at Usk. In life-changing moments that prove fortunate for all concerned, a black gentleman catches up with the policeman.

In the words of the men who lived it:

> 'Nunno, nunno,' he shouted, 'not that man.' The policeman removed his hand, courteously proffered his apologies to Shouldice and moved off through the crowd in search of someone who had robbed the coloured man on the train. And the four most wanted men in Britain moved through the barrier towards the streets of Liverpool.[400]

When the getaway is discovered at Usk telegrams are wired urgently to ports (as far north as Stranraer and Larne) and train stations. Minuted records – *Reports Escape of Four of the Interned Irish. George Geraghty, Joseph McGrath, Herbert Mellowes, Frank Shouldice* – sent from Usk Prison to the Home Office suggest keeping 'a quiet watch on premises occupied by the Irish National Relief Committee'[401] and the Effra Road home in Brixton of a known Irish sympathiser. The Governor notifies the Assistant Commissioner of Prisons, New Scotland Yard, Under-Secretary at Dublin Castle, local county police and stations in Cardiff and Newport. Descriptions of each man are posted in the national newspapers:

> George Geraghty (40), dark complexion, heavy dark moustache, weight 11 ½ stone, 6ft in height; Joseph

McGrath (28), clean shaven, pale complexion, loose lipped and drawls, 6ft in height, 12 stone; Herbert Mellowes (28), clean shaven, hair long and light brown, pale complexion, wears glasses, his overcoat is rather too long for him, 10 stone; Frank Shouldice (25), round boyish face, fresh complexion, appears shy, has little Irish accent, 6ft in height, 12 stone. The others have much accent.

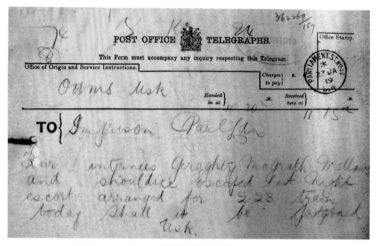

Telegram from HMP Usk following escape
(Courtesy British National Archives, Kew)

Despite this notice the jailbreak is remarkably under-reported in the national press. The *Nottingham Evening Post* suggests ingratitude shown by the escapees, who, 'during their stay at Usk they had as political prisoners received many privileges and considerable latitude was allowed them.'[402] The *Lancashire Evening Post* goes one better and says that the four men 'were captured when entraining for Liverpool.'[403]

Geraghty and McGrath are smuggled back to Ireland by a local IRB man. Shouldice and Mellowes have to wait a few days, twice changing their Liverpool hideouts before they join a designated ship as seamen. Their boat is searched by detectives before leaving port but nothing is discovered.

Grandpa's diary for 1919 has but two entries for January.

Left Usk with Joe McG., Barney M. and Geo G!!

28.1.19 – Left L. for Éire (in bottom of boat) with B. Mellowes.

The Secretary of State personally calls the Prison Commission demanding an explanation. Governor Young escapes reprimand but will be replaced by October. According to a memo to the Home Office:[404]

> If he erred, it was on excessive reliance on the word of these men, which had been faithfully kept for 7 months.

Governor Young appears to take the escape personally, citing a pledge made by prisoners through McGrath that if cells remained open until 10.00 pm 'our conduct in the future will not be different from what it has been up to the present.'[405]

A handwritten entry from the Home Office notes:

> We have up till now found that the Sinn Féiners kept to their word of honour. Apparently they are deteriorating.[406]

HMP Usk closes a few years after the escape and reopens as a borstal 15 years later. In more recent times it has served, like Arbour Hill, as a custodial prison for sex offenders. Usk currently has about 250 inmates, about double the complement since Grandpa's time. Approaching from Maryport Street its squat red sandstone design is immediately evocative of times past. The main entrance arch, now disused, presents a cast iron portcullis-style grille with two five-sided towers either side.

I request permission to see the inside of the prison but HMP Usk cites 'internal restructuring/staff movements' and is unable to accommodate me. It's almost comical how desperate I am to get into the institution Grandpa was determined to get out of. With a little help however I gain access to the grounds via the new, modern entrance. It's not quite the same as breaking into the very jail Grandpa escaped from but reversing his footsteps 97 years later is an exhilarating and emotional path.

Front entrance to HMP Usk (photo by the author)

The prison feels larger inside than it looks from the street. Designed by Thomas Henry Wyatt using a panopticon plan HMP Usk opened in 1844, operating the Pentonville design – similar to Mountjoy – with three wings that converge like spokes into a central atrium. One block contains full-door cells complete with a serving hatch and spy-hole. Prison officers stationed at the central area have a clear view of each cell doorway. The doors are surprisingly low. Despite various modernisations the jail appears as you might imagine it looked a century ago. A spiral staircase twists upwards like a two-storey corkscrew, latticed iron railings run along each landing. Sound travels harshly here, bouncing off the ceiling and back but inmates and wardens alike don't seem to notice.

Stone-breaking used to be the main activity for prisoners. Usk also housed a temporary scaffold, an infirmary, iron baths and a disinfector. The exercise yard at the back is now more modern, ringed by a high wire fence. Locals like to walk their dogs in the surrounding fields so the jail's recreation area is blocked from public view by black canvas sheets. At night, sodium lights bathe the yard in orange-yellow light.

The Governor and staff used to live inside the walls before the Governor was rehoused just outside the perimeter wall. Escorted through a series of locked gates the constant jangle of wardens' keys is an aural reminder of liberty withheld. I am led out along the former women's prison where Grandpa and his 19 comrades were located. In a narrow avenue of daylight between buildings they constructed a handball alley and drove the rubber ball with repetitive force at the prison wall. This is where they passed time, sang rebel songs, grew weak from 'flu and mourned the passing of Dick Coleman. I am led along the perimeter wall, which looms 18½ foot high. On a freezing January night they pitched their rope ladder and Grandpa, last man out, unballasted, took the swaying rope from over the wall, clambered up and out.

Surprisingly, very few archive records remain of Usk Prison. I visit the Court Sessions building next door, which also serves as Usk Town Hall. Fortunately, the Court Sessions has unearthed the prison's old admittance book, a heavy leather-bound ledger with the names of those incarcerated there at the turn of the century. Turning the pages to June 1918 I find Joseph McGrath, Barney Mellowes, George Geraghty and Frank Shouldice. Other recognisable names too – Con O'Donovan, Richard Coleman. All the names and details are registered in red ink. Pausing at Prisoner #36 I trace Grandpa's entry across the ledger's open spine to the last column on the facing page. Everything present and correct until, on closer inspection, added in pencil, as though it might hopefully be corrected at a later date:

HMP Usk today, from rear (photo by the author)

Escaped, 20/1/19.

What happened there in an icy winter's night in 1919 sent jitters throughout the British prison system. With tension running high between the Prison Commission and the Home Office, the prison governors feel their understaffed officers are being left to administer bad policy shaped by political expediency. The escape delays the transfer of Irish prisoners from Usk to Gloucester but when it goes ahead the prisoners refuse to hand up personal monies on arrival as the authorities would expect them. These are small but significant pockets of resistance. Gloucester Governor H.J. Pearce asks for clear direction from the Prison Commission. The response is typically ambiguous. 'You should try and persuade them to give up the cash. If they refuse, you must allow them to have it.'[407]

On February 3, 1919 Pearce reports that the rebellious streak shown by incoming Usk prisoners has spread to Irish prisoners already resident. Writing to the Prison Commission he says:

> They have evidently talked the matter over and I am of the opinion that they will all refuse to sign the supplementary book in future. The only thing in my mind against the internees having their money is that in case of escape it would help them to get away. Every precaution is adopted against such a course, but Gloucester is probably no more immune from escape than any other prison.[408]

Register Number.	NAME.		TRADE OR OCCUPATION.	Religion and Birth Place.	REMARKS.
	Surname.	Christian Name.			
36	Shouldice	Frank	nil	R.C. Co Mayo	Escaped 22/1/19
37	Geraghty	George	Builder	R.C. Roscommon	Escaped 22/1/19

HMP Usk admissions book – notes Frank Shouldice
and George Geraghty "Escaped 22/1/19")

The very same day Eamon de Valera, Sean McGarry and Sean Milroy literally walk out of Lincoln Jail as the operation hatched by Collins and Boland comes to fruition. The escape of seven 'German Plot' prisoners in a fortnight is a huge embarrassment to the authorities, particularly the flight of such a high profile prisoner as de Valera. All efforts at recapture are fruitless.

The Prison Commission responds to the embarrassment with a detailed internal review, following which it reports back to the Secretary of State.

> The Commissioners are of the opinion that the escape of the Irish Internees from Usk Prison should have induced the Governor to have examined, with particular care and perspicacity, any means by which these men could contrive egress from the Prison. [409]

Responsibility for the escape lies clearly with the escapees.

> It has evidently been a fixed practice on the part of these men to beguile the Prison Authorities with an assumed good behaviour and quietness of demeanour. The lessons of Usk and Lincoln show that these men cannot be trusted and if escape is to be prevented, military assistance, both inside and outside the walls is essential.

The remaining 'German Plot' internees, still without any prospect of trial, are increasingly restless. On February 12, 1919 the Secretary of State requests Army Council support 'at the prisons where the Sinn Féin prisoners are interned.' The War Office, having previously said it could not spare soldiers because of the demands of the Western Front, now says it cannot spare soldiers because the war is over. It responds to the Secretary of State:

> Apart from the question of the great depletion of the military forces which has taken place and is daily taking place owing to demobilization, the Army Council object in principle to the employment of military forces except for the purpose of assisting the Police, or the Warders of one of his Majesty's prisons in maintaining order therein, as indicated in the King's regulations. [410]

Violent flare-ups are reported elsewhere. At HMP Reading the Irish contingent includes MP Lawrence Ginnell, now a full member of the Sinn Féin party and jailed for land agitation. The Prison Commission warns Edward Troup, Senior official at the Home Office, of perceptible cracks within the prison system.[411]

> I think S. of S. should see these reports, in order that he may be able to tell Mr MacPherson how great the difficulties are of keeping these Irish interned in present conditions. It is worst at Reading, owing to the presence of Ginnell, but Governors and staffs elsewhere are feeling the strain too. The present arrangements cannot last much longer. There must be either discipline or release.

The War Cabinet decides to release Ginnell, W.T. Cosgrave and several others but the fate of the 'German Plot' prisoners is in the balance. From initial acceptance at the height of the war, questions are mounting about the legal basis for their detention.

The Spanish 'flu' death in Gloucester of Pierce McCann, Sinn Féin MP for Tipperary East, is the final straw. The issue is raised by Capt. William Benn, MP of Leith, who castigates MacPherson for what he describes as 'the bogus German plot of 1917'.

> *Benn*: Take the case of Mr Pierce McCann . . . I took care to find out what sort of a man Mr McCann was. He was elected by a large majority and returned as a member of this House. He was an active opponent of the English. He was arrested without a charge and he died in prison.
>
> *MacPherson*: I did not arrest him.
>
> *Benn*: What is the good of the Chief Secretary saying he did not arrest him? It is the Administration I am attacking, and the Right Honourable Gentleman is merely one of a number of transient and embarrassed phantoms.[412]

Rather than allow a reprise of the enthusiastic 1917 homecoming, a War cabinet meeting that same day decides to 'gradually' set the internees free. The first batch accompanies Pierce McCann's body across the Irish Sea. With war ended in Europe the pretence of Sinn Féin collaboration with Germany is loosely abandoned by Home Secretary Shortt. Fraying at the edges he tells the House of Commons:

> I do not propose to go into the question, which has been argued ad nauseum in this House, as to whether there was a German plot, or what these people are in prison for. They are in prison because they are dangerous people.[413]

The Directorate of Intelligence wraps up its close censorship of the 'German Plotters.' It feels it has gained little from the exercise but makes an interesting observation:

> As far as it is possible to judge from correspondence, the cohesion and unity of purpose which was so marked a feature of the Sinn Féin movement prior to the General Election is perceptibly changing and diversity of opinion is in many cases apparent.
>
> A certain number of extremists, whose letters are invariable hostile and abusive in tone, appear prepared to go to any lengths, more for the sake of revenging themselves on England than for the furtherance of the good of Ireland.[414]

If Lloyd George's intention was to influence the general election by deporting Sinn Féin's leadership the 'German Plot' is an unmitigated disaster. Like so many strategies for Ireland co-cobbled together by the cabinet and Home Office, it has the opposite effect. Thirty-five of 73 Sinn Féin MPs are held in British prisons when elected. And when those incarcerated are released from jail every Sinn Féin MP intends to take his seat not at the House of Commons but in Dáil Éireann at the Mansion House in Dublin.

29.

*'Your kindness in remembering me may
bring trouble to your door'*
– Lawrence Ginnell, MP to Henry Dixon, 7 July 1919

Politically, the Usk and Lincoln jailbreaks mortify the authorities and reignite public scepticism about the origins of the 'German Plot'. The whole scheme is so discredited that any serious attempt to recapture the seven escapees would expose Lloyd George and Chief Secretary Shortt to greater scrutiny, even ridicule.

Two months after Armistice Day the first Dáil convenes at the Mansion House on Dawson Street, a signal rejection of Westminster's role in Ireland. It coincides with the shooting dead in Soloheadbeg, County Tipperary of two RIC officers, effectively marking a resumption of military resistance post-Rising and the beginning of the War of Independence.

Frank's clandestine return to Ireland in the bottom of a boat at the start of 1919 means he effectively joins Jack 'on the run'. The brothers remain wary, never knowing when RIC officers, 'G' men or military might pounce. The family home in Ballaghaderreen is frequently raided and Jack's souvenir prison cap from Lewes is pilfered during one unheralded visit. The only safe place Jack can meet his wife Eily is in the vestry after Mass in Fairview Church, a rendezvous facilitated by parish priest Fr Walter McDonald.

Jack and Harry Boland have already established a pattern of moving to different places, sheltering in safe houses. A dawn raid by police at the Boland house in Marino causes hushed pandemonium upstairs. Avowedly in protection of her modesty Mrs Boland detains detectives at the front door while Jack and Harry clamber up an attic ladder to the roof. Jack relives the close call in his account to the Bureau:

We went along inside the balcony to the end house, where fortunately we found the attic roof door there was not locked. We let ourselves in as quietly as we could with the intention of returning without arousing the occupants but must have made some noise as the good lady of the house happened to be getting up and hearing something – she said afterwards that she thought it was cats – came up and Harry, whom she knew, declared ourselves before she might faint – which she nearly did – at the sight of two dishevelled characters in shirts and trousers and bootless. When matters were explained she brought us downstairs and gave us a cup of tea.

Strangely, Dublin Castle's secret files now held at the UK's National Archives in Kew tell very little about Frank's movements during this period. Special Branch reports end in 1917 but considering he broke out of Usk it seems unlikely that such an intense level of surveillance would have simply tailed off. The authorities are struggling to cope with the broader emergence of militant nationalism, of which both brothers are card-carrying members. The inexorable drift into full-scale guerrilla war is just a matter of time.

Following Pierce McCann's death the Irish internees are released without fanfare by the Home Office. A number of them accompany McCann's coffin on the mailboat. Jack, Harry Boland, Michael Collins and P.J. O'Hanlon await its arrival at Dún Laoghaire pier where it is draped in a tricolour. It is the closing chapter of the 'German Plot', a scheme John Dillon describes as 'one of the basest and most unscrupulous political tricks that I ever remember in my political career.'[415]

With the general amnesty declared Frank feels it should be safe enough to go to a service for McCann at the Pro-Cathedral in Dublin. It's the first time he meets many ex-Usk prisoners since the getaway and he is named in press reports with George Geraghty, Barney Mellowes and Joe McGrath as 'the Sinn Féiners who escaped from Usk'[416] Sean McGarry and Sean Milroy who escaped from Lincoln with de Valera also attend.

While the religious ceremony is dignified the procession to Kingsbridge (now Heuston Station) is not without incident. Three RAF officers aboard a motorbike and sidecar cut through the sad cortege at Parliament Street. Incited by 'this indiscreet act'[417] the mourners close in on the vehicle and the RAF personnel take flight. The motorcycle is tossed into the Liffey and the funeral resumes course for Thurles, County Tipperary.

Of course much is going on beneath the surface and, like most things of import, there is no mention of McCann's funeral in Grandpa's diary. Sinn Féin's abstentionist policy and the creation of the first Dáil corresponds with the establishment of a shadow government in Ireland. Departments established by the Dáil function as the unofficial state with the assistance of local Sinn Féin clubs.

Jack continues to work as Secretary of the Leinster GAA Council but is appointed by the shadow Department of Justice to preside over Republican courts, a clandestine judicial system that operates cheek-by-jowl with the official British-administered court system. Judges and court clerks are appointed as honorary positions and work without salary. He tells the Bureau:

> (We) sat with other Justices at regular intervals at 41 Parnell Square and other Centres and decisions of courts were in the main faithfully carried out. We had our own Republican Police, of course, who saw that where opposition occurred the Courts decisions were observed.

In Mayo John P. McPhillips does not say how exactly the rule of law was upheld but maintains the Republican Courts' decisions were final.

> It was decided by the first Dáil and Courts that ranches would be made available for tillage to suit the needs of smallholders in the congested districts at the prevailing locality price per acre. Under the command of Frank Shouldice we enforced this new law of the land. There were several attempts to prevent this new law from functioning but the farmers with their ploughs and

horses carried on while the Volunteers defended them against the police.[418]

The populace is told that from now on all grievances will be dealt with at the Republican Courts. Dissenters are warned not to attend the Crown courts. A notice placed by the IRA North Mayo Brigade in a Belmullet chapel is found by the local RIC and forwarded to the Under-Secretary. The notice states:

> Any person who takes part in proceedings in an Enemy Court either as Plaintiff, Defendant, Witness or otherwise unless with a special written permission of the Minister for Home Affairs (Austin Stack) will be deemed guilty of assisting the enemy in time of war and will be dealt with accordingly.
>
> – O/C Police, North Mayo Brigade[419]

Dropping plans to start a farm Frank decides to open up a mobile cinema. Before doing so he approaches parish priest Fr. Gildea, now based in Foxford. It seems strange that someone involved in armed insurrection feels obliged to seek a blessing to open a cinema but it's a portent of the shift in institutional power set to occur post-independence.

> 1.4.19 – Lr from Fr G. Doesn't approve of pictures in BD – except a few winter months. Suggests summer season in Enniscrone.

It's hardly a relaxed time but within this fast-changing picture Frank and Cissie O'Kelly get to pick up where they left off before Usk.

> 20.4.19 – Glorious day – a bit breezy. Out with COK.

Frank asks Jack and Jim about their interest in the cinema venture and sets about procuring a projector. Who knows what Grandpa omits from his diary lest it is seized – we have no diary for 1918 – but it's obvious that between many blank pages other activities are left to the imagination.

22.4.18 – Ag obair 'plotting.'

23.4.18 – Ag obair arís. Breezy + fine. From Paddy R. to go to S'ford. Replied unable to go. Cancelling job for 'Mayo'. Out with COK.

With Fr Gildea's nod he cycles to Enniscrone and meets with a local committee to agree rental for the town hall at 3 shillings 10d weekly. Surgery on his troublesome knee lays him up for a week but he's soon back on his feet. Plans for the cinema almost go awry when the projector is found to be missing essential parts but after a frantic night's improvisation it's all set for a grand opening.

29.6.19 – Enniscrone. Opening cinema. 'De Luxe Annie!!' After terrible work we got all parts. Borrowed screws. Blacksmith made key. Good house and crowded dance after. COK, Ena, Willie C, Molly S and C came from BD.

Through the entire first week he's nervously watching the box office. Monday night is disappointing. Tuesday is dark and Wednesday and Thursday aren't much better. 'Small house during week, but crowd not here yet,' says the budding entrepreneur, hoping for tidal changes in the resort's summer season. By the third week of July he clears £4 profit.

He also goes into business in Ballaghaderreen, buying a second-hand printing press for £55 and tendering for contracts. From modest beginnings he gets small jobs from local GAA clubs and drama groups in Carracastle, Swinford, Ballymote, Lisacul, Frenchpark, Castlerea, Tubbercurry and Gurteen. He also gets some printing orders from Sinn Féin, including 2,000 handbills (for £13) and a run of summons forms for Republican courts. He covers the region by car and bicycle although driving country roads is no picnic. A day trip to Bundoran is interrupted by six punctures en route. 'Home 2.30 am,' he notes flatly.

Whatever Fr. Gildea's business acumen, the box office picks up in Enniscrone. Takings for the week ending July 18 amount to a healthy £36-2/-9d.

27.8.19 – Best week house cinema.

Given that many of Grandpa's activities are under the radar the travelling cinema feels more like a parallel universe, possibly even a front. He expands the operation by booking the hall in Ballaghaderreen for four weeks, then has a look at opportunities in Ballymote and Crossmolina. But while the management of a travelling cinema presents a romantic notion, the times are fraught with danger.

Although he and Jack were both involved in IRA training camps they don't see much of each other these days. They communicate mainly by message and letter and many of the Dublin locations they frequent are under surveillance. Jack takes to wearing disguises to get around the city unhindered.

The Strand Cinema in Enniscrone is holding its own with an 8.30 screening every night and two shows on Sunday. Frank takes out advertisements in the *Western People* announcing himself as Manager and makes a big effort at promotion. It feels as though things are returning to normal when in fact the opposite is the case.

Showtime!

RIC barracks throughout Mayo and Roscommon are under constant attack and Volunteers – now the Irish Republican Army – are an armed and trained proposition. The level of drilling and training is monitored with genuine alarm by RIC County Inspectors throughout the country.

Frank teams up with Alec McCabe of the IRA's South Sligo Brigade to destroy the courthouse in Ballaghaderreen. It seems that most of Mayo is aflame through 1920 – in addition to ambushes on police and soldiers, RIC barracks are destroyed in Deergrove, Cloonthumper, Carrowkennedy (April 3), Bellacorick (April 20), Bohola (May 12) and Culleens (July 1).[420] In August the RIC Barracks at Ballyvary – between Bohola and Castlebar – is raided and its weapons stolen.

As Jack notes:

> The tempo of activities increased all over the country, raids and arrests became more numerous, occupied Police Barracks were being attacked and usually captured or vacated with the result that the Police Forces were unable to cope with the I.R.A.[421]

Frank is a member of the IRA's East Mayo Brigade but the brigades treat county boundaries as semi-permeable. His own brigade covers a vast area from Kiltimagh to the Sligo border, taking in Foxford, Swinford, Ballaghaderreen, Kilkelly, Charlestown, Frenchpark and as far south as Ballyhaunis. As he guardedly tells the MSP interview, 'I was moving about.' Then he takes part in burning down the Enniscrone coastguard station in County Sligo, an operation carried out by the North Mayo Brigade.

The attack takes place about 8.30 pm on August 26, 1920 when a group of between 100 and 150 men raid the station. The haul is significant – four rifles, 11 pistols, 2,000 rounds of ammunition and bayonets. Three suspects – William O'Neill, James Dowd and Joseph Kelly (unrelated to Joe O'Kelly) – are later arrested. At the court-martial held in Belfast a month later, Chief Officer Thomas Livermore testifies:

> On my way back to the station . . . a motor car, containing nine or ten men, passed me, going in the direction of the station. I had this car in view and saw it draw up at the station and the occupants alight. I was then suddenly surrounded by six or seven men, all armed with revolvers. One of these men said, 'Hands up, Governor' and covered me with his revolver. None of the accused was in this party.

Livermore and his wife Alice – who would also testify – were given a few minutes to gather their most prized (and portable) belongings. The coastguard station was then burnt to the ground.

O'Neill gets three months but Dowd and Kelly are convicted of arson and sentenced to one year hard labour.

Three days later, the recently vacated Ballyglass coastguard station is also set alight. An RIC patrol happens upon the dispersing rebels with Sergeant Richard Norris estimating he saw 'about 50 men.' Two Belmullet locals – James Kilroy (later a TD) and Daniel Dixon – are apprehended and sentenced to three years imprisonment for their part in the action.

The authorities, in turn, target quasi-nationalist bodies like the Gaelic League and GAA and try to suppress *An t-Óglach*, the Irish Republican Army newspaper. However the escalation of IRA activity is starkly revealed by government records which show that 517 police barracks were destroyed by July 1920. Up to June that year 41 policemen were killed and 50 injured; yet in July alone the corresponding figures were 15 killed and 30 injured.[422]

A confidential memo from General Officer Commanding-in-Chief Nevil Macready to Sir Hamar Greenwood, the last Chief Secretary of Ireland, fears that prosecutions and arms seizures are 'merely a drop in the ocean to the number of men (and women) who are connected with the carrying of arms.' It's a drift that won't be arrested by the Restoration of Order in Ireland Act in August, 1920. Macready tries to make sense of how the British administration in Ireland has effectively lost control.

> Sinn Féin in my opinion has gained ground from the point of view of obtaining more adherents throughout the country, either from fear or conviction. Nearly every day one sees in the papers that the Sinn Féin Police are able to round up malefactors where the R.I.C. are powerless and that of course is merely because the Sinn Féiners have now at their disposal the very men who formerly were used by the R.I.C. to get their information, that is, the loafers and hangers about in the various towns and villages.[423]

Directives are issued to shopkeepers, such as a letter circulated by the IRA's Sligo Brigade 6th Battalion advising that 'the Trade Department of Dáil Éireann have decreed that the following goods of British manufacture be banned', namely, biscuits, margarine, soaps ('including Ruiso Lux and other powders'), medicated wines, jams, marmalades, ointments and more.

> You are hereby warned that if any of the above goods are exposed for sale in your premises after this date you will be fined a sum not exceeding £20.
>
> The sale of English tobaccos, cigarettes and Bass ale should not be encouraged at the present juncture.[424]

Of course waging this type of campaign costs money and administering the Dáil's shadow government includes generating funds through the National Loan at home and abroad – particularly in the United States – as well the collection of taxes. Publicans in North Mayo, and throughout the country, are notified the following year that 'a tax will be levied on stout and beer' to the tune of five shillings per kiln and 20 shillings per barrel. According to a letter from Óglaigh na h-Éireann's North Mayo Brigade, 'it is optional for traders to increases the retail prices by one penny per bottle or pint to cover above tax.'[425]

It's unclear what role Grandpa plays in this and the answers won't be found in his diaries. As he is described as 'working in the collection of the Dáil loan' he was questioned years later during his application for the Military Services Pension.

> Q: Had you ever any prisoners to arrest or fines to collect?
>
> FS: No. I had not.

Tensions ratchet considerably when the Black and Tans arrive in March to try shore up gaps left by the retreating RIC. The growing capacity of the IRA to hit and run fosters a cycle of attack and reprisal. Facing an unknown enemy the fear and indiscipline of Black and Tans and then the Auxiliaries ensures widespread support for the IRA. Lloyd George hands over total authority to British military command in Ireland, effectively returning the country to the type of autocracy spearheaded disastrously by General Maxwell four years earlier.

Despite the turmoil around them Frank's relationship with Cissie blossoms. His travelling cinema is up and running, as is his small printing operation in Ballaghaderreen. Business is good. Johnny O'Grady, a local 18-year-old manages the print jobs when Frank is on the road.

The 1920 diary is sporadic at best with names of films and mention of an unsuccessful recall to the Mayo senior county football panel. Apart from a reference to a hunger-strike in Mountjoy (April 14) there is no mention made of IRA activities or incidents anywhere in the country until Wednesday, September 1:

> 1.9.20 – Shooting at BD. 2 Peelers + 1 civilian.

Amid the mayhem, Thursday offers Ballaghaderreen's film buffs a suitably titled double-bill – *Conquered Hearts* and *Southern Justice*.

> 3.9.20 – BD wrecked Thurs morning. Flannery's burned. Tom + Beirne's partly. Other places broken up by Black + Tans. Terrible night.

Over the next days he stays in O'Kelly's house where he is held up and searched before being let go. Reprisals are anticipated when an RIC officer is assaulted in town and relieved of his revolver. Some locals leave town but the backlash does not materialise.

Entries are increasingly cryptic.

> 14.10.20 – Dip at pier today. Weather ok. Reply ó Fhrainc. Lorry out of order. Wire Bernie, BD.

> 16.10.20 – In to town but no lorry. Wire from B. Frainc 'can't come'.

In October, news filters back from London that Terence MacSwiney, another ex-Frongoch internee, dies in Brixton Prison after a hunger-strike lasting 74 days. His funeral service in Cork draws massive crowds and sympathetic international attention.

In November, Frank's print business in Ballaghaderreen is raided for the third time. RIC officers find an old union poster for the ILP&TU, 'No Munitions of War', advocating a wartime boycott by railway workers of Dublin-manufactured munitions. More tellingly, they also find printed summons forms for Republican Courts, raffle tickets for Sinn Féin clubs and IRA-related stationery. As owner of the print works Frank is arrested and taken to Boyle military barracks. Johnny O'Grady is arrested too. The printing press is seized.

The family's upheaval is soon overshadowed by calamitous events in Dublin. Jack's many hats enable him to set up fundraisers for the INAAVDF, which provides assistance for Republican prisoners and their families. Operating from his Leinster GAA Council office at 68 O'Connell Street he acts as a liaison between the Dublin Brigade and the Dependents' Fund. In his capacity as Secretary of the Leinster Council he organises a Gaelic football challenge at Croke Park between Dublin and Tipperary to raise funds. 'We were rather unfortunate in the date selected,' he reflects.

On the morning of the match British intelligence agents in Dublin are eliminated by Michael Collins' elite squad. Jack and INAAVDF organisers hear of the assassinations and, fearing retaliation from the military, are in a quandary whether to go ahead with the match or postpone it. They decide to continue as planned. About 10,000 spectators make their way for Croke Park.

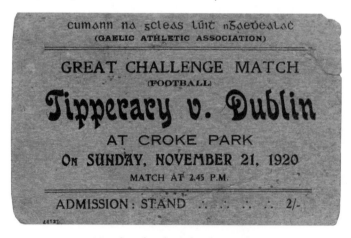

Match ticket for 'Bloody Sunday'

He tells the Bureau of Military History:

> The game was fixed to take place about 3pm. A good
> crowd attended and the game had only started when
> the trouble began. An airplane, rare at that time, flew
> over the grounds and returned, apparently to report
> or give some signal to the Black and Tans and Auxil-
> iaries. We had not long to wait for the game was not
> in progress more than 15 minutes when lorries of the
> raiders swooped down on the grounds and without any
> warning burst their way to the railings surrounding the
> playing pitch, opened fire on the people on the far side
> and on the players. [426]

Fifteen civilians, including 24-year-old Tipperary footballer
Michael Hogan, were killed and scores injured in the panic. Jack
was detained for questioning by a drunk officer before being sent
on his way by a senior Auxiliary officer who 'appeared to be dis-
gusted with the whole business.'

Receipts of £160 were handed to the Dependents' Fund but
the day became engraved in national history as the first 'Bloody
Sunday'. Frank, who had played football at Croke Park and often
went training there, gets the news in fragments at his solitary cell
in Boyle Barracks. 'Shooting at Croke Park', he writes tersely, and
it's as much as he can say.

It is quite ironic that he occupies a cell in the RIC barracks
where his father Sgt Henry Shouldice was once stationed. For an
active Irish Volunteer the personal legacy of having a father in
the police force does Grandpa no favours in 1920/21. Compiling
'The History of Frank Shouldice' has been a long and frustrating
exercise for RIC officers in County Roscommon, particularly for
Head Constable John A. Kearney. Despite the diligence of their
pursuit Frank has eluded them time and again. And now, through
incriminating slips of paper found at his printing business, they
finally have him. He recalls being severely beaten at Boyle and the
memory of that uniformed assault sticks with him for the rest of
his life. 'I received a beating up at the hand of the military around

the Christmas, at the instigation I understand of the local RIC,' he submits on his Military Service Pension application.

He strongly suspects the beating is ordered by Constable Kearney and makes the point of identifying the officer. From January to April that year criminal prosecutions were taken against 221 Crown forces personnel; 69 of the accused were RIC officers.[427] Kearney's name appears all over the confidential police files Grandpa never saw – curiously, when stationed in Tralee in 1916 the same officer reportedly displayed genuine compassion when Roger Casement was his prisoner.[428]

Grandpa spends five months in Boyle, most of it in solitary confinement in Cell #1. He worries about the prospects of the travelling cinema and the print company and asks Bertie to try keep both enterprises going. Neither venture will survive for long.

Coming into winter, the stone barracks – since splendidly renovated and acquired by Roscommon County Council – is unbearably cold. The unheated cell measures 9 x 4½ ft. Christmas comes and goes and Frank is still locked up in Boyle. Whatever the discomfort of his incarceration there is no let-up in the violence outside. He writes to his mother in January 1921 when she is due to visit.

> I wrote you a few days ago about coming tomorrow but now I understand <u>all</u> visits are stopped. I'm afraid you won't have this in time . . . no further news yet but as I told you am expecting court martial next week. Tell B. drop me a line as to how they get on every Sun. also if here's any printing news.[429]

The case against him and Johnny O'Grady is finally heard on March 10, 1921 at a court-martial in Athlone. The four arresting officers are called as witnesses. Whatever about publishing republican stationary Shouldice and O'Grady are charged for printing the posters for the Independent Labour Party and Trade Union (ILP&TU). Afterwards, they are returned to Boyle. Locked up for most of the day – he calculates they get less than 20 minutes exercise per day – he draws on his experiences at Frongoch and Usk to formulate a complaint to the prison authorities.

Four of us are confined in un-heated cells with conse-
quently so little opportunity of exercising or even keeping ourselves warm in this cold weather, the results
naturally are stomach disorders, headaches, colds etc
and possibly a permanent undermining of health.

If this is merely a question of shortage of sentries or in-
curring extra duties on them I am prepared (as I'm sure
my comrades are also) to give a guarantee that even
with one policeman I would carry on just the same as
in their (sentries) presence in whatever area was pre-
scribed for exercise.[430]

There is no change in the regime and five days after the trial
they get an early knock. He scribbles a quick note for Bertie.

Got called this morning 5.30 and told pack up. Don't
know where to and no word of sentence. Maybe it's internment. J. Grady is off also.

Bi bi now in haste. Feeling in the pink and ready for a
change of air. Best love to all. Will send word soon as
poss. Keep things moving – and cinema if you can for
summer.[431]

Shouldice, now 28, is sentenced to two years imprisonment
with hard labour; the 18-year-old O'Grady receives one year with
hard labour. The pair are transferred to Mountjoy Prison in Dublin where, as prisoners #169 and #155, they refuse to wear prison
clothing and demand political status. The Mountjoy admission
book notes no distinguishing marks on Frank but notes that Johnny
has a 'scar, right cheek' and specifies that they are not to be granted
'any amelioration.'[432] The cells are, again, bare and unheated.

They are locked up for 22 hours of the day and are not allowed
receive parcels although Ena does manage to visit him. Their sentence prompts a strong letter of support from ILP&TU. Congress
Secretary Thomas Johnson writes to the *Irish Independent* saying
that this was the public position taken by the ILP&TU the previous year with paid advertisements using the same wording in both

Irish and English newspapers. The railway boycott had been well publicised, leading Johnson to state:

> Whatever may have been thought of the wisdom or unwisdom of the action of the railwaymen, there has never been any suggestion that their act was criminal. How the printing of a poster appealing for funds in their support could be construed as a crime passes comprehension.[433]

Whether they know it or not, the pair's incarceration is raised at the House of Commons when Durham Liberal MP Samuel Galbraith questions Attorney-General Denis Henry.[434]

> *Galbraith*: . . . whether two men – named Frank Shouldice and John O'Grady – were sentenced at Athlone to imprisonment with hard labour for two years and one year respectively; whether their offence was the printing of a poster in connection with the refusal of Irish railwaymen last summer to carry munitions of war and asking for funds to help to support the dismissed men; and whether similar posters and advertisements were at the same time displayed openly throughout Ireland and the fund openly collected without interference by the police?
>
> *Henry*: The answer to the first part of the question is in the affirmative. With regard to the second part, Shouldice and O'Grady were also charged with printing forms of summonses for use in connection with the so-called Republican courts. In the circumstance the remainder of the question does not arise.

And so begins Grandpa's third and final incarceration.

30

*'Well you must sit tight for the present – there
doesn't seem to be anything else to do'*
– Frank Shouldice to his mother,
Christina, 23 August 1921

Brixton is the seventh institution to provide Frank with a temporary home at His Majesty's pleasure. The prison, opened in 1820 and by the turn of the century served as remand jail for all of London. To discourage escape attempts its 17-foot brick outer boundary wall is raised by three feet

Transferred from Mountjoy, Shouldice and O'Grady are first held in Pentonville Prison, then Wormwood Scrubs. They are incorrectly categorised as regular convicts and instructed to wear prison issue clothing. No post is allowed in or out.

Held for several weeks they are told to gather their belongings a third time. Both men are then chained before another transfer is made, this time to HMP Brixton. Frank faces the same military court sentence handed down to Terence MacSwiney the previous August, two years with hard labour for possession of seditious material.

By the time they walk to their cells MacSwiney is buried seven months in St. Finbarr's Cemetery in Cork, the tenacity of his protest and its ultimate sacrifice carried in headlines around the world. Prisoner No. 4225 writes to his mother, sounding like the enthusiastic correspondent of a penal travelogue.

Still another change!

Pentonville was interesting enough for a <u>short</u> experience and of course you bet we aren't sorry to return to the old ways by coming here. However even in the other jails the food was an improvement on M'joy and is still better here I understand and satisfactory (as far as one can expect in these places, of course)

You see when for the past weeks when in P'ville and The Scrubbs they were good enough to <u>clothe</u> as well as board me – so all my own duds were lying up; I had enough baggage to carry in one hand when moving around on the end of a chain you may bet. You needn't have been expecting a lr from me in the other gaols – as barrin' the official notification I wouldn't have been entitled to a lr for about 2 mos – in or out.[435]

I'll be in the best of form DV and as fit as when Ena was in on her visit at Mjoy – when she was apparently fairly satisfied with my form and you know she's not easily pleased!!! We are back in our own togs again and we were sure a comical lot of 'guys,' as Uncle Sam would say, in the <u>other garb!</u> But you get used to all these little things eventually and you know I was never given to worrying unduly over the ups and downs of this life!

I expect the cinema and printing are at a standstill as a result. I will write Bert about these things after tomorrow. We are allowed a lr daily and I'm writing you first – will write Ena tomorrow –

Hope Cissie is A1. Will write her in a few days. Besides the daily lrs 2 visits weekly are allowed so we'll be alright as soon as Ena looks up some of the friends to drop in.[436]

Following Grandpa's footsteps down Jebb Lane 94 years later is another strange, evocative experience. I have an appointment at the prison with Chris Impey of National Prison Radio who is researching Brixton's history. Under pressure to make Stansted in time I carry a holdall with me for my onward flight home that same evening. It is hardly a comparison but it dawns on me that Grandpa came through here with his possessions in one arm while keeping the prison chain slack with the other.

Just as urban sprawl has engulfed this former Surrey country-side into London SW2, the area within boundary walls has since built up to the point of severe congestion. The inmate population, first intended for 175 prisoners, now numbers around 800, operating mainly as a Category C training prison, the first resettlement prison in the U.K.

It's no longer maximum security but absolutely nothing can be brought inside. That includes mobile phones, cameras, USB sticks and anything that might be adapted as a makeshift weapon. The security guard behind a glass partition at the front gate does not like to see me arrive with a holdall. 'We thought you was staying with us Mr S!' he jests with a mock grimace. Before entering the prison I am photographed – 'Face the camera please Mr S!' – and biometrics readings taken from my right and left index finger – helpfully identified as 'your trigger finger' by the guard.

Although UK prisons started taking photographs of incoming prisoners as early as 1871, there are no pictorial records of Frank at Brixton. Jack was photographed entering Dartmoor but otherwise the Irish prisoners were not processed in the same manner as regular convicts.

Upon clearance at the gate, the path ahead is now negotiated through a series of electronic doors operated remotely and heavy metal doors with brass locks opened by big old-fashioned keys. We walk through and emerge left of the entrance arch, the Governor's former house immediately in front of us. 'Your grandfather would have come through the main entrance,' says Chris, 'and the Governor's house is the first thing he would have seen.'

The house is a hexagonal structure designed to convey a sense that every corner of the prison falls under the Governor's watching eye. The former quarters are now occupied by the appropriately named Clink Restaurant. The menu includes fresh bread daily from the Bad Boy's Bakery established in-house by TV chef Gordon Ramsey. The prison, then and now, was a place for religious observances.

> We have a nice little chapel here and besides the usual
> Sun. Mass (and Benediction after dinner) we have

prayers 3 times weekly – and generally weekly Communion! So you see our souls as well as our bodies are well looked after here.[437]

The wooden-raftered Catholic oratory has been converted into legal consultation rooms; hemmed in at the centre of the complex a former Church of England high-ceilinged chapel is now a multi-faith facility complete with a blue crescent moon mural facing Mecca.

Originally built four storeys high the landscape is urban sepia. High walls of weathered brick under looping razor wire. From any vantage point tin roofs and metal window grilles fill the view. Visually, like any prison from that era, efforts at modernization appear little more than cosmetic. A parcel of space has been converted into a five-a-side astro soccer pitch but walking through a series of locked gates and inter-connecting high wire fences it still feels very claustrophobic. Brixton's Victorian credentials remain intact.

Apart from the astro the only glimpse of colour is a patch of grass dabbed across the fenced-in exercise yard. Sandwiched between A Wing and the multi-faith centre this is the same space Grandpa wrote about in 1921.

> We do a bit of running round our yard every morning lately and am getting rid of some of the softness which we put up during the heatwave! Grand weather – a second summer in fact but not quite as overpowering as earlier in the season.[438]

If the hexagonal house conveyed a sense of being observed, the psychological nudge has been replaced by televisual reality. The all-seeing eye is now a multiplicity of discreetly placed 360-degree security cameras which put you on view wherever you go.

On the day I visit Brixton a group of prisoners gathers on steps in the exercise yard, basking like cats in the sunshine that floods over the rooftop of Wing A. Encouraged by fellow-inmates, the exercise area turns into an outdoor gymnasium of push-ups and pull-ups. It's a cross between exertion and relaxation. Something to do. A few prisoners jog the oblong track inside the fence. Others walk it.

The unseasonably high April temperatures that greet us catch an echo in Frank's letters.

> I'm quite as tanned as ever at E'crone!! Am feeling A1 and enjoying this spot as well as can be expected. This heatwave has helped to reduce our 'washing bill' considerably – down to a shirt, 1 pair of sox & 1 hakf weekly now and if this continues the sox will be struck off the list also!! As some of the boys have done already.[439]

In fact the summer of 1921 leaves the prisoners sweltering in London. Frank remarks to his mother that 'I struck two extremes on this trip all right – my winter quarters in Boyle and here!'[440] Temperatures in July hit 32 degrees but in a concrete den like this there is no breeze, the heat trapped, like the captives within.

> It has been necessary to discard everything possible during past while in order to keep middling cool. Today and yest are an improvement – not quite as baking and oppressive! We had a nice breeze and a little rain yest evg and it was quite a welcome change to us. Great hopes just now that things will be settled up in the near future – let's hope they continue satisfactorily . . . am feeling A1. I'm sure it's a great relief all over at home 'cease fire' sounded and the curfew withdrawn.

> Has it been very hot there? Never came across anything like it is here before – very much in the nature of an oven. They've been discharging big guns last few nights up into the air trying to burst clouds – but I don't think it has worked very satisfactorily! It would be very nice indeed if one could bring down a shower whenever necessary but it will be a more difficult job than that to control the elements I'm thinking![441]

Food parcels don't fare so well either.

> Just got your pcl today and the butter was in a very sad state.[442]

Back home, a truce has been declared. Just a few miles from where Grandpa is doing time, de Valera enters negotiations with Lloyd George at Downing Street. It will not be lost on Republican prisoners that Dev escaped England as a fugitive only to return as an international statesman. His experience is not all that unusual – by the time the Dáil's first Executive Council forms, every cabinet member will have spent some time in prison.

Republican Court.
KILGLASS.

The Parish Court, Kilglass, will sit at
ENNISCRONE,
On THURSDAY, 22nd SEPTEMBER
at 12 noon,
and every second Thursday from that date at the same hour. Summonses, etc, can be had on application to
A. BURKE, Clerk of the Court,
Carrowhubbick, Enniscrone.

Republican Courts advertised in Western People, 17 September 1921

Through the calmer end of a very fraught summer Jack continues to serve as Justice in the Republican Courts, mainly at 41 Parnell Square. The capacity of Sinn Féin to operate a shadow legal system reaches audacious new levels when court sessions are openly advertised in the local press. The RIC takes exception when the *Western People* announces that a Republican Court will be held in Kilglass on September 22 'and every second Thursday from that date at the same hour.' Regular court sessions are also held in Ballymote and Sligo town and in selected centres all over the country.

These courts supplant, then replace, the Crown's civil authority, ruling on everything from neighbourly disputes to pubs serving after hours. On September 22 at Loftus Hall in Ballymote, for example, of 23 cases heard by the Republican court 15 are civilian cases (including a trespass of cattle) and five publicans in the town are summoned by the Republican police.

The RIC Inspector in County Sligo reports the Sinn Féin Republican court being held in Enniscrone 'in a shed belonging to Thomas Kennedy,' a local carpenter. 'It is impossible at present to obtain any statement or information in the locality as the people say they are afraid of the 'gunmen,' he advises in a report forwarded to the Under-Secretary.[443]

In secret correspondence the County Inspector's Office concedes to Dublin Castle that 'Republican Courts are now displacing the King's Courts all over the country.'[444]

The RIC and DMP are powerless to do anything about it. With a growing sense of impotence RIC Special Branch at Dublin Castle brings it to the attention of the Under-Secretary:

> The members of the I.R.A. in many places have already been in charge and control for some time. The truce is being used to strengthen their position. The non-interference in these 'acts of Government' is tantamount to recognising the Irish Republic.[445]

Officially, the truce holds but it's clear who is calling the shots. Police Sergeant Kennedy in Louisburgh, County Mayo reports to HQ in August that the local courthouse was 'taken over by the IRA for a dance.' Parish priest Fr Healy had refused use of the national school so the IRA 'executed some slight repairs to the doors and walls' of the courthouse and advertised a dance Sunday evening. His colleague Constable Donnellan is not impressed.

> The action of these people was very high handed and when I saw the Court House on Monday it was in a dirty filthy condition. Should I hear of a repition (sic) of this conduct being arranged I shall ask to have it stopped.[446]

RIC Divisional Headquarters in Athlone is understandably disillusioned at its loss of authority. Typifying developments nationally, the RIC Divisional Commissioner reports:

> A party of 150 I.R.A. under the command of Patrick Cassidy, Gortanure, and Patrick McLoughlin, Charlestown, County Mayo, who were in uniform, marched through the town of Ballaghaderreen, County Roscommon.
>
> I report this to you as a breach of the 'Truce' and a provocative display of Force. There were no such displays

prior to the 'Truce' in this division. I shall be glad to know what action is taken.[447]

As President of the East Mayo Sinn Féin Executive, Jack proposes to a public meeting in Swinford that Lawrence Ginnell represent Ireland at the upcoming Peace Conference. Frank, who has taken up studying Irish in Brixton, is glad to see some movement in the right direction.

> There seems to be good hopes for the conference just now – perhaps I may have to be sending for my brown suit shortly for travelling purposes! One never knows and 'tis as well to be optimistic. I was celebrating my 29th birthday on Sat! Hope it will be my last in circs such as these![448]

Anglo-Irish negotiations do not officially start until October but even the lead-up feels protracted and difficult, dragging on for months through a half-baked summer. For Grandpa and others there is nothing to do but wait. According to William Murphy, prior to declaration of the truce, a total of 6,129 Irish men and women are either interned or in prison in Britain and Ireland directly because of the hostilities.[449]

The Irish Republican Army uses the cessation to prepare for further conflict. It's an obvious breach of the truce and no large town is immune. In Ballaghaderreen Frank's imprisonment simply means that someone else steps in to oversee Volunteer training and drilling. The RIC's Divisional Command in Athlone is told that 'an IRA Training Camp was established at St. Mary's Hall, Ballaghaderreen' and defended by 'two sentries, armed with rifles and fixed bayonets.' It submits its report to the RIC Special Branch noting the additional use of a vacant house at Kilfree Junction 'as a training camp.' According to the report 50 Volunteers are trained intensively on 'instruction in the use of arms, methods of ambush and drill' by two IRA officers visiting from Dublin. The report on 'IRA Training Camps – Ballymote District' concludes:

> When first party of 50 have finished their course of instruction they will be replaced by another batch of

same number, and so on until all the IRA Volunteers of the locality receive training.[450]

The report is forwarded to the Under-Secretary with a note added by the RIC County Inspector that 'the number of these training centres is rapidly increasing'[451] Another vacant house in Kilmovee is identified as an IRA training camp for men from Lisacul, Loughglynn, Crossard and Ballaghaderreen with an emphasis on 'bombing, musketry and ambulance work.'[452]

Posters start appearing in shop windows around Boyle – and elsewhere – with an edict from Dáil Éireann signed by the 'Chief of Republican Police'.

Emigration (Shipping and Emigration Agents) Regulation

Dáil Éireann has decided that no Citizens of the Irish Republic shall leave Ireland for the purpose of settling abroad without having first obtained Permit from the Minister of Home Affairs.[453]

Outraged, an RIC officer at Boyle brings this to the Divisional headquarters in Athlone. Before passing it on to Dublin Castle, a senior officer in Athlone remarks:

It seems plain that, even during the truce, the Republican party is neglecting no effort to take over the administration of the country. If this is allowed no one can blame the people for regarding them as the legitimate government. I imagine during the negotiations all such activity should be suspended.

The RIC Inspector in Dublin Castle adds his own impression before he forwards it to the Under-Secretary.

The I.R.A. are acting as if they had already established a Republic.[454]

The Irish contingent at Brixton whittles away, slowly and unpredictably. Individual cases are reviewed on what prisoners feel is an *ad hoc* basis. Since Shouldice and O'Grady's arrival, the num-

bers drop from 17 to nine. The anticipation of release, every prisoner's obsession, sets in, particularly in the run-up to Christmas.
Then, suddenly, everything appears to simply stop. Back home
Cissie, too, is left waiting, once again. There are no letters from
her in his Brixton collection. Whether correspondence got lost or
Cissie simply could not put herself through another tense waiting
game is not clear. However from his references to her in other letters home it seems Cissie has withdrawn somewhat from the front
line.

Frank hears that Tadhg Barry, his co-pallbearer for Dick Coleman at Usk, 'an old pal of mine in "18"', has passed away. 'We don't
notice the time slipping around here,' he tells his mother. 'Looking
out for fresh news or "crises" every now and then.'[455]

Christina and Lily have specially constructed a new box to
transport eggs from the West of Ireland to London. A high casualty rate in December suggests Frank is either getting weary of the
effort or hopeful that release is imminent. Reports of agreement
reached between Irish and British negotiators on December 6 suggests a breakthrough but the details are vague and the stakes never
higher.

> Looking out for 'developments' during past week.
> Things have been happening sure enough and let's hope
> this will be the last epistle I'll have to pen from here!
>
> I got Lily's note today and both her pcls arrived in due
> course. The eggs were a bit battered about tho' – 4
> or 5 being broken in transit – so you see even those
> egg boxes are not proof against the knocking around
> they get en route! It's a matter of chance I suppose as
> sometimes they come thro' safe enough! She needn't
> trouble about butter this week as I've plenty on hands.
> I'll return egg box today – but don't trouble sending
> any more – just at present, at any rate.[456]

The weeks roll on and he becomes resigned to spending Christmas with 384 others who make up the prisoner population in Brixton. It will be the third occasion he will spend the festive season
behind bars. But formative details of the Treaty have emerged,

thrashed out miles closer to Brixton than to faraway Ballaghader-reen. Ratification in Dublin is another month away.

> I see we're definitely fixed here for the Xmas <u>at least</u>. What will happen after 3 Jan is hard to say but I expect another month or so should see us out – and meantime we're not going to worry!
>
> Surely things seem to be going topsy-turvy in the Dáil. It's not very pleasant reading for any of us – old crowd – but I think G Duffy put it best so far. Since it <u>has</u> been signed the best that could be done is to ratify – I imagine.
>
> Hope you'll make the most of the festive season – and all have a happy time.[457]

When the Treaty passes acrimoniously 64/57 in the Dáil the Irish prisoners are no longer under British dominion. As the British administration completes its evacuation from 26 counties in January, 1922 Frank and Johnny O'Grady are taken on remand from Brixton. They are going back to Ireland but not quite going home just yet.

There is no fanfare of jubilant crowds massing at the port this time, no all-night vigil at North Wall. They arrive back to a country bearing the jagged scars of war and now about to plunge itself into internecine strife. They are both remanded with 183 other political prisoners at Mountjoy Prison and await their final release.

31.

'Open the prison doors and the convict cells!'
– *Freeman's Journal,* 11 January 1922

With an unintentionally neat sense of timing the curtain rises
at the Abbey Theatre for the premiere of T.C. Murray's
new play, *Aftermath.* The Treaty has been ratified in Dublin and
London and the diplomatic process towards independence is underway. British troops are photographed dismantling fortifications
at Dublin Castle and military barracks throughout the country are
also emptying out. If the *Freeman's Journal* is preparing for the big
moment, its editorial on January 12 starts the countdown.

> The evacuation has begun.
>
> Kits are being packed and arrangements completed
> which will mean the end, in a short time, of the Army
> of Occupation.[458]

Several thousand Irish political prisoners are still held captive
– including 40 under death sentence – but the official handover
from British to Irish civil authority means their time too has come.
Under general amnesty Irish prisoners emerge into daylight from
Pentonville, Winchester, Dartmoor, Exeter, Gloucester, Maidstone,
Ipswich, Dorchester, Durham, Birmingham, Carlisle, Bedford,
Bristol, Cardiff, Carmarthen, Carnarvon, Hull, Leicester, Lincoln,
Liverpool, Canterbury, Preston, Oxford, Nottingham, Northamp-
ton, Plymouth, Swansea, Shepton Mallett, Newcastle, Portsmouth,
Worcester, Shrewsbury, Perth and Wormwood Scrubs.

Grandpa and Johnny O'Grady are already remanded to Mountjoy where a crowd now gathers at the prison gates.

The process of liberation was a slow and tedious one. The prisoners were released in small batches at intervals of an hour or even more, between 4.30 and 10 p.m.

The first inkling the crowd had that something was afoot inside the gaol was the sound of cheering. The cry was taken up by those inside. The clanging of bolts as the doors inside were being unlocked was the signal for an outburst of enthusiasm The big gate was then flung open and as the first twenty of the released men filed through a thunderous cheer broke out.[459]

Shouldice and O'Grady are freed from captivity. For Grandpa it's all over. Walking from prison for the last time he takes a train from Dublin and makes his way home to Ballaghaderreen. After so many disruptive years it's time to spend with his mother Christina, and rejoin Jack, Ena, Bertie and Lily. It's also time to start over with Cissie. The businesses he built up – the travelling cinema and the print shop – are no more. His funds are very low, he has nothing left to invest and paid work is extremely hard to come by. .

Frank is very fortunate to be offered a position as Intelligence Officer in the National Army newly formed by Michael Collins and Arthur Griffith. After years of attrition he might want to put some distance between himself and military life but it's a badly needed job so he joins Army Intelligence staff at Oriel House. Deep differences over the Treaty are already driving hard lines between those for and against and he observes the rapid polarisation of former comrades. Unless calmer voices prevail it is a matter of course that State forces will move to subdue anti-Treaty forces. He sees it coming and the inevitability of it all sickens him. Grandpa will not take sides and after a couple of months he resigns from the army.

Q: Was it because of the Split came you left it?

FS: Yes. I left it (at) the time of the Split.[460]

Jack makes the same decision. 'When the Civil War started I gave it up,' he tells the Military Service Pensions interview. 'I washed my hands of the whole thing.'

All over the country the guerrilla brigades that operated so successfully against the British military have now splintered into rival camps and are taking on each other. The atrocities of wartime do not end with British withdrawal.

> 28.6.22 – Republican rebellion. Attack of 4 Courts by Dáil forces. Fighting in Dn etc Thurs/Fri/Sat. Bridges out all over. Bad work.

> 6.7.22 – War and rumours of war all over . . no papers, letters or such like!

> 9.7.22 – More war. BD mined in several places. Attack expected. J Dillon's private residence taken over by Reps, wind up amongst town folk. Out by nights. No biz doing.

> 23.7.22 – Shops closed for past week or more. Wed. Barracks evacuated and burned. Troops taking to country. No fight in BD. So far after all.

Harry Boland sides with the anti-Treaty forces and the family house the brothers know so well – 15 The Crescent in Marino – is a regular target for government raids. Coincidentally, it's where Bram Stoker, author of *Dracula*, grew up. The same house is the unlikely repository of priceless Russian Tsarist jewels. In an astonishing story told by Kathleen Boland to the Bureau of Military History, the jewels were offered as collateral to a cash loan from Sinn Féin on a fundraising trip to the U.S. in 1920.

> Harry brought home the jewels that he had received on behalf of the Irish Republic from the representative of the revolutionary government of Russia in New York – a man called Martens – this man had apparently been empowered by his government to borrow money on the security of the jewels and our representatives in America agreed to lend twenty thousand dollars on them.[461]

Harry took the bag home where his mother stashed the diamonds, sapphires and rubies up the kitchen chimney.

> We kept the jewels in the house. During the various raids by the Free State soldiers during the civil war, my mother carried them around on her person and afterwards we made various hiding places for them . . .

The value of the jewels is estimated at $25,000 – worth about ten times as much today. While it seems incongruous that the Russian crown jewels would end up in a hidey-hole in Marino, Boland was going to return them to Collins when they met at the Gresham Hotel. In a precursor to their Civil War split, they got into a physical fight which ended with Collins throwing the jewels back at Boland.

A few short years later, in his dying hours, Harry asks his sister Kathleen to keep the Tsarist jewels safe until de Valera gets into power.

> In that way we held them secure and in 1938, when de Valera had passed the Constitution and had recovered the ports, we considered Harry's wishes were fulfilled . . . (we) . . asked him (de Valera) to take possession of them.

The jewels were finally returned to Moscow in 1950 after the loan reportedly repaid to the Irish state.[462]

Aghast at how rapidly hard-won Irish independence is falling asunder, Frank and Jack feel they played their part and want no more of it. While it all sounds a bit anti-climactic after hectic, dramatic years making history they are ready for calmer times. Not that things have settled at all. Frank, Jack, Ena and Bertie can see all around them the fruits of their labour unravelling. Even though Grandpa considers himself 'a Dev man' he is not prepared to take up against those he fought alongside. He seems determined to move on and almost turns his back on the appalling realities that surround him.

When Harry Boland is gunned down in Skerries it's a tragedy so close to home that it doesn't even get a mention in his diary. Amid the bedlam it's time to keep the head down and get their old jobs back. The brothers seek reinstatement to the Civil Service.

On November 1, 1922 Frank goes back to work at the Department of Local Government where he rejoins his work chum Tom McKenna. Jack is reinstated to the fisheries section at the Department of Agriculture.

Frank is not personally involved in the Civil War but his friends are. As Dominic Price illustrates in *The Flame and the Candle*, the National Army does not distinguish itself in County Mayo and it draws strong criticism for general indiscipline among its troops. Five days after going back to the Civil Service Frank complains in writing to General Sean MacEoin about the conduct of Commandant McGoohan 'who was very much under the influence of drink and absolutely incapable of carrying fire arms, not to mention effecting any discipline over his men. Instead of inspiring a sense of security and safety in the breast of the average man or woman, as any National Army should', his actions were 'only bringing it into disgrace and making the name of the National Army, in the West, a byword in the mouths of their own countrymen.'[463]

Three days into the New Year and a pre-dawn raid by Free State troops leads to fatal injuries sustained by local IRA Brigade member Tom Flannery. Grandpa helps Joe Flannery retrieve his cousin's body from Dublin.

> 3.1.23 – Raid by troops at 3.30 a.m. Tom F wounded Brought to B'mote, Boyle and Portobello
>
> 6.1.23 – To Boyle with Joe F. thence to Dn for body. Got it at Portobello.
>
> 8.1.23 – Funeral at Kilcolman . . pistols and firing party next to one another huge funeral!
>
> 2.2.23 – Senators and govt officials houses going up every other day. Terrible destruction.

On April 2, 1923 – coincidentally, Easter Monday – Frank marries Cissie in Ballaghaderreen. Their car journey back to Dublin is hampered by 'umpteen punctures' so they don't get home until 5.00 a.m. Honeymoon takes them to London, Paris, Toulouse and Barcelona and they leave the wedding photographs until August. When they stop off in London I wonder if he takes Cissie to Jebb Avenue to see Brixton from the outside, even to sate his own curiosity. Or to Wandsworth or Wormwood Scrubs or Pentonville, the scenes of what are fast becoming the earlier chapters of a previous life.

Civil war shudders to a fitful conclusion. The time to rebuild has come. A minor promotion to Lower Executive Officer follows for him and Tom McKenna. Frank and Cissie buy a piano for £57. Outside the smaller details of Grandpa's diary, Jack's tenure as Secretary of the Leinster GAA Board comes to an end. Bigger news at home though on January 14, 1924.

> Our first arrived at 7.45 this morning. Had Dr Acton just in time and all went well. 9½ lbs.

Following a difficult pregnancy, Cissie gives birth to a daughter. 'Baby squealing away with lusty lungs!' A week later they christen their daughter Rita, after a favourite

Frank and Cissie's wedding day (top), the occasion recorded in a photographic studio four months later

aunt of Cissie's. The early months are complicated by the discovery of what he calls a 'rupture' which leaves the baby in frequent pain.

> 22.3.24 – Rita is howling same. Wants soother. Nurse took it off her – bad!

The child isn't well enough to travel so Grandpa goes home to Ballaghaderreen for Easter on his own. He puts a deposit down for a house in Marino (priced at £425) and Rita's condition improves, which gives everybody a lift.

> 10.8.24 – Rita Óg v stout and in great form! 15 ½ lbs.

She turns one year 'fine and fat and well (TG)'. A cable arrives at the house to say Cissie has been left $2,500 by a relative in America. 'Glee!' writes Grandpa. Grandpa's erratic use of exclamation marks is hard to decipher but three marks certainly denote something really special. The story of the transatlantic windfall is not over.

> 5.2.25 – Further wire from home saying 20,000 dollars!! Consternation!!!

Cissie goes to a solicitor and is told that $2,500 is the correct sum. While Grandpa is fixing the carpet on the stairs another cable arrives in Marino.

'*Clareville', Dollymount, 1930*

> 7.2.25 – More wires. They state from home that two cables come giving C's portion as 20,000 dollars!!!

The timing is perfect, the largesse almost miraculous. Deciding to move house they put a deposit on 'Clareville', a seafront house in Dollymount which is priced at £925 ('afraid we went too high at £900. However <u>it is</u> a good house').

The release of 19 republican prisoners from Mountjoy at the end of 1925 is one of few references made to political events. The family spends Christmas 1926 in Ballaghaderreen where the town is speckled with snow. Relatives and neighbours call in with their kids so it's a 'full house' bursting with energy and noise. With an air of Piagetian curiosity Grandpa watches the baby grow – 'Rita making great attempts to walk – partly successful' – yet while they have been blessed with good fortune health issues are arising with increasing regularity. In February 1927 Cissie has to have an operation on her womb. Her family in Ballaghaderreen takes care of the child.

> 4.3.27 – C. pretty weak. Bad form this evening. Thinks operation not successful!

With Cissie in convalescence the news from Ballaghaderreen is not good. Aunt Rita is in decline.

> 26.3.27 – Rita Óg still in country. Auntie Rita not too well tho' and it looks as if she will not last too long – pretty weak and coughing a good deal.

But the bad news spreads to both Ritas when the child is also feverish and clearly out-of-sorts.

> 23.4.27 – Rita Óg sick with stomach and Aunty Rita middling fair but wasted.

Cissie goes west to tend to the baby. On arrival, she wires urgently for Frank to follow.

> 26.4.27 – Rita Óg very weak. Went on night train – met by Joe at Kilfree. Found her low enough. Had some convulsions – and now lying in a semi-conscious state!

It rains continuously, night into day. Rita shows no improvement and they take her to a doctor in Charlestown. Meningitis is diagnosed and little solace offered. On May 3, 1927 it all ends.

> 3.5.27 – Rita Óg died today at about 12.45. Terrible blow and a shock for everyone.

They bury the child in Kilcolman cemetery, previously the setting for big shows of revolutionary defiance. This time there is only defeat, the plaintive service carried out in 'glorious warm'. Grandpa's heartbreak over his baby daughter is characteristically terse. On occasion however he allows himself further room, letting his thoughts roam and corralling them into a spare page of his diary.

> Wore new tweed suit for first time on my run to BD for poor Rita Óg's burial! She had a short illness and (TG) practically painless death! Started with stomach complaint – developed into slight convulsions and then meningitis. When the latter was evident we were better pleased she to go. Had been perfectly healthy since Xmas and apparently looked like a 5 or 6 year old instead of 3. Was the centre of admiring eyes in BD and a tremendous favourite – her looks and C apparently attracting attention everywhere they went. Able to talk well and very wise. It is very hard indeed but we must bear the decrees of the Almighty who has taken her to himself. All in BD, also Sutton and C. are deeply affected.

Rita, aged 3

Forlorn, Grandpa and Cissie return to Dollymount. He goes back to work and Cissie, still unwell from her operation, grieves privately at home. The postscript to this huge tragedy comes when Grandpa gets a payment from the Irish People's Assurance Company, the firm set up by his former comrades in Frongoch. He has paid £13 into Rita's policy; upon the child's death the company pays out £6. 'Desperate crowd of swindlers these Irish cos!!' he writes bitterly.

Aunt Rita dies at the end of the month. Cissie, still uncomfortable from major surgery, takes the train back to Ballaghaderreen for the funeral, 19 days after burying her daughter.

> 23.5.27 – May has been an unlucky month for us. Rita Óg passed away 3rd and Rita O'Kelly 23rd. The two little pals will now share company again DV!

It is clear that Rita's death takes a huge personal toll on Cissie. Her deteriorating spirit becomes a cause of concern to her husband who sees her 'very disappointed and very bad form'. The operation at the Mater was, as she originally suspected, unsuccessful. She has to return to the Rotunda for a second procedure in August.

Periodically, Grandpa considers the depth of their loss. On an undated page, he probes the cruel larceny that reduces 'Clareville' to a childless silence.

> 20.6.27 – A bit shook lately. Not right since Rita Óg's death.

> 19.7.27 – Haymaking again. I miss little Rita from the loads of hay.

Cissie emerges from the Rotunda much improved. Her spirits lift over the next weeks but as year's end approaches they feel Rita's absence with an ache, particularly when they return to Ballaghaderreen for Christmas.

> 26.12.27 – Tons of wren boys as usual. Otherwise things much quieter than usual.

At the end of the year there can only be one event that prompts reflection.

> Meningitis started with stomach trouble. Only 8 days ill. Died in BD, buried Kilcolman aged 3 years 3 months. Was a perfect little beauty and great favourite. Fair curls and big blue eyes. Had been in BD since Xmas and thriving apace! Very tall tho' not lanky and quite healthy. Her death came as a huge surprise to all and was a severe blow to us indeed.

He closes the diary and brings 1927 to a close.

32.

'Let Fate do her worst, there are moments of joy
Bright dreams of the past she can never destroy'
– Prisoner #1836 JD King in Frongoch, 23 December 1916

The next years meld together through incidents great and small, a kaleidoscope of the everyday, a host of commemorations, sporting events and funerals punctuated by an increasing slate of blank pages and, occasionally, new arrivals.

He is still playing football at a very high level and often goes up to Jones Road (Croke Park) for a run. Through 1927 he plays a number of National League games with Mayo before beating Sligo in a disputed championship replay ('fell thro' after 15 mins, Sligo refusing to continue when a goal we got was not disallowed!!') only to lose to Galway by a point in the Connacht semi-final. He plays League games the following year and wants to keep going but at 35 he feels age catching up with him, gradually dropping from senior to junior football and then from inter-county player to Mayo supporter.

Some years are missed out – or the diaries got lost – including 1931, the year my Dad was born. Grandpa always refers to his son as Frank Óg. After the trauma of losing Rita, it's evident that anything health-related, even a minor complaint, triggers alarm bells for both Cissie and Frank.

> 8.2.33 – Frank Óg has got down several teeth lately with eye ones included – in good form otherwise TG. Is about height of dining table now and well able to trot around.

28.9.33 – F Óg going great guns and throwing his weight about. In great form TG. .

9.10.33 – F Óg has chest cold and cough these days.

18.11.33 – F Óg going strong and growing big. Shouting hello or how do do! Now BiBi. Cheerio. Which with dada, mama and baba comprise his vocabulary to date.

For Frank and Jack, it is a feature – and grievance – of their working lives that staying neutral through the Civil War costs them in terms of career advancement. Regardless of their contributions during the War of Independence they find themselves overlooked for promotion when new opportunities arise in the Civil Service. They suspect cronyism when they see favour shown to individuals associated with whatever side of the Treaty is in the ascendancy at a given time.

13.6.34 – Jack has apparently been turned down for major staff post. E was in to see Joe Boland and told him a few home truths.

There is little indication that Grandpa's desk job adds any great meaning to his life, other than providing a means to support his family. He also enjoys Tom McKenna's company, the carefree young socialite trimming his sails to adjust to Frank's married, fatherly status. By Christmas, life in Dollymount seems to have settled into domestic contentment.

Cissie and Frank Óg in London

26.12.34 – F Óg had his final Santa Claus Xmas and saw to his stockings etc being hung up. Enjoying himself A1 with aeroplanes, motors, balls etc and is charmed with the decorations and coloured lights – which we have since the Congress time! Very happy Xmas at Clareville TG.

Donkey express – Frank Óg with his cousin Eddie, 1936

Then in April, inexplicably, Tom McKenna dies. The diary entry offers no hint of cause. He is several years younger and after the funeral in Glasnevin Frank repairs to Hedigan's pub where he stays until 1.00 a.m. His departed friend had shown himself to be a considerate and thoughtful ally through prison days, apologising at one point for mentioning his upcoming holiday while Grandpa languished in Usk.[464] Through various spells of incarceration Tom reliably sent reading material, cigarettes, chewing gum, searching Dublin high and low without complaint for the particular and the peculiar – such as a Spanish grammar book and an elusive spool of macramé thread.

In Hedigan's Grandpa might have considered Tom's musings about their nights out drinking.

> Well Dear Frank, this was the first dance I had since we parted and it brought back fond memories of many pleasant nights we spent together and DV history will repeat itself in that respect. Dancing loses one of its

most pleasant associations when there isn't an occasional exodus – (is that the word?) – from the dance hall followed by an almost mechanical visit to the nearest pub or hip pocket. Such visits alone have not the same pleasing, soothing and exhilarating effect as in the days of yore.[465]

Had Grandpa fished through his store of kept letters he would have found one from Tom McKenna during the Frongoch days, a simple statement, heartfelt and true. Up at Hedigan's one would imagine Tom's words echoing under the sad salute of a raised glass.

> I very seldom see any of our old crowd now. I do not like the idea of 'knocking around' on my 'own' and spend most of my time in the club. I really miss you very much and when I drop in to have a drink by myself – Charlie Gaffney style – I invariable think of the many pleasant nights we had together and drink to your health.[466]

Each year Clery's Restaurant in O'Connell Street hosts the War of Independence annual dinner, attracting upwards of 500 people. As Grandpa turns 43, the family takes a brief holiday in Blackpool. The exuberance of their four-year-old son delights and exhausts him.

Frank, Frank Óg and Cissie snapped by a photographer on O'Connell Street

26.6.35 – F Óg enjoying himself tip top and in good
form but a bit of a nuisance at times.

Life at the office is quieter without Tom. Grandpa's promotion
comes belatedly but he is named Acting Higher Executive level
and must await the 'long overdue' formal appointment. Bertie is
married – life is moving on. Frank and Cissie mark their 15th anniversary with a drive to Glendalough with Frank Óg, Jack and
Eily. Jim visits from New York in 1938, 'looking A1' and talking of
coming home for good five years after retirement.

The eruption of World War Two brings rationing and scarcity
and reawakens fears of mass destruction across the Continent –
peace in Europe lasting just two decades. The family moves from
Dollymount to a bigger house in Hollybrook Park in the summer
of 1940. While war engulfs much of the globe, 1941 is a year of
late awards in Dublin – Frank receives his '1916 medal' and, after
a five-year delay, is finally confirmed, as a Higher Executive Officer (HEO). The occasion is marked at Scotch House (a pub since
demolished). He gets an electric train set for his son's birthday but
is less forgiving when it comes to school results.

13.12.41 – F Óg hols. Did not do so good at exam this
year! Not applying himself. Too many toys.

Two years later his mother Christina, aged 88, passes away in
Ballaghaderreen. Frank Óg switches to boarding school in Clongowes Wood College in Clane, County Kildare. Occasionally during term he gets home for a football match or concert and it is on
a visit home with a school pal on October 17, 1948 that Dad finds
his mother Cissie on the dining room floor, struck down by a brain
haemorrhage. Panicked, he tries to lift her inert body into an easy
chair but there's absolutely nothing he can do. Dazed with shock
he struggles to absorb what has happened.

17.10.48 – C died suddenly, RIP. About 5.10pm! Tessa
& Padraig Lenihan originally in house. F Óg up for Bee-
cham concert in Royal. We arrived out about 5.15 but

TG F Óg had been out earlier 2.30 and saw her well. Dreadful shock indeed. RIP.

A funeral mass is held in St. Anthony's, Clontarf before the hearse drives west to Ballaghaderreen for High Mass. Cissie is buried in Kilcolman beside her little girl, Rita. Father and son stay over before returning home to Dublin. Then it's back to boarding school where Dad's classmates meet him at the doorway and offer teenage condolence. Miserable with heartbreak he later ascends the stairs to what were Spartan sleeping quarters in the school dormitory. The 16-year-old feels the chill and confusion of abruptly losing his mother. He climbs into bed, pulls up the blanket only to discover the soothing welcome of a hot water bottle – considered a luxury at the time – placed under covers at the end of his bed. Dad guesses it was left there by a particularly kind Jesuit teacher. Nothing is ever said but the compassion of the gesture stayed with him ever since.

Grandpa tries to make up for his son's loss. On his birthday in November he sends a parcel to Clongowes with 'chocs, fruit and pencil flashlamp for birthday. F Óg 17 years.'

Father and son return to Ballaghaderreen for Christmas but Dad's miserable year doesn't get any better when he has a minor road collision on the way home with a drunk driver in Longford. The following Easter Grandpa attends the Easter commemorations alone. Dad's Leaving Cert results open the doors to UCD ('very good considering circs of past year'). By way of reward father and son take the ferry and train for Twickenham ('F Óg is the main instigator!') to see Ireland lose 3-0 to England. Excluding the childhood trip to Blackpool it is Dad's first real trip abroad.

Two Franks in Clongowes, 1948

October 1951 is the third anniversary of Cissie's passing. Jim stops off in Dublin on a world trip but there is no more talk of moving back to Ireland. Another friend visits from the United States. Dillie Power, originally from Dublin, returns from Chicago on a trip home. 'Looking very well,' observes Grandpa, suitably impressed.

He takes her to Croke Park for the Oireachtas final where Wexford beat Kilkenny by a point. He finds that he enjoys her company and they arrange to meet again.

> 3.11.51 – Met Dillie and went for run to Howth. Walked around cliff. Grand day. To Annie Wade's at night and very enjoyable hooley. Dillie's last night here. Home at 4.30 am!!

Dillie Power

Dillie heads south to connect with the cruise liner taking her back across the Atlantic from Cobh. Grandpa confesses to 'feeling flat after very enjoyable week!' Even from his diary however there is a palpable sense of change. She has only left and he writes an uncharacteristically 'long epistle' to her in New York. Ten days later he gets her reply and is happy to part with seven shillings and four pence to send a 21-word telegram. Unfortunately we don't know the exact formula of those 21 words but the transatlantic wire appears to have the desired effect.

A Christmas parcel brings a Ronson lighter from America and a leather wallet for Frank Óg. Grandpa rings in the New Year at 'the bells with Jack, Eily + F Óg.' Love is in the air.

> 20.1.52 – Told F Óg re D. who is making preparations for return home.

It all happens very quickly but Grandpa and Dillie plan to get married. Dillie, a widow with four sons, lost her husband Frank

338

years earlier. Her son, Frank Junior, was killed fighting the Japanese Army in the Palau Islands, a sacrifice marked by a personalised letter from President Franklin D. Roosevelt. As Dillie would later like to put it, 'I lost two Franks and I got two Franks!'

It's four years since Cissie died and the proposed new arrangement is a lot for Frank Óg to take in. Jim Shouldice is in town and he brings Dad down to Ballaghaderreen for the day. It is the last time Grandpa will see his older brother – Jim dies suddenly in Nice, France in January, '54, where he is buried in the city cemetery.

Whatever fresh optimism Dillie's visit has stirred, the New Year begins ominously with Bertie diagnosed with cancer and nephew Fr Sean also hospitalised. Before Dillie leaves Chicago – she will sail from New York to Cobh on the *Mauritania* via Southampton – Bertie's condition worsens. Aged 57 he dies in March and it's back to Ballaghaderreen with Frank Óg, Ena, Jack, Eily and a recuperating Fr. Sean for yet another funeral at Kilcolman.

Dillie arrives in Cobh in April, home in time for an Old IRA commemorative parade at the GPO. She and Frank marry on June 2, 1952 in a morning ceremony at St. Theresa's, Donore Avenue. They go for breakfast and then set out for Connemara. Despite these bright moments it seems the frequency of death is gathering pace near and far. A two-month-old grandchild of Dillie's suffers a cot death in Chicago and then Grandpa hears that George Geraghty of Roscommon, his fellow Usk escapee, has passed away.

Frank Óg presses ahead with his Masters' degree studies ('Doubtful where it will lead!' queries Grandpa) and in November

Dillie and Frank at Hollybrook

his 21ˢᵗ birthday party takes place at home in Hollybrook. Grandpa observes it, making an entry in his diary:

> 22.11.52 – F Óg's birthday (21ˢᵗ) party. Very busy all week! About 50 present and all went well. Broke up after 4 am. Plenty of dancing – 3 pianists and F Óg .. lots of presents for F Óg.

'Tall and fair' Jean Kelly

The biggest present that night was Dad being introduced to Jean Kelly, a liaison craftily arranged by Una and Maureen Meehan who double up as Mam's pals/Dad's cousins. 'Nice young girl, tall and fair', notes Grandpa. Frank and Jean, my parents, would marry five years later.

The Easter commemorations continue and Grandpa retires from the Civil Service, aged 60. His work colleagues present him with a bag of golf clubs at a farewell do in Scotch House. The prospect of retirement does not traumatise him.

> 9.5.53 – Last day in Oifig. Marvellous warm sunshine but cool breeze in evening. A very inviting week to go out on pension!!

With the number of 1916 veterans already whittled down there are fewer and fewer survivors to mark anniversaries of the historic occasion. Only the old reliables like Jack, Tom Sheerin, Eamonn Dore, Frank Burke remain with whom to share memories.

> 14.3.54 – Mass in Berkeley Road for old 'F' Co. deceased. At Gers and the Westerns cship match. Latter won. Very cold.

Dillie persuades Frank to take a cruise with her to the United States. Newly-retired he is glad for the opportunity. In April they make for New York from Southampton on the USS 'United States'.

> 20.4.54 – Splendid vessel but a long way to our quarters from dining room and deck. Trying to find our way around this monster ship – it is difficult! I wonder what the Queen M. is like! We are clocking 800 odd miles per day. D. still not so good or eating as she might. Full of foreigners – a lot of Germans – some from Cyprus – Japanese and a smaller sprinkling of English and Scotch and American. Not quite as sociable a company as one would like.

The vastness and energy of New York beguiles, his curiosity about America oozing from every pore. The city enthrals him ('a tremendous place . . absolutely dazzling at night . . . lights, lights, light sparkling everywhere and the buildings towering away up in the sky and the crowds rushing hither and thither like an ant heap!').

They take a train onwards to Illinois. Somewhat wide-eyed he finds the service from Grand Central to Chicago a step up from the Dublin/Ballaghaderreen line with a jump-off at Kilfree Junction.

> Tips, tips, everywhere! If a cove just looks at your baggage or tells you the way he expects a tip!! Same on liner. Fellows, bell boys, cleaners, bar waiters gets $240 a month and overtime and unlimited tips!! Can drive in Cadillacs on shore and pay $50 for shoes etc – so bar attendant told us.

They meet Dillie's sons and their families and the cultural education continues with a trip to a local baseball game in Toledo. Grandpa's take on American life is sharply perceptive, sometimes comical.

> Fine stadium – all seated as is the fashion here. Game over at 8.15pm. Floodlit. Entrance $1 and 10 cents (tax). Locals won. All around under stand and at back

are places for refreshments. Hot dogs, pea nuts, candies, beer, minerals etc which do a great biz.

American kids, he observes, 'have the life of Riley – all attentions, toys and choice of food' while the novelty of television is another discovery.

> You don't have to go out at all here. TV with games!
> Boxing, wrestling, plays, sketches, films mostly English
> or old USA ones. Film people don't allow current re-
> leases to TV for a few years! It's going all day to late at
> night – but the continual boosting of all kinds of prod-
> ucts, including motor cars, is tiresome. Advertising +
> ballyhoo are tops in this country. It's a fine art!

The world's a wonder but by the end of the trip he's had enough. Dillie will make a couple of trips back to family in Chicago but Grandpa doesn't travel abroad again. At home he goes to numerous sports events with Jack. The brothers enjoy playing golf, Frank twice winning the Murray Cup open handicap event at St. Anne's. The game holds its own fascination for him, once marking with schoolboy delight a diary entry:

Jean and Dillie

24.3.35 – Hole in one at 5th in St Annes!!!

He and Jack make regular trips across town to the National Stadium for boxing tournaments. He also takes in rugby internationals at Lansdowne Road, marvelling at the All Blacks in 1935 as well as an occasional soccer international at Dalymount Park and shooting a few frames at the local billiard hall in Fairview.

On April 24, 1955 the veterans walk together in sunshine past the GPO for the Easter Parade. On a bracing January day in 1958 he and Jack go to watch Mayo play a challenge match in the newly-opened O'Toole Park in Crumlin. Jack picks up a serious chill and ends up confined to bed, leading to a bout of pleurisy and pneumonia. He's fit enough by April for the Easter Parade with Frank, Tom Sheerin, Eamon Dore and others. For the first time Grandpa does not attend the annual dinner in Clery's. And for the first time, at the age of 65, he is about to become a grandfather when Ronan Francis Shouldice is born.

> 21.7.58 – Young son born to Jean + F Óg at about 3 am! 7lbs 12 ozs. Both well, saw them this evening about 5.30. Thro' Guinness with F O'Neill from USA! Lá breagh.

In September he travels down the west to Mayo and Sligo, stopping in Swinford and Enniscrone.

> 22.9.58 – Met Kilgallon where I stayed long ago when forming Vols in 1918!!

> 30.11.58 – Parade to Church St. for 1ˢᵗ Battn. Mass for dead members. Small crowd.

Ronan's arrival, like when Frank Óg was born, gives Grandpa a deep sense of contentment. It's most obvious at Christmas when he reviews the year. His thoughts dust down of the ironies of life, the drip-drip impact of the mundane interspersed with moments of quiet, almost radiant, wonder. Despite various losses and the growing prevalence of health concerns the day, and the year, ends well.

> 25.12.58 – Lá breagh. We had a nice quiet little party of our own. F Óg + family stayed over. Had white Xmas tree with lights. Pretty.

His dog, a collie called Bran, starts roaming so he is relocated down the country and replaced by a corgi-terrier, also named Bran. When Bran II disappears and no trace can be found at the pound it's time to 'give up idea of keeping a dog at Hollybrook!!'

A telephone is installed at home in February, 1959. The first bill arrives four months later for a princely £5.98.

In the same year he attends a service for Dan Hannigan ('an old friend who helped us in Liverpool after Usk escape and arranged passage to Dublin. R.I.P.'). The Easter commemorative march is shorter than usual – from the Customs House to the G.P.O. – but he enjoys the day with Jack, Tom Sheerin, Sean Byrne and Maurice Collins.

> 26.6.59 – Up at 3.30 to hear heavyweight boxing from New York. Bit of a fiasco Johansen awarded fight after knocking Patterson down five times in Round 3.

Dillie makes a trip to Chicago – by plane this time – but most of the passengers are airsick on a 'bumpy' flight back to Dublin.

> 15.10.59 – 67 today. Paint brushes from F Óg & Jean! Cig tobac ó D!! Picking blackberries with D. in Howth. Lovely sunny day. Supper at North Star hotel and to Abbey after. 'The Country Boy' by Mayoman John Murphy. Very good + enjoyed it. Feeling good enough but the old sciatica or rheumatism is troublesome.

Jack's wife Eily passes away in September, 1960 and the following January Mam gives birth to 'a bonny little girl', my sister, Darina.

> 29.1.61 – Baby girl born to Jean + F Óg at midday. 8 lbs. Both well. Wet + cold weather + raining. Over to see Jean + baby. Doing nicely!

The 45th anniversary of the Rising is marked by an evening parade. He meets up with Tom Sheerin, Eamon Dore, Frank Burke and Maurice Collins amongst others. 'Good turn out of old pals,' he writes. The GAA League Final in May that year he sees a very special talent shine in the shape of Kerry midfielder Mick O'Connell.

> 14.5.61 – Outstanding, best performance I have seen of perfect gaelic f'ball!!

Dillie makes another visit to Chicago in '62, the year Frank turns 70. 'Feeling pretty good on the whole,' he considers. An increase to his Military Services Pension has been delayed for over a year but is eventually sorted out. It's the kind of bureaucratic pedantry he has little patience for.

Limited prospects at the I.C.I. and high unemployment prompt Dad to look for work opportunity abroad. Grandpa would not discourage him but the entry in his diary suggests a hint of alarm.

3.5.63 – F Óg for interview re job in Australia!!!

There is no entry for when I am born but Grandpa has other things on his mind. Dillie is unwell and when he picks up a chill himself he is ordered to bed. Everything changes dramatically when Dillie is rushed to the Bons Secours for a blood transfusion. She is haemorrhaging and the cause cannot be traced.

30.5.63 – 3rd transfusion for D. Took Jean + Frank III over to children's clinic for TB injection! Lovely warm day.

13.6.63 – F Óg to London for doctor exam in Australia job!!

Grandpa at his office

The prognosis from the Bons Secours is dismal. Both Dillie's kidneys are infected and surgery is ruled out. She cannot keep food or liquids down and is steadily losing weight. There is a helplessness about the course ahead. Rather than go home to an empty house Grandpa stays over with Dad and Mam most nights.

> 4.7.63 – D anointed tonight, very low. Mise stayed in Dollymount. Further blood transfusion and feeding by drip injection.

> 5.7.63 D – had a fair night – not quite as low as yest. DV perhaps she may pull thro' but I'm afraid not!

> 10.7.63 – D very poorly – and by all accounts declining!

Dillie's brother Jim arrives from Chicago on July 14. Grandpa collects him from the airport. He can only stay for three days, by which stage medical advice excludes any possibility of recovery.

> 19.7.63 – Poor D apparently recognised she was low. Looked appealingly at me and threw her arms about me saying 'Oh Frank'!! She was really suffering a lot of discomfort – bed sores etc – and passing into coma was a welcome relief.

> D very restless and apparently fading. Recognised me tho' – but back was sore from continuous lying on it. Spoke very little. Left hospital at 10pm when night nurse came on. She was very low!

> 20.7.63 – D died peacefully at 7.30pm in the Bons Secours. She was unconscious from about midnight last night. R.I.P. F Óg and I were present at end!

It is a month before Grandpa reopens his diary.

33.

'If friends thou hast and their adoption tried,
Grapple them to thy soul with links of steel'
– Ned Boland, Frongoch, 24 December 1916

Dillie's farewell is a bodyblow. Grandpa's world is receding and there isn't much anyone can do. He and Jack, now both widowers, continue to take in GAA and boxing matches but there is no mistaking the vacuum left behind.

> 13.9.63 – Making some apple jelly. As per Dillie's custom!
>
> 15.9.63 – To Kildare to see Daly's. Lovely warm sunny day but sad journey without D.
>
> 18.9.63 – To Knock via Kildare with Peg, Lucy and Dolly. Glorious warm sunny day. All that was required was poor Dillie's company which we all missed so much. RIP.
>
> 28.10.63 – D's birthday!!

Even his trips west have lost some of their lustre. Ballaghaderreen is still home but while he likes the drive, he feels a little different about the destination.

> 30.10.63 – Ballagh seems to be the same old place except for the fact that I don't know more than a couple of folk there!! A lot of my pals dead or gone away and new names on most of the houses etc or at least a big percentage.

In March the following year he finally retires from St. Anne's golf club. Jack is hospitalised with a perforated ulcer, then a stroke.

Grandpa visits him regularly. Then, most unwelcome family news from Ballaghaderreen. Ena, a staunch ally in difficult times, suffers a heart attack and is taken to a nursing home in Kiltimagh.

Dad leaves his insurance clerk job in search of something better. He and Mam try their luck with a grocery store on Vernon Avenue in Clontarf. Grandpa takes a cursory interest in the shop but the enterprise does not work out. When the shop is put up for auction nobody comes to bid. Dad gets temporary work in the fruit markets but after just five months work there also dries up. It seems that Canberra, at the other end of the world, values Dad's Master's degree more than prospective employers at home. The Australian Government offers him residence and a full-time position as a departmental economist. The family's passage will be paid for and a house provided as well as various incentives as part of the government's drive to populate the country with graduates from Britain and Ireland. One of Dad's close friends, a solicitor, accepts the offer and takes his family on the big journey.

It's a radical proposition and a tempting alternative to 1960's Dublin. Emerging Australia feels like an open book and the broad, bright uncertainties are part of its appeal. Mam is prepared to go, although not hugely enthusiastic about living at such a great distance from her own parents, Alo and Jean Kelly. And as things now stand, emigrating would leave Grandpa very much alone. This becomes the critical and decisive factor.

Instead of moving from Dublin to Canberra, the family makes a shorter trip from Dollymount to Clontarf. We will move in with Grandpa and Australia is left to another lifetime. The new arrangement seems to shake Grandpa from the languor of Dillie's passing. The house needs to be adapted, the roof redone. Starting 1965 with new-found vigour admits 'house in a mess this few months . . . dividing top (R) bedroom into two for self, bed and sitting, when Frank Óg + clan come!'

But Jack is not getting any better and remains in hospital. Although there are ten years between them there is an unmistakable closeness expressed through a mutual love of sport, song and The West. Both are reserved men but quite different in character – Jack more outgoing; Frank more private. The vibrancy of those days and nights together in North King Street and subsequent experiences through the War of Independence make Frank's repeated visits to Jack's bedside more and more difficult.

> 25.1.65 – Churchill died (age 90!). RIP. Jack still weak and low! In to see Jack yest morning in Hume St. Very low still and we are afraid the end is not far off unfortunately!

That same week Roger Casement's body is exhumed at Pentonville and reinterred in Glasnevin cemetery after lying in state for five days in Arbour Hill. Tens of thousands of people visit to pay their respects before a state funeral.

> 15.2.65 – Jack died. RIP. Last night.

Like Jack, Casement is laid to rest in Glasnevin.

Jack's son Chris recalls the funeral service in Fairview. The vestry at the back of the church was where Jack and Eily could meet when Jack was 'on-the-run'. Chris remembers clearly seeing two aged men in the car park in close confab that day, Eamon de Valera and W.T. Cosgrave, two former Civil War adversaries brought together to honour a neutral friend.

> 18.2.65 – Burial after 10am mass. Large crowd of old comrades etc incl. Pres de Valera, W.T. Cosgrove etc etc. Met E. Dore, F. Burke, self, T. Sheerin went in for parade at Marlboro St. Cold but dry and sunny. Very impressive turnout army etc! Everybody pleased with return of Casement remains for which we have been trying for nearly half century!!

Piaras Béaslaí, former Vice-Commandant, 1st Battalion, Dublin Brigade – gives the eulogy at Jack's funeral. In his contribution to Jack's Military Service Pension application Béaslaí states quite simply, 'It is not too much to say that he and the men under his command sustained the brunt of the enemy's attacks.'

Others, like Oscar Traynor and Fionnán Lynch, are equally effusive in their witness statements about the former Lieutenant.

> There are very few men indeed in the country who can
> boast of such a proud record as Jack Shouldice had pre-
> truce and I am can say with intimate knowledge that
> if he joined the National Army in 1922 he could have
> got a very high military rank. He preferred, however,
> to refrain from taking sides in the Civil War – Fionnán
> Lynch TD[467]

Béaslaí himself passes away in June, the event marked by a
sizeable state funeral. When the Four Courts garrison holds its
next meeting only ten veterans show up. Before the year is out
Ena is also gone. Grandpa must make another sad trip back to Ballaghaderreen where from a family of a dozen children only he and
Lily remain. Ena joins Cissie and three-year-old Rita in the family
plot at Kilcolman, the cemetery on the edge of town

That September Jack's son Chris kindly presents Frank with
Jack's unused ticket for the All-Ireland football final. He's always
stood on the terraces but from relative luxury, a seat in the Hogan
Stand, Grandpa, a football purist and ever the westerner, watches
Galway beat Mick O'Connell's Kerry 0-12 to 0-9.

> 26.9.65 – On Hogan Stand with ticket of Jack's (from
> Chris). RIP. First time up there for final!! Good. Match
> not a classic – rugged and a bit rowdy.

He will go to many more matches in Croke Park yet. In previous years he would take his son Frank Óg, lifting him over the
heavy iron turnstile in time-honoured fashion, just as my father
would lift me. Many seasons later Grandpa takes me with him,
parking his Hillman Imp in Fairview and lifting me over the turnstile. If it's not too crowded I can take the seat beside him, a narrow
wooden bench divided by thin metal rails; if the stand is packed his
knee can be my perch.

In keeping with the times going to matches in Croke Park is a
monochrome, no-frills experience. Merchandising has yet to hit
popular sport – unless you count GAA sombreros and papier ma-
ché hats that run in the rain. People generally do their eating at

home – travelling fans excepted – while the only county jerseys on view are those worn by players out on the pitch.

We go to Sunday matches regardless of who is playing but despite every human exhortation, he will not see Mayo lift Sam Maguire after 1951. Grandpa is a studiously passionate spectator and will not be distracted by wicker basket women in white shopcoats extolling Maxi Twist with lime and raspberry topping. As they plug their wares the white shopcoats discover that Grandpa has no time for such diversion. This is Croke Park after all, not Toledo.

As I get bigger Grandpa gets weaker so the turnstile is no longer negotiable. My Dad will take me instead and Grandpa will tune in at home on the wireless. The radio, a chunky old Bush transistor, provides an essential connection to the world outside with sports rivalling news for importance and meaning. His inter-county football days with Geraldines, Dublin and Mayo were special but he also loved hurling, Muhummad Ali and handball, the popularity of which in Ballaghaderreen was memorably evoked by John Healy in *No One Shouted Stop.*

Coming up to the 50th anniversary of the Easter Rising there is a curiosity among the surviving veterans as to how the event will be commemorated. In the run-up to the anniversary Grandpa is photographed by the *Irish Times, The Sunday Times* and *Irish Press.* Then, something unexpected:

10.3.66 – Nelson's Pillar blown up!! Nobody hurt!!

On St. Patrick's Day there is a special commemoration near North King Street.

17.3.66 – At pageant in Cuckoo Lane. Easter Week.
About 14 of us (survivors) were there.

In fact they are a little chuffed at the level of attention and the fulsome effort put into remembering the origins of the Irish Republic. The national event is a military parade past the GPO on Easter Sunday, April 10. Surrounded by Grandpa and erstwhile veterans President de Valera opens the Garden of Remembrance a day later in Parnell Square, appropriately enough, at noon.

*Likely lads on Church Street, 1964. The North King Street garrison –
(L-R) J. O'Connor, T. Sheerin, M. Flanagan, F. Shouldice, P. Béaslaí,
J. Shouldice, P. Lynch, M. Collins, E. Morkham & Mrs Morkham
(Courtesy Sunday Times)*

De Valera and Sean Lemass reopen a restored Kilmainham Jail and other sites around the city are marked with wreaths and plaques. The GAA stages its own full-scale pageant (Aiséiri) at Croke Park directed by Tomás MacAnna with Ray McAnally playing Padraig Pearse ('very good but cold night!!'). Religious services follow at Arbour Hill, Dublin Castle and the Capuchin friary on Church Street. In pelting rain de Valera unveils Edward Delaney's bronze sculpture of Thomas Davis on Dame Street while a half-drowned children's choir gurgles its way through 'A Nation Once Again'.

It may feel strange for Grandpa to visit de Valera at Áras an Uachtaráin but he seems to enjoy the occasion with Tom Sheerin, Patrick O'Hanlon's family and a few others.

In May he is invited to Boyle, County Roscommon for the unveiling of the Pearse plaque in the town square, not far from the barracks where he remembers being beaten up by the police. Grandpa, a man of few words is kindly asked by Editor of the *Roscommon Herald* Miceál O'Callaghan to mark the occasion. He replies:

May I say I was greatly honoured to be asked to do so but at the risk of appearing churlish I must explain that my immediate reaction was to say, regrettably, no!

I have never aspired, unfortunately perhaps, to the art of public speaking and, realising my own inadequacy would prefer if someone more practiced in it were called on to make it, which is customary at such events. To be quite candid I was never made fill the role of public speaker, nor indeed have I ever been called on to do so. I'm afraid I belong with the 'back room' boys and I am now too old to change!

To learn that I am the last surviving Roscommon man of the Dublin 1916 garrisons surprised me and gives the event a special significance (for me), though I have often been puzzled as to whether, as a BD man, I rate as a citizen of Roscommon or Mayo!! However this is only of academic interest in the honouring of one of the outstanding men of our generation!

Unveiling at Boyle, 1966 – Frank and Alec McCabe in centre
(Courtesy Roscommon Herald/Barry Feely)

The Editor replies graciously:

> Dear Mr Shouldice,
>
> Very many thanks for your acceptance of our invitation. You need have no worry about the oration for in deference to your wishes we have decided to get somebody else to that part of it and would be honoured if you would do the actual unveiling of the plague without having to say anything.[468]

Dad and Ronan travel to Boyle with him and he joins old IRA comrade Alec McCabe for the unveiling. They go on to Ballaghaderreen and return home to Dublin afterwards. The Pearse plaque remains at the former courthouse in Boyle. Through his diaries Grandpa makes very few additional comments about the passing of former Volunteers but in a fast-changing world the cumulative effect of steadily losing comrades takes its toll.

> June 4, 1966 – Fionnán Lynch our captain – F. Company died. RIP.

He goes to his former captain's funeral with Tom Sheerin, Sean O'Brien and Seamus Brennan. The following month Joe O'Kelly passes away, further chipping the deep connection with his home town, Ballaghaderreen. He enjoys meeting the children of former comrades – 'Lunch at McKee Barracks with Maurice Collins and 3 sons!' – and should not be faulted for clerical errors, even if he is two weeks late on my younger brother Killian's arrival.

> 9.10.66 – Killian born. Both ok (TG) 3rd boy!

Six days later he notes he is in his 74th year. 'TG all fairly well,' he writes. Bloody Sunday in Derry in 1972 troubles him and he loses another friend when Eamonn Dore passes away. However the survivors are not averse to an arthritic knees-up. For the few that remain the memories are rich and the ties are binding. They adapt to the present by reliving the past, enjoying the quiet respect of good company.

5.10.72 – Tom Sheerin's 80th. Whisked out there by
Tom's son with Sean Byrne. Home near 3 a.m.

On April 24 he goes to Dublin Castle for the 58th Anniversary
Mass of the Rising. Dev is there. It will be the last 1916 commemoration Grandpa will attend. He meets Tom at the funeral of Maurice Collins, another good friend and ex-Frongoch internee. When
Frank and Tom look around they can't but notice the pews gapped
by absent comrades. What is there to do but make a revolutionary
shrug and face forward.

By the end of summer he feels the pains in his legs. 'Cannot
walk,' he writes. 'Only poorly.' His diary entries are now sporadic.
On September 9 he notes, 'Legs and feet bad now. Was to go into
Mater for a night.'

A week later he re-drafts his will. The pages afterwards are
blank.

*U.S. President John F. Kennedy honours Easter Rising commemorations
at Arbour Hill, 1966 (Courtesy RTÉ Stills Library)*

34.

After 83 years it ends very quickly. One Friday evening in December Ronan rattles a few pebbles against the Grandpa's window upstairs. If you had no front door key or were stuck outside Grandpa was the gatekeeper. Lifting the heavy frame sash window he would drop keys below so we could let ourselves in.

On this occasion Ronan gets no response although Grandpa's light is on. After gaining entry Ronan checks upstairs and finds Grandpa on the floor, oblivious to the cigarette burnt ash-long to his fingertips. He's talking quite coherently to someone who isn't there, Tom Sheerin, his old mucker from Rising and Frongoch days. They fought side-by-side, were arrested together, imprisoned together – Frank and Tom have seen it all but recent years have led to more muted affairs, usually meeting up to bid farewell to a passing comrade. And then in October Tom himself shuffles on, leaving Frank behind for the first time.

During Easter Week Grandpa came to know death intimately. Men he shot when the South Staffordshire regiment attempted to storm Reilly's Fort. Friends he and Tom lost at the barricades. Years later when he carried Dick Coleman's coffin through a Welsh jail. Close friends like Harry Boland cut down in Civil War. All of this before the shooting finally stopped.

And then through the vagaries of peace time losing his daughter, Rita. His wife, Cissie. His second wife, Dillie and his brothers Jack, Bertie, Jim and sister Ena. If he feels the spectre of his own time coming maybe he feels he is ready to rejoin Tom Sheerin. They have much to talk about; they always will.

Dad and Ronan help Grandpa to bed. He's calmer and able to rest but the following day Dad feels he must send for the parish priest. Grandpa is given the last rites before being taken to St Mary's Hospital in Phoenix Park. St Mary's was once a hospital for the National Army before it became a residential home. Grandpa's youngest sister Lily had previously stayed there and whenever we visited her we found the institutional greeting bleak and austere. It has since been renovated with bright new quarters, unrecognisable from the dismal grey Victorian residence it once was.

Lily is not Grandpa's only connection with St. Mary's. Jack's eldest son, Father Sean Shouldice, worked there with TB patients before succumbing to Hodgkinson's aged just 31. Fr. Sean, revered far and wide in his short life span, lies buried in St Mary's under a Celtic Cross paid for by the donations of grateful patients. Nineteen years previous Grandpa attended the blessing of the Cross and noted it in one of the miniature diaries he kept irregularly since 1917.

> 11.11.55 – At St Mary's in evening. Blessing of statue
> over Fr Sean's grave. Terrible wet + cold day.

It is doubtful that any of these thoughts cross his mind as the ambulance drives up North Circular Road that Saturday afternoon. Ronan accompanies him. There is no siren, no flashing light, no urgent need to make the hospital at breakneck speed. Grandpa regards the roof interior, confused and a little disorientated. He is taken by stretcher-trolley into St. Mary's and made comfortable. Dad gets over to the hospital later and returns again early on Sunday morning to find no change in Grandpa's condition.

Our mother Jean is in the Rotunda Hospital that same week. Mam is about to bear an unexpected fifth child. All four of us, ranging in age from eight years to 15 are thrilled at the prospect but we are thrown by Grandpa's sudden absence and uncertain about what is to come.

When the phone rings around noon on Sunday we don't know whether to expect a curtain closing or a bright unveiling. Dad takes the call and we stand at the stairs, listening in. He replaces the receiver quietly, turns to us and says, 'The Da is dead.'

Then he goes outside, walks slowly to an old elm tree at the end of the garden and weeps. It is the first time I've seen Dad crying. We stand watching from the window, torn, wondering should we race down to him or leave him be. When he comes back in we hug him and make tea. Over a numb table he says arrangements will have to be made. A classified ad will have to be put in the paper. Kirwan's undertakers in Fairview will be notified. Busy taking care of the afterlife Dad rings the Rotunda to see how Mam is faring. We can all go in later to visit.

The house feels a bit strange over the next couple of days. Even if Dad had lived there since 1940 Hollybrook Park was very much Grandpa's house. Built almost a century earlier the street was only given numbers in 1955. Arguably just bricks and mortar but the space within is full of significance to our family, most happily as the place where Dad celebrated his 21st and first met Mam.

It is, like any family home, where each of us will experience particular moments, mark significant occasions. The place where life's tremors are absorbed and cushioned. In between events of great consequence – like when Dad, at 16, found his stricken mother, Cissie – there is custom and there is ritual. At each day's end Grandpa does his rounds – a nightly check on each of his grandchildren. A gentle tap, the door cracked ajar:

Oíche mhaith. Codladh sámh.

His checks completed he would shuffle to his quarters at the top corner of the house. He has two rooms – a sort of living room adjoining the bedroom. The living room is heated by a gas fire. For day-to-day living he has a plug-in kettle to make tea, a small fridge and a two-ring cooker on which he stews apples, his speciality. The apples come from what we call 'the orchard' – three apple trees and a spectacularly under-performing pear tree. Grandpa would spoon stewed apples on Jacob's crackers for each of us who would steal up to his room at night. But now he is gone. We approach his room tentatively, almost knocking on the door, half-expecting him to call out in reply.

Tar isteach!

The rooms have gathered a slight mustiness, a tincture of age, as if in his last days his physical movement slowed enough to leave the air within undisturbed. In earlier years he used to join us for family dinner in the evening when Dad got home from work. With his mobility in decline he takes to using a wooden walking stick with a rubber bung at the end for grip. Our new collie Rover goes wild at the mere sight of the stick, transformed from placidity into a furry snarl circling a traditional adversary. Grandpa and Rover will not become friends.

But he is facing other obstacles. Shuffling from his room he sometimes finds my younger brother Killian and I sprawled on the floor, the carpet at the top of the stairs congested with high-revving Matchbox cars. Or when model soldiers turn the landing into a battleground he can hear us imitate the fricative energy of machine guns. Or the sibilant trajectory of a lone rifleman, bullets ricocheting off imaginary street corners. Plagiarised from countless films, the last gasp of a miniature plastic infantryman: *'I don't think I'm going to make it . . .'*

Pistols at dawn

Grandpa is never curious about us 'playing soldiers'. We are too young to imagine what he has seen. He is not old enough to forget what he'd rather not remember. When he finds his way impeded he is not averse to clearing away entire armies with his walking stick, impervious to howls of protest underfoot.

As the staircase becomes more of a challenge he needs advance warning so he can negotiate a descent in time for dinner. Eventually he is just as happy to have meals brought up to his room. Even though he is not a gaelgóir the greeting to the tray bearer – be it Ronan, Darina, me or Killian – is usually made in Irish.

Dinner, Grandpa.
Go raibh míle maith agat.

And now the serving tray hangs idle in the kitchen. There is nobody upstairs to bring it to. And there is no Mam at home making dinner. She is still in the Rotunda and the news is not good. We are told that Mam needs to rest and there is no baby. We are grappling with the contradictory properties of the word 'stillborn'. It doesn't seem like a valid explanation for what she has gone through but our enthusiastic plans to put new names to a vote have been put on hold. We will remain a family of six.

The funeral passes off in Glasnevin where Grandpa is buried in a plot beside his second wife, Dillie. A tricolour, guns, blackbirds. Relatives journey from the West and somehow in Mam's absence sandwiches miraculously appear on the kitchen table. It is also my cousin Matthew's 12th birthday and after Glasnevin my Auntie Maureen whisks me and Killian out to Malahide. We don't really feel like going to a party but once we get there we find consolation in sweets, cake and Pepsi.

When the drama is well and truly over Dad brings us to The Night Owl restaurant in Fairview (long gone) for an evening meal. I have no memory of it. It feels like an awful lot has happened in a short space of time. In just one week everything has become so different. A house that was going to get bigger and noisier got smaller, quieter. Gradually, the heavy black ceramic phone at the foot of the stairs stops ringing. After so much activity, things are slowing down. We miss Mam and we want her back. And we miss Grandpa but he is gone.

Struck by a cruel double-blow my Dad begins the painful and emotive trawl through his father's belongings. Anybody who has been through this will recognise the dear familiarity of a particular shirt, coat, hat. All saturated with memory and meaning. Small cherished items from everyday use, each identifiably and evocatively Grandpa's. Clip-on braces. His walking stick. His glasses. Condor plug tobacco Penknife. Pipe.

It is 1974 but a calendar on the wall of Grandpa's room marks the fiftieth anniversary of The Rising. I recall its picture of Padraig Pearse – in profile, as ever – phoenix-like and incombustible over the jagged lick of orange-red flames. Dad sifts through Grandpa's personal effects, sorting out what has been left behind. He sets aside his GAA medals, medals and ribbons from the Easter Rising and the Tan War. They sit there like clues. It makes sense, even to an 11-year-old, that he allowed Padraig Pearse keep an eye out long after the commemorative calendar ran out of days.

Padraig Pearse calendar

Although Grandpa attended numerous commemorations and various public events he preferred let the essential details of his journey remain vague. To some extent he left us all in the dark and prompts his son to strike a match in the shadows. It is so fortunate that he kept his letters and diaries together and stored them all in an old leather suitcase. Decades later the old case and its contents will become my guide to tracing the past. Finding the people he and Jack knew; the people who knew them. Through this search I find myself saddened on occasion, frequently entertained, occasionally jolted and even stunned. Grandpa illuminates the way and reminds me what it means to carry out a labour of love.

Paul O'Brien's description of him as a sniper conjures up an image that will not go away. Joseph E.A. Connell Jnr. notes the same proficiency in *Dublin in Rebellion*, describing Grandpa as 'a very effective sniper, firing from a perch on the Jameson's Tower.'[469]

That capacity for clinical efficiency jars with the mental picture of my grandfather, the soft timbre of whose voice never left the precincts of the West. A sniper with a fixed eye, steady hand and a cold, measurable heartbeat all betrayed in later years by the infirmities of age. Eyes that water, hands that tremor. A heart that stopped.

It is hardly surprising that corporeal frailty tricks us into underestimating experience, the vast reservoir of a life previously lived. I have a clear image of Grandpa's slow ambulatory descent, his breath laboured, right hand leaning heavily into the banisters for support. But this former Dublin and Mayo footballer did not always move and breathe like that.

Prison wall at Usk, scaled by rope ladder (photo by the author)

Following his trail will take me to Usk Prison in Wales where I stand shaded by the 18½-foot wall he scaled alone almost a century ago. He was the one to offer ballast so that three others could get away. And then he hauled himself up a vertical brick wall to freedom. Looking upwards my eyes are blinded by sunshine spilling over the high parapet. I feel a smile encroaching my lips, a lump forming in my throat.

The extraordinary reality of Grandpa's past again takes me back, attempting to connect these revelations to what I already know. A series of rewrites scribble constantly through my mind. Archives, libraries, academic studies, witness statements, historians, official papers, interviews and publications all offer their own alibis. Interrogating what I remember reveals memory can be an unreliable witness but truth itself can be a conjuror when plain facts are plainly remarkable.

In making up lost ground I am reminded that Grandpa is not the only participant who speaks so seldom of the War of Independence. Men and women who went out in Easter Week usually review the past with a reserve that belies their hand in shaping it. They may have been central characters – and very proud of the achievement – but they do not wish to be the story. Michael O'Flanagan, who fought alongside Grandpa and Jack in North King Street and was then interned in Frongoch, put it very simply:

> I have no regrets. The years I spent and the people I met in the national movement – life would not have been life without it.[470]

For years those who survived 1916 and the War of Independence often found themselves treated as some sort of anachronism, their marches through Dublin streets observed by onlookers more often in mute curiosity than warm appreciation. Gratitude for their sacrifice was seldom, if ever, expressed.

> 17.3.49 – Republic of Ireland celebrations but six counties still missing!!

Having wrested autonomy from the world's leading colonial power, the newly-declared Republic had to prove itself worthy, even capable, of handling its own destiny. For years the veterans marched past the very spot where Pearse proclaimed the ideals of the Republic. Could those aspirations actually be delivered?

Years after my grandfather died I sought out for interview all the surviving veterans I could find. Physically frail, the memories of Easter Week burned brightly for these men but they could not hide a sense of disappointment. They were part of a 26-county state riven by civil war politics, monopolised by the Catholic Church and beset by unemployment, emigration and poverty both extreme and widespread. It left an abiding impression that any personal satisfaction they had about the formation of an Irish state was tempered by the sour fruits of their achievement. The men and women marching past the GPO could be forgiven for wondering if independence was everything it was cracked up to be.

Ongoing argument over legacy will never be settled. Rival groups and political parties will each claim to be natural successors to the unpopular minority that changed the course of Irish history. Even the 50th anniversary of The Rising was preceded by an angry demonstration against the imprisonment of republican prisoners by the Irish state. Six years later I accompany my Dad on a protest enraged by another Bloody Sunday, the murder of 14 civilians by British paratroopers in Derry. In response, the British embassy at Merrion Square is burnt to the ground. Surviving veterans from 1916 watch as it happens – and what would they make of where we are now?

It is not coincidental that Tom Sheerin did not provide testimony to the Bureau of Military History. Neither did George Geraghty or Barney Mellowes, lesser-known names who pledged themselves, body and soul, to achieving national freedom. They did not seek attention or approval and by shunning the limelight afterwards they chose to let the record stand for itself. Grandpa's significant legacy would probably surprise even himself.

They might remember all too clearly when they found themselves exposed to open hostility on the streets of Dublin immediately after The Rising. Spat upon by jeering crowds only to be chaired shoulder high eight months later, they got a first-hand introduction to the fickle humours of public affection. Some of them were deeply scored by the experience.

It is likely that witnessing such a faltering sense of loyalty among countrymen and women inclined them firmly towards caution, even distrust of the community at large. If they ever needed somebody to count on they had each other. Faithful comrades who had already proved their worth.

One hundred years ago a group of ordinary men and women demanded change, a demand that shook, then re-designed, the corridors of power. The preference of these modest revolutionaries to let their actions do the talking makes it harder to gauge their individual contributions but that's probably the way they want it. What they did, they did together; everything they gave us, they leave behind.

Frank and Jack Shouldice, 1964

365

Appendix

Dealing with such a copious amount of material the Directorate of Military Intelligence developed their own shorthand at decoding the letters that came before them at Usk Prison and from other 'German Plot' prisoners. They produce a virtual lexicon for reference, described as 'key code words' and nicknames by which the novice censor can make sense of incoming material.

Most of the terms relate to Sinn Féin (SF) elections and law.

Official Explanation Prisoners' Phrases

Police – Traveller, Leap people, Black boys, Black pigs, Bloodhounds, Cossacks, Mr Hockey

Prison – H.H. Hotel, King George's Hotel

Imprisonment – French leave

New to Jail – New potatoes

SF meetings – Dancing class

SF committee – Board of Directors, Football team, Hurling team

SF organisation – Co-operative society

SF business – Insurance business

SF candidate – Manager

SF leaders – Main pipes

SF propaganda – Missionary work

Keeping SF interests alive – Weeding the plot

Canvassing for SF – Wheat growing

SF meeting – Football, Jawbone

Harcourt Street (Sinn Féin HQ) – Dublin House

People with SF sympathies – Oat growing, Flax growing

Sinn Féiner – Hottentots

Temperate Sinn Féiners – Juniors

SF becoming more popular – Barometer rising

A part of the country not in favour of SF or where the organisation has not yet commenced its activities – Area of virgin soil

Election results – Cricket final

Votes – Marks

Electors – Buyers

A public meeting – Concert

A constituency – Farm, Garden

A candidate – Farmer

Work a constituency – Handle a superintendency

Fighting a constituency – Buying a property

Election agent – Debt collector, Labour leader

Arrested – Lifted

Avoid arrest – Escaping the flue

Visitors – Police raids

Ill – In danger of arrest

Trouble – Music

Conscription – Notice of eviction, Miss Con

Labour Party – Nurses

Arms or ammunition – Oats

Gun – Fishing rod

Ammunition – Grass seed

English – Huns

Soldiers – Carrots

Transportation and acquisition of arms or ammunition – Fishing trade

Election – Big market, Examination

Big Push – Easter Rising (1916)

Prepared to go to the length of fighting – Learning how to save turf

Larry's House – Mansion House

Nicknames

Sir Edward Carson – The White Chief of Bigotry

John Dillon – Colorado Jack, Honest John, The Melancholly Humbug, The Peacock, The Pedlar, Ballaghaderreen Jack, Grey John

Darrell Figgis – Sacred Egotist, Red Admiral of the North

Lord French – The Primitive Man, Mighty Atom, St. Patrick II, The Frenchman, The French Cook

Eoin MacNeill – Eoin the Uncertain, Eoin of the Bakers

William O'Brien – The Lame Man

T.P. O'Connor – Tay Pay

Edward Shortt – Ananias, Longshort

Governor Young of Usk Prison – The First Gentleman

ENDNOTES

1   'The Pride of Petravore (Eileen Óg)' by Percy French
2   *Crossfire: The Battle of the Four Courts*, 1916 by Paul O'Brien, New Island
3   Eamonn Ó Duibhir, BMH Statement #1403
4   'Policing Famine Ireland' in *Eire-Ireland*, by W.J. Lowe, xxix, no. 4 (Winter 1994)
5   *– ibid –*
6   Patrick Cassidy, BMH Statement #1017
7   Seamus Doyle, BMH Statement #166
8   Royal Commission on the Rebellion in Ireland, 26.6.16
9   NLI, DMP Chief-Commissioner to Under-Secretary Nathan, 16.4.18
10 NLI, CSO/JD/2/1, DMP, 1.6.16
11 NLI, CSO/JD/2/21 DMP, 29.6.16
12 NLI, CSO/JD/2/16, DMP 22.6.16
13 NLI, Ms 26,182, Joseph Brennan Papers
14 *Irish Volunteer*, 22.4.16
15 'The Easter Rising', BBC Home Service, Tx 21.1.66
16 NLI DMP to Chief Secretary's Office, 20.4.16
17 *Sunday Independent* 23.4.16
18 Jack Shouldice, BMH Statement #162
19 'The Easter Rising', BBC Home Service, Tx 21.1.66
20 Kathleen Boland, BMH Statement #586
21 Gerald Doyle, BMH Statement #1511
22 Mort Ó Conaill, BMH Statement #804
23 Sean Prendergast, BMH Statement #755
24 Garry Houlihan, BMH Statement #328
25 NLI, Ms 26,193, Joseph Brennan Papers
26 RTÉ 'They Remember 1916: Piaras Beaslaí', 6.4.56
27 Liam Archer, BMH Statement #819
28 WNAC Radio, Boston interview, 1966

29 Garry Houlihan, BMH Statement #328

30 Patrick O'Hanlon to BMH, 26.12.35

31 NLI, Ms 26,193, Joseph Brennan Papers

32 *Hansard*, House of Lords, 26.4.16

33 *Evening Herald*, 25.4/3.5.16

34 Patrick J. Kelly, BMH Statement #781

35 Michael O'Flanagan, BMH Statement #800

36 Charles Shelley, BMH Statement #870

37 NLI, Ms 26,193

38 NLI, Ms 49,810, Lawrence Ginnell Papers

39 *An t-Óglach,* Vol. 14, No. 18, 15.5.26

40 Con O'Donovan, BMH Statement #1750

41 *Irish Independent*, 5.5.16

42 *Irish Life*, 12.5.16

43 *Hansard*, House of Lords, 11.5.16

44 WNAC Radio, Boston interview, 1966

45 Gen. Maxwell to Field Marshal French, Home Forces Irish Command, 25.5.16

46 Liam O'Doherty, BMH Statement #689

47 William Scully, BMH, 11.11.35

48 John J. Scollan, BMH Statement #318

49 Sean Prendergast, BMH Statement #755

50 NLI, Ms 22,251 Patrick Rankin

51 Harry Colley, BMH Statement #1687

52 *Catch and Kick* by Eoghan Corry, Poolbeg Press, 1989

53 – *ibid* –

54 Ignatius Callander, BMH Statement #923

55 *Evening Herald*, 25.4/3.5.16

56 NA (Kew), WO 141/21

57 'The Easter Rising', BBC Home Service, Tx 21.1.66

58 Gen. Maxwell to Field Marshal French, Home Forces Irish Command, 25.5.16

59 RTÉ 'They Remember 1916: Piaras Beaslaí', 6.4.56

60 Jack Shouldice, BMH Statement #679

61 Robert Holland, BMH Statement #371

62 Patrick Rankin, BMH Statement #163

63 FS to Mother, 27.6.16, Private Collection

64 War Office to Gen Byne, Irish Command HQ, Parkgate May 22, 1916

65 NLI, Ms 49,632/26, Sankey Papers 1916-18, 23.5.16

66 Joseph V. Lawless, BMH Statement #1043

67 Liam Tannam, BMH Statement #242

68 Frank Burke, BMH Statement #694

69 *Hansard*, House of Commons, 11.5.16

70 Patrick Colgan, BMH Statement #850

71 Patrick Rankin, BMH Statement #163

72 *Hansard*, House of Commons, 3.5.16

73 *– ibid –*

74 Field Marshal French to Gen. Maxwell, 3.5.16, TCD Letters 1916

75 *Hansard*, House of Commons, 3.5.16

76 *Hansard*, House of Commons, 20.4.16

77 NLI, Ms 26,196 Joseph Brennan Papers, 30.6.16

78 'The Easter Rising', BBC Home Service, Tx 21.1.66

79 *Hansard*, House of Commons, 9.5.16

80 *Manchester Guardian*, 7.5.16

81 ES to FS, 15.5.16, Private Collection

82 Mother to FS, 18.5.16, Private Collection

83 ES to FS, 25.5.16, Private Collection

84 Sheila O'Regan to FS, 22.5.16, Private Collection

85 *Hansard*, House of Commons, 11.5.16

86 *Hansard*, House of Commons, 17.5.16

87 BMH 1913-21, #CD 196/2/1

88 NA (Kew), Dartmoor admissions record, Doc. 311980/34,

89 Lord Lt. Wimborne to Gen Maxwell, 1.5.16, TCD Letters 1916

90 NLI, Ms 24,334, Irish National Aid Association and Volunteer Dependants' Fund Papers

91 Tom McKenna to FS, 29.5.16, Private Collection

92 FS to Mother, 23.6.16, Private Collection

93 FS to Mother, 23.5.16, Private Collection

94 Tom McKenna to FS, 1.6.16

95 WNAC Radio, Boston interview, 1966

96 Ignatius Callender, BMH Statement, #923

97 *Hansard*, House of Commons, 3.5.16

98 Major Ivor Price, Director Military Intelligence in Ireland, 10.4.16

99 *Hansard*, House of Lords, 11.5.16

100 *Hansard*, House of Lords, 26.4.16

101 NLI, Ms 26,008, Joseph Brennan Papers, 22.5.16

102 *Hansard*, House of Commons, 17.5.16

103 *Irish Independent*, 4.5.16

104 *Hansard*, House of Lords, 11.5.16

105 Liam Tannam, BMH Statement #242

106 Royal Commission on the Rebellion in Ireland, 26.6.16

107 *Hansard*, House of Commons, 22.5.16

108 Jim Shouldice telegram, 13.5.16, Private Collection

109 Jim Shouldice to JS, 7.5.16, Private Collection

110 Jim Shouldice to FS, 29.5.16, Private Collection

111 Jim Shouldice to FS, 16.6.16, Private Collection

112 Maire Merriman to FS, 30.4.16, Private Collection

113 Patrick Rankin, BMH Statement #163

114 Aggie/Tess to FS, 7.6.16, Private Collection

115 TCD Letters 1916, P106/120 (24); 26.5.16

116 TCD Letters 1916, P106/120 (20); 28.5.16

117 TCD Letters 1916, Office of Chief Commission of Police to Nancy O'Rahilly, 19.6.16

118 *Hansard*, House of Commons, 17.5.16

119 Gen. Maxwell to Secretary of State for War, HQ Irish Command, 25.5.16

120 *Daily Mail*, 13.5.16

121 WNAC Radio, Boston interview, 1966

122 Gen. Maxwell to Field-Marshal French, 16.5.16, TCD Letters 1916

123 *Guardian*, 11.1.2001

124 *The Easter Rebellion* by Max Caulfield, Gill and Macmillan, 1995; 294

125 *Hansard*, House of Commons, 20.7.16

126 *Hansard*, House of Commons, 26.7.16

127 Thomas Doyle, BMH Statement #1041

128 FS to Mother, 23.5.16, Private Collection

129 Robert Holland, BMH Statement #371

130 – *ibid* –

131 *Irish Independent*, 4.5.16

132 Patrick Rankin, BMH Statement #163

133 Frank Hardiman, BMH Statement #406

134 Joseph McCarthy, BMH Statement #1497

135 *Hansard*, House of Commons 31.5.16

136 NLI MS 49,632/26, Sankey Papers 1916-18, 12.6.16

137 *Hansard*, House of Commons, 1.6.16

138 Sankey Papers 1916-18, NLI MS 49,632/26, HO to Sankey, 8.6.16

139 – *ibid* –

140 Sankey Papers 1916-18, NLI MS 49,632/26, Broderick to Sankey, 3.6.16

141 Sankey Papers 1916-18, NLI MS 49,632/26, Sankey to Pim, 10.6.16

142 *Hansard*, House of Commons, 25.7.16

143 US State Dept., Index 763.72114/2123, 25.10.16

144 ES to FS, 24.6.16, Private Collection

145 NLI, Ms 24,324 Irish National Aid Association &U Volunteer Dependants' Fund Papesr

146 *Joe Stanley: Printer of the Rising* by Tom Reilly, Bandon, 2005

147 NLI 13A 2066, 'Official Report of Ill-Treatment of Irish Prisoners of War Interned at Frongoch Internment Camp'

148 BS to FS, 28.6.16, Private Collection

149 NLI, Ms n.2736, p1638, Frongoch Internment Camp: Irish Prisoners of War, Minute Book, June 11-July 10, 1916

150 Christina Shouldice to BS, 22.6.16, Private Collection

151 NLI, Ms 24,366, Irish National Aid Association & Volunteer Dependents' Fund Papers

152 NLI, Ms n.2736, p1638, Frongoch Internment Camp: Irish Prisoners of War, Minute Book, June 11-July 10, 1916

153 ES to FS, 11.6.16, Private Collection

154 Collins to Mollie Woods, TCD 1916 Letters, 24.6.16

155 FS to Mother 23.6.16, Private Collection

156 Patrick Rankin, BMH Statement #163

157 Sheila O'Regan to FS, 26.7.16, Private Collection

158 ES to FS, 29.10.16, Private Collection

159 ES to FS, 25.5.16, Private Collection

160 NA, Kew, CO 904/214/26, File 405

161 – *ibid* –

162 – *ibid* –

163 – *ibid* –

164 *Irish Independent*, 5.5.16

165 NA, Kew, CO 904/214/26, File 405

166 – *ibid* –

167 – *ibid* –

168 – *ibid* –

169 – *ibid* –

170 – *ibid* –

171 NLI, Ms 26,188, Joseph Brennan Papers, Johnstone to Chalmers, 22.7.16

172 NLI, Ms 26,188, Joseph Brennan Papers

173 NLI, Joseph Brennan Papers

174 NLI, Ms 26,196 Joseph Brennan Papers, 26.6.16

175 Sean Prendergast, BMH Statement #755

176 Joseph Good, BMH Statement #338

177 BS to FS, 7.7.16, Private Collection

178 ES to FS, 4.7.26, Private Collection

179 NLI, Ms 24,366

180 FS to Mother, 10.7.16, Private Collection

181 FS to Mother, 17.7.16, Private Collection

182 NLI, Ms 24,362

183 Mort Ó Conaill, BMH Statement #804

184 Michael Lynch, BMH Statement #511

185 *Hansard*, House of Commons, 22.11.16

186 *Harry Boland's Irish Revolution* by David Fitzpatrick, Cork University Press

187 HB letter to Ned Boland, 14.12.16

188 NA (Kew) HO 144/1463/319502, Ireland (Insurrection): Irish Civil Servants suspended for complicity in the Rebellion of 1916

189 FS to Mother, 26.10.16, Private Collection

190 NHIC to FS, 16.10.16, Private Collection

191 NLI, Ms 49,632/26 John Sankey Papers

192 – *ibid* –

193 – *ibid* –

194 NLI, INAAVDF, Letter from Prisoner #1459, 5.7.16

195 Joe Lawless, BMH Statement #1043

196 Joseph McCarthy, BMH Statement #1497

197 NZ Truth, 12.3.21

198 Sean Nunan, BMH Statement #1744

199 *Cambrian News*, 28.7.16

200 FS to Mother, 17.7.16, Private Collection

201 FS to Mother, 29.7.16, Private Collection

202 NLI, MS 24,366

203 Joe Lawless, BMH Statement #1043

204 Eamonn Dore, BMH Statement #153

205 NLI, Ms 24,450

206 Michael W. O'Reilly, BMH Statement #886

207 Home Office to Commdt, Frongoch, 9.10.16, TCD 1916 Letters

208 M. Collins to J. Ryan, 2.9.16, TCD 1916 Letters

209 Frank Hardiman, BMH Statement #406

210 FS Diary note 18.7.16, Private Collection

211 FS to Mother, 5.9.16, Private Collection

212 NLI, Neville Chamberlain to Samuel, 27.6.16

213 NLI, POS 8,541, RIC 6.6.16

214 NLI, Ms 26,196 Joseph Brennan Papers, 12.7.16

215 NLI, Ms 26,196 Joseph Brennan Papers, 12.7.16

216 BS to FS, 3.8.16, Private Collection

217 NLI, DMP to Under-Secretary, 20.11.16

218 Jack Shouldice, BMH Statement #679

219 ES to FS, 8.8.16, Private Collection

220 Jim Shouldice to FS, 16.8.16, Private Collection

221 NA, Kew, Home Office memo, 3.10.16, Doc. 311980/26

222 Letter HMP Dartmoor to Home Office, 1.7.16

223 FS to Mother, 5.9.16, Private Collection

224 Jim Shouldice telegram, 2.9.16, Private Collection

225 ES to FS, 8.9.16, Private Collection

226 NLI 46,074, Frongoch Favourite, 17.8.16

227 ES to FS, 27.9.16, Private Collection

228 Máire Merriman to FS, 4.10.16

229 Sorcha to FS, 30.10.16, Private Collection

230 *Irish Migrants in Modern Wales* by Paul O'Leary, Liverpool University Press, 2004

231 *South Wales Weekly Post*, 12.8.16

232 *Fron-goch Camp 1916 and the Birth of the IRA* by Lyn Ebenezer, Carreg Gwalch

233 NLI, Ms 24324, Art Ó Briain Papers

234 US State Dept., Index 763.72114/2123, 25.10.16

235 Thomas Doyle, BMH Statement #1041

236 NLI 24,324, Irish National Aid Association and Volunteer Dependants' Fund Papers.

237 FS to Mother, 12.10.16 Private Collection

238 Lily to FS, 30.9.16, Private Collection

239 FS to Mother, 3.10.16, Private Collection

240 Lily to FS, 26.10.16, Private Collection

241 NLI, MS 15,533

242 Thomas Doyle, BMH Statement #1041

243 Comdt. Joseph McCarthy, BMH Statement #1497

244 *Hansard*, House of Commons, 19.12.16

245 BS to FS, 18.9.16, Private Collection

246 NLI, Ms 24,463, Irish National Aid Association & Volunteer Dependants' Fund Papers

247 NLI Ms 24,450

248 FS to Eamonn Dore, 30.4.61, Personal Collection

249 NLI Ms 15,533

250 NLI, Ms 24,463, Irish National Aid Association & Volunteer Dependants' Fund Papers

251 *Hansard*, House of Commons, 22.11.16

252 *Hansard*, House of Commons, 29.11.16

253 NLI, Ms 24,366, Irish National Aid Association & Volunteer Dependents' Fund Papers

254 NLI, *Cork Free Press*, 11.11.16

255 *North Wales Chronicle*, 1.12.16

256 Summary of Evidence, Frongoch 10.11.16, Private Collection

257 *Irish Independent*, 27.11.16

258 ES to FS, 1.12.16, Private Collection

259 *Irish Independent*, 28.11.16

260 FS to Mother, 30.11.16, Private Collection

261 *Hansard*, House of Commons, 4.12.16

262 *Hansard*, House of Commons, 29.11.16

263 *Hansard*, House of Commons, 14.11.16

264 *Hansard*, House of Commons, 14.12.16

265 NLI, Ms 24,366, Irish National Aid Association & Volunteer Dependents' Fund Papers

266 *Liverpool Daily Post*, 21.12.16

267 *Yr Adsain*, 19.12.16

268 *With the Irish in Frongoch* by W.J. Brennan-Whitmore, Mercier Press, 2013

269 *Hansard*, House of Commons, 31.12.16

270 Gerald Doyle, BMH Statement #1511

271 JS letter to Mother, 14.12.16, Private Collection Chris Shouldice

272 JS letter to Bertie, 14.12.16 Private Collection Chris Shouldice

273 FS to Mother, 7.12.16, Private Collection

274 *Hansard*, House of Commons, 19.12.16

275 – ibid –

276 NLI, Under-Secretary to Chief Secretary, Telegram 22.12.16

277 Seamus Ua Caoimhanaigh, BMH Statement #889

278 Sean Nunan interview, RTE, 1964

279 *Irish Independent*, 26.12.16

280 – ibid –

281 NLI, MS 49,356/1, INAAVDF

282 Telegram 23.12.16, Private Collection

283 NA, Kew, 18890/48, Prison Commission to Gov, HMP Maidstone, 5.12.16;

284 JS to Bureau Military History, Dublin

285 JS to Mother, 14.12.17, Private Collection Chris Shouldice

286 Excerpt from HMP Lewes conditions for Irish prisoners, 1916/17.

287 *Hansard*, Irish Prisoners, 14.12.16

288 JS to Mother, 20.2.17, Private Collection

289 FS to HB, 23.1.17, Private Collection

290 NA, Kew, CO 904/214/26, File 405

291 – ibid –

292 JS to FS, 14.3.17, Private Collection, Chris Shouldice

293 *Cork Free Press*, 11.11.16

294 NLI, MS Joseph Brennan Papers

295 *Hansard*, Irish Prisoners (Release), 31.12.16

296 JS to FS, Easter 1917

297 JS to BMH

298 JOK to FS, 11.5.17, Private Collection

299 JS to Mother, 6.4.17, Private Collection

300 NA, Kew 311980/4, 17.5.16

301 NA, Kew 311980/4, 22.5.16
302 NA, Kew 311980/14, 27.6.16
303 NA, Kew, Prison Commission to Home Office, 27.3.17
304 NA, Kew, HO 311,980, HO to Prison Commission, 29.6.16
305 – *ibid* –
306 De Valera to Governor, HMP Lewes 29.5.17
307 De Valera to Governor, HMP Lewes, 3.6.17
308 JS to ES, 14.4.17, Private Collection
309 ES to FS, 29.10.16, Private Collection
310 NA, Kew, WO 0625, 8.4.17
311 Irish Command HQ to Chief Commissioner, DMP 12.4.17
312 NA, Kew; CO 904/214/26
313 NA, Kew, HMP Lewes to Home Office, 6.6.17,
314 NA, Kew, Prison Commission, 6.6.17
315 NA, Kew, Prison Commission to Home Office, 6.6.17
316 NA, Kew, HMP Lewes to Prison commission, 6.6.17,
317 *Harry Boland's Irish Revolution* by David Fitzpatrick, Cork University
    Press, pp. 56-68, 2004
318 NA, Kew; CO 904/214/26, p28
319 NA, Kew CO 904/214/26, Irish Command HQ to Under-Secretary,
    23.6.17;
320 NA, Kew, Dublin Castle to GPO, 26.6.17, 14835/S
321 JS BMH statement
322 NLI, MS 49,356/1/1
323 NA, Kew; CO 904/214/26
324 – *ibid* –
325 – *ibid* –
326 Ena to Jim, 3.8.17, Private Collection
327 *Western People*, 'Service in Ballaghaderreen, 19.9.64
328 Military Service Pension, Frank Shouldice, 34 SP/22322
329 Military Service Pension, Jack Shouldice, 34 SP/22323
330 *Western People*, 'Service in Ballaghaderreen, 19.9.64
331 NLI, MS 23,500, Irish National Aid Association and Volunteer
    Dependants' Fund Papers
332 NLI, MS 24,359, Irish National Aid Association and Volunteer
    Dependants' Fund Papers
333 NA, Kew, CO 904/214/26, File 405, Irish Army Command #17837,
    21.1.18
334 JOK to FS, 14.11.17, Private Collection
335 Irish Command HQ to Under-Secretary, Dublin Castle, 2.5.18
336 NA, Kew WO 35/95/28
337 Special Branch to Chief Secretary Duke, 26.2.18

338 NA, Kew, Provost Marshal, Col FHG Stanton, HQ Parkgate, 22.2.17

339 NA, Kew, Issued by Lt-Gen Mahon, CMA, 7.3.18

340 NA, Kew, Irish Command, Parkgate to Asst Under-Secretary, 23.5.17

341 Micheál Ó Droignáin, BMH Statement #1718

342 *Hansard*, Arrests in Ireland, 26.2.17

343 NA, Kew, J O'Doherty to Lieut-Gen. Mahon, Commanding-in-Chief the Forces Ireland, 12.3.17

344 FS Notes, 22.6.18, Personal Collection

345 Christina Shouldice to Reading/Gloucester Prisons, 4.6.18, Private Collection

346 Ward, A., 'Lloyd Ward, Lloyd George and the 1918 Irish Conscription Crisis', (1974), *The Historical Journal* XVII

347 *Hansard*, Government of Ireland, 5.11.18

348 *Hansard*, House of Lords, , 20.6.20

349 Kathleen Boland to FS, 17.6.18, Private Collection

350 Home Office to Under-Secretary, Dublin, 22.5.18

351 FS 22.6.18, Private Correspondence

352 *Llanelly Star*, 31.8.18

353 *Cambria Daily Leader*, 25.5.18

354 Chief Secretary's Office to Christina Shouldice, #14906, 3.6.18, Private Collection

355 Christina Shouldice to FS c/o Usk Governor, 6.6.18, Private Collection

356 ES to FS, 21.5.18, Private Collection

357 NA, Kew, Prison Commission to Secretary of State, #362269, 20.5.18

358 War Office to Home Office, 23.5.18

359 Memo on Prison Commissioners, #36229, Home Office May 1918

360 NA, Kew; HMP Usk to Home Office, 23.5.18

361 Cissie to FS, 22.6.18, Private Collection

362 NLI, 48,910, Ginnell Papers, Griffith to Dixon, 13.8.18

363 Tom McKenna to FS, 13.6.18, Private Collection

364 Tom McKenna to FS, 9.10.18, Private Collection

365 ES to FS, 7.6.18, Private Collection

366 *Roscommon Herald*, 9.9.18

367 NA, Kew, #362269, Directorate of Military Intelligence

368 NA Kew, HO 362269 / 185, 26.11.18

369 NA, Kew, #362269, Directorate of Military Intelligence

370 – *ibid* –

371 Bertie to FS, 12.6.18, Private Collection

372 Bertie to FS, 12.7.18, Private Collection

373 Sheila O'Regan to FS, 17.6.18, Private Collection

374 Alfred O'Kelly to FS, 12.7.18, Private Collection

375 FS to Mother, 30.7.18, Private Collection

376 FS to Mother, 12.9.18, Private Collection

377 Cissie to FS, 28.7.18, Private Collection

378 Cissie to FS, 11.7.18, Private Collection

379 Cissie to FS, 21.11.18, Private Collection

380 Cissie to FS, August 1918 (undated), Private Collection

381 Kathleen Boland to FS, 7.6.18, Private Collection

382 ES to FS, 3.6.18, Private Collection

383 NLI, 48,910, Ginnell Papers, O'Donovan to Dixon, 3.8.18

384 FS to Mother, 7.8.18, Private Collection

385 NLI, 48,910, Ginnell Papers, O'Donovan to Dixon, 23.8.18

386 ES to FS, 1.10.18, Private Collection

387 ES to FS, 18.10.18, Private Collection

388 Tom McKenna to FS, 13.10.18, Private Collection

389 ES to FS, 26.10.18, Private Collection

390 NLI, 48,910, Ginnell Papers, O'Reilly to Dixon, 10.1.19

391 Governor Young, HMP Usk to Christina Shouldice, 8.11.18, Private Collection

392 FS to Home Secretary, telegram 13.12.18, Private Collection

393 NLI, 48,910, Ginnell Papers, Lawless to Dixon, 3.1.19

394 FS to Cissie, 14.12.18, Private Collection

395 JS to FS, 21.12.18, Private Collection

396 NA, Kew, #362269, Directorate of Military Intelligence

397 Cissie to FS, 25.12.18, Private Collection

398 FS to Mother, 13.1.19, Private Collection

399 Anvil Books, *Sworn to be Free: Complete Book of IRA Jailbreaks 1918-21*, 1971

400 'The Break-Out from Usk Jail' by Frank Shouldice and George Geraghty, from *IRA Jailbreaks, 1918–1921*, Mercier Press, 2011

401 NA Kew, 362269/157, Gov Young to Home Office, 23.1.19,

402 *Nottingham Evening Post*, 23.1.19

403 *Lancashire Evening Post*, 29.1.19

404 NA Kew, 362269/19, Prison Commission to Home Office, 7.2.19

405 NA Kew, 362269/157, Gov Young to Home Office, 23.1.19

406 NA, Kew 362269, HO Minutes, 29.1.19

407 NA, Kew, ML Waller at HO to Irish Office, 28.1.19

408 NA Kew, 362269/162, HMP Gloucester to Prison Commission, 3.2.19

409 NA, Kew, #362269/163a, Prison Commission to Home Office, 11.2.19

410 War Office to Secretary of State, 17.2.19

411 NA, Kew #326629/172, Prison Commission to E. Troup, Home Office, 3.2.19

412 War Emergency Laws Continuance Bill, *Hansard*, 4.3.20

413 *Hansard*, 14.11.18

414 Directorate of Military Intelligence – Postal Censorship, 9th and Final Report, NA, Kew

415 *Hansard*, Government of Ireland, 5.11.18

416 *Derry Journal*, March 10, 1919

417 *– ibid –*

418 *Western People*, 'Service in Ballaghaderreen, 19.9.64

419 NA, Kew 76S / 45707RIC, Belmullet to Inspector-General,

420 *The Men Will Talk To Me: Mayo Interviews by Ernie O'Malley*, Mercier Press, 2014

421 Jack Shouldice BMH Statement #679

422 NA, Kew, CO 904/188

423 NA, Kew, CO 904/188

424 NLI Bishop St., MFA 54/80, Box 155

425 NLI Bishop St., MFA 54/80, Box 155

426 Jack Shouldice, BMH Statement #679

427 *Hansard*, House of Commons, 19.4.21

428 *District Inspector John A Kearney* by Donal J. O'Sullivan, Trafford Books, Canada

429 FS to Mother, (undated) Jan 1921, Private Collection

430 FS to Boyle Prison Authority, 21.3.21, Private Collection

431 FS to Bertie, 15.3.21, Private Collection

432 Mountjoy Prison, Admission Records 1922

433 *Irish Independent*, 15.4.21

434 *Hansard*, 20.4.21

435 FS to Mother, 8.6.21, Private Collection

436 FS to Mother, 29.5.21, Private Collection

437 FS to Mother, 8.6.21, Private Collection

438 FS to Mother, 26.9.21, Private Collection

439 FS to Mother 21.6.21, Private Collection

440 FS to Mother, 30.7.21, Private Collection

441 FS to Mother, 14.7.21, Private Collection

442 FS to Mother, 8.7.21, Private Collection

443 NLI Bishop St, MFA 54/80, Box 155; RIC ref CO 904/155

444 NLI Bishop St, MFA 54/80, Box 155; RIC ref CO 904/155

445 NA, Kew 76S/45,519, RIC Dublin Office, 30.9.21

446 NA, Kew, RIC Louisburgh, 29.8.21

447 NA, Kew, DC/S/898, RIC Athlone, 22.10.21

448 FS to Mother, 17.10.21, Private Collection

449 *Political Imprisonment and the Irish, 1912-1921*, by William Murphy, Oxford University Press

450 NLI Bishop St., MFA 54/80, Box 155, #490

451 NLI Bishop St., MFA 54/80, Box 155

452 NA, Kew 79S / 45762, RIC Special Branch to Dublin Castle,

453 NLI Bishop St., MFA 54/134, Reel 137

454 NLI Bishop St, MFA 54/80, #472, Box 155

455 FS to Mother, 23.11.21, Private Collection

456 FS to Mother, 10.12.21, Private Collection

457 FS to Mother, 23.12.21, Private Collection

458 *Freeman's Journal*, 12.1.22

459 *Freeman's Journal*, 13.1.22

460 FS Military Service Pension interview, 34 SP/22322

461 Kathleen O'Donovan, Statement #586 to BMH

462 *Harry Boland's Irish Revolution* by David Fitzpatrick, Cork University Press

463 *The Flame and the Candle* by Dominic Price, Collins Press, 2012

464 TMcK to FS, 26.7.18. Private collection

465 T McK to FS, 19.6.16, Private Collection

466 TMcK to FS, 12.7.16, Private Collection

467 Jack Shouldice MSP application

468 M. O'Callaghan to FS, 16.5.66

469 *Dublin in Rebellion* by Joseph EA Connell Jnr,, Lilliput Press, 2009

470 Michael O'Flanagan, BMH Statement #800

INDEX